Easy Access Britain

The Guide to Accessible Places to Stay and Visit

visit**Britain**™

Contents

USEFUL INDEXES
A full list of indexes, including
by accessible rating, place name
and display advertisers can be
found on page

KEY TO SYMBOLS
Inside back-cover flap

VisitBritain

VisitBritain is the organisation created to market Britain
to the rest of the world, and England to the British.

Formed by the merger of the British Tourist Authority
and the English Tourism Council, its mission is to build
the value of tourism by creating world-class destination
brands and marketing campaigns.

It will also build partnerships with – and provide
insights to – other organisations which have a stake in
British and English tourism.

Tourism for All UK

TFA UK is the UK's central source
of holiday and travel information
for people with access requirements.

It is a registered charity which liaises
with government and industry bodies.

The guide that
gives you more

This accessible guide is packed with information from where to stay, to how to get there and what to see and do. **In fact, everything you need to know to enjoy Britain.**

Quality accommodation

Choose from a wide range of quality-assessed accommodation to suit all budgets and tastes: this guide contains a comprehensive listing of hotels, bed and breakfast accommodation, self-catering properties and camping and caravan parks, all of which offer accessible accommodation. Look for the accessible and quality ratings in each entry.

Great days out

Every region has its own unique attractions – in each section we highlight a selection of interesting ideas, all of which are accessible. For even more ideas go online at visitBritain.com.

You'll also find useful contacts including regional tourism organisations and Tourist Information Centres.

National organisations and travel

Need general advice, equipment hire or the best way to reach your destination? Turn to the back of the guide for some really useful contacts and invaluable information.

Useful indexes

Indexes at the back of the guide make it easy to find accommodation that matches your requirements.

The British Museum, London

The seafront at Broadstairs, Kent

How to use
this guide

This essential guide for the traveller with accessible needs offers a great choice of accommodation throughout Britain.

Each property in England and Scotland has been awarded an accessible category according to strict criteria. Access Statements are available for properties in Wales. In addition, the quality of the accommodation has been assessed to nationally agreed standards, so that you can book in confidence.

Detailed accommodation entries include descriptions, prices and facilities. Listings include contact details only.

Finding accommodation is easy
Regional entries
The guide is divided into regional sections and accommodation is listed alphabetically by place name within each region.

Colour maps
Use the colour maps starting on page 22 to pinpoint the location of all detailed accommodation. Then refer to the place index at the back to find the page number.

Indexes
The indexes will help you find the right accommodation if you have a particular requirement, for example, a hearing or visual rating, or a specific facility such as a level entry shower. If you know the name of the establishment, turn straight to the property index for the page number.

Tourism for All UK

Finding suitable accommodation for holidays or to visit relatives is not always easy, especially if you have to seek out ground floor rooms, a step free entrance and all facilities on one level, or large print menus and colour contrast in the bathroom.

Proprietors can sometimes be unaware of accessible needs resulting in disappointment on arrival when you find numerous steps to encounter and you are unable to seat a wheelchair at the dining room table.

For those needing accurate advice, help is at hand.

All-round service

Tourism for All UK (formerly known as Holiday Care) provides information that helps thousands of people arrange a successful holiday or trip every year. This includes equipment hire, respite care centres, accessible attractions, financial help, activity and children's holidays information as well as advice on accommodation.

Tourism for All is the UK's central source of holiday and travel information for people with access requirements.

Finding accommodation

For help in finding suitable accommodation or to make a booking call the Tourism For All reservations line. You may also be able to take advantage of special offers at hotels throughout the UK and overseas. (Note, if you use this service all accommodation in the UK will be assessed by VisitBritain or Tourism for All. Quality ratings for overseas properties are usually based on self-reporting or member's recommendation.)

Making friends

Consider joining the Tourism for All UK 'Friends of TFA' scheme. Members share information and experiences and receive a regular newsletter which highlights new accessible accommodation, attractions and places to go. Membership also gives special discounts on publications and accommodation.

Above Carrie-Ann Fleming, Tourism For All UK (front right) with members of the Board outside the call centre in Kendal

tourismforall

Tourism for All is the UK's central source of holiday and travel information for people with access requirements.

information helpline
0845 124 9971

reservations 0845 124 9973
(lines open 9-5 Mon-Fri)

f (01539) 735567

e info@tourismforall.org.uk

w tourismforall.org.uk

or write to
Tourism for All UK, c/o Vitalise,
Shap Road Industrial Estate,
Kendal LA9 6NZ

TFA UK is a registered charity, No 279169 and Company Limited by Guarantee No 01466822

Tourism for All UK (TFA) is a charity, formed in 1979. Working with the national tourist boards it has helped to develop the National Accessible Scheme run by VisitBritain, by which accommodation is assessed and rated. The organisation also works with government, speaks at tourism related conferences, promotes good practice and offers consultancy on all kinds of tourism-related access issues.

Improved accessibility throughout the tourism industry is actively encouraged by Tourism for All. Where good practise is established – such as in Chester, and through Cheshire for All, or by Brighton who recently undertook a destination audit, looking at the whole visitor experience from a disabled person's point of view – the charity seeks to celebrate and promote the achievement.

Membership of TFA by local government and industry bodies is an indicator of their commitment to observe their obligations under the Disability Discrimination Act. (Many of these are advertisers in this guide.) Corporate Patrons also support the charity's aims, and include Accor Hotels, InterContinental Hotels, Choice Hotels, Hand Picked Hotels, VisitBritain and the Wales Tourist Board.

National
Accessible Scheme

England

Accommodation is assessed under VisitBritain's National Accessible Scheme, which includes standards useful for hearing and visually impaired guests in addition to standards useful for guests with mobility impairment.

Accommodation taking part in this scheme will display one or more of the mobility, visual or hearing symbols shown opposite.

When you see one of the symbols, you can be sure that the accommodation and core facilities have been thoroughly assessed against demanding criteria. If you have additional needs or special requirements we strongly recommend that you make sure these can be met by your chosen establishment before you confirm your booking.

Scotland

All kinds of accommodation are assessed by VisitScotland Quality Advisors, based on criteria drawn up with the co-operation of organisations who deal with wheelchair users. This is part of the VisitScotland grading schemes. Criteria can be found on visitscotland.com. Accessibility is checked every three years. Entries show one of three symbols.

Category 1
Accessible to a wheelchair user travelling independently.

Category 2
Accessible to a wheelchair user travelling with assistance.

Category 3
Accessible to a wheelchair user able to walk a few paces and up a maximum of three steps.

Wales

Owners of all types of accommodation in Wales are required to have a full Access Statement and were invited to join the National Accessible Scheme in autumn 2006.

England

Mobility Impairment Symbols

 Typically suitable for a person with sufficient mobility to climb a flight of steps but who would benefit from fixtures and fittings to aid balance.

 Typically suitable for a person with restricted walking ability and for those who may need to use a wheelchair some of the time and can negotiate a maximum of three steps.

 Typically suitable for a person who depends on the use of a wheelchair and transfers unaided to and from the wheelchair in a seated position. This person may be an independent traveller.

 Typically suitable for a person who depends on the use of a wheelchair in a seated position. This person also requires personal/mechanical assistance to aid transfer (eg carer, hoist).

 Access Exceptional is awarded to establishments that meet the requirements of independent wheelchair users or assisted wheelchair users shown above and also fulfil more demanding requirements with reference to the British Standards BS8300:2001.

 ## Visual Impairment Symbols
Typically provides key additional services and facilities to meet the needs of visually impaired guests.

 Typically provides a higher level of additional services and facilities to meet the needs of visually impaired guests.

Hearing Impairment Symbols

Typically provides key additional services and facilities to meet the needs of guests with hearing impairment.

 Typically provides a higher level of additional services and facilities to meet the needs of guests with hearing impairment.

The criteria VisitBritain and national/regional tourism organisations have adopted do not necessarily conform to British Standards or to Building Regulations. They reflect what the organisations understand to be acceptable to meet the practical needs of guests with special mobility or sensory needs and encourage the industry to increase access to all.

Ratings and awards
at a glance

Reliable, rigorous, easy to use – look out for the following ratings and awards to help you choose with confidence:

Ratings made easy

★	Simple, practical, no frills
★★	Well presented and well run
★★★	Good level of quality and comfort
★★★★	Excellent standard throughout
★★★★★	Exceptional with a degree of luxury

For more details of the national tourist board quality assessment schemes, see page 306

Star ratings

Establishments are awarded a rating of one to five stars based on a combination of quality of facilities and services provided. Put simply, **the more stars, the higher the quality and the greater the range of facilities and level of service**.

The range of accommodation within this guide differs greatly in style, so to help you make your choice, the rating scheme also includes categories that give an indication of the type of establishment. Descriptions of these can be found overleaf.

The process to arrive at a star rating is very thorough to ensure that when you book accommodation you can be confident it will meet your expectations. National tourist board assessors visit establishments annually and work to strict criteria to rate the available facilities and service.

A quality score is awarded for every aspect of the experience. For **hotels and bed and breakfast** accommodation this includes the comfort of the bed, the quality of the breakfast and dinner and, most importantly, the cleanliness. For **self-catering** properties the assessors also take into consideration the layout and design of the accommodation, the ease of use of all the appliances, the range and quality of the kitchen equipment, and the variety and presentation of the visitor information provided. **Camping and caravan park** assessments are based on the quality, cleanliness, maintenance and conditions of the facilities provided. The warmth of welcome and the level of care that each establishment offers its guests are noted, and places that go the extra mile to make every stay a special one will be rewarded with high scores for quality.

All the national assessing bodies (VisitBritain, VisitScotland, Visit Wales and the AA*) now operate to a common set of standards for rating each category of accommodation, giving holidaymakers and travellers a clear guide on exactly what to expect at each level. An explanation of the star ratings can be found on pages 306-309.

*The AA does not assess self-catering properties.

Gold and Silver Awards

These Enjoy England awards are highly prized by proprietors and are only given to hotels and bed and breakfast accommodation offering the highest levels of quality within their star rating, particularly in areas of housekeeping, service and hospitality, bedrooms, bathrooms and food.

Classifications explained

The following classifications will help you decide which type of accommodation is right for you, whether you are seeking a non-stop, city-buzz holiday; a quiet weekend away; a home-from-home break or camping fun for all the family in England, Scotland and Wales.

Hotels

Hotel	A minimum of six bedrooms, but more likely to have over 20.
Small Hotel	A maximum of 20 bedrooms and likely to be more personally run.
Country House Hotel	Set in ample grounds or gardens, in a rural or semi-rural location, with the emphasis on peace and quiet.
Town House Hotel	In a city or town-centre location, high quality with a distinctive and individual style. Maximum of 50 bedrooms, with a high ratio of staff to guests. Possibly no dinner served, but room service available. Might not have a dining room, so breakfast may be served in the bedrooms.
Metro Hotel	A city or town-centre hotel offering full hotel services, but no dinner. Located within easy walking distance of a range of places to eat. Can be of any size.
Budget Hotel	Part of a large branded hotel group, offering limited services. A Budget Hotel is not awarded a star rating.

Guest Accommodation

Guest Accommodation	Encompassing a wide range of establishments from one-room bed and breakfasts to larger properties, which may offer dinner and hold an alcohol licence.
Bed and Breakfast	Accommodating no more than six people, the owners of these establishments welcome you into their home as a special guest.
Guest House	Generally comprising more than three rooms. Dinner is unlikely to be available (if it is, it will need to be booked in advance). May possibly be licensed.
Farmhouse	Bed and breakfast, and sometimes dinner, but always on a farm.
Restaurant with Rooms	A licensed restaurant is the main business but there will be a small number of bedrooms, with all the facilities you would expect, and breakfast the following morning.
Inn	Pubs with rooms, and many with restaurants as well.

Self Catering

| **Self Catering** | Choose from cosy country cottages, smart town-centre apartments, seaside villas, grand country houses for large family gatherings, and even quirky conversions of windmills, railway carriages and lighthouses. Most take bookings by the week, generally from a Friday or Saturday, but short breaks are increasingly offered, particularly outside the main season. |

Self Catering

Choose from cosy country cottages, smart town-centre apartments, seaside villas, grand country houses for large family gatherings, and even quirky conversions of windmills, railway carriages and lighthouses. Most take bookings by the week, generally from a Friday or Saturday, but short breaks are increasingly offered, particularly outside the main season.

Serviced Apartments

City-centre serviced apartments are an excellent alternative to hotel accommodation, offering hotel services such as daily cleaning, concierge and business centre services, but with a kitchen and lounge area that allow you to eat in and relax when you choose. A telephone and Internet access tend to be standard. Prices are generally based on the property, so they often represent excellent value for money for families and larger groups. Serviced apartments tend to accept bookings for any length of period, and many are operated by agencies whose in-depth knowledge and choice of properties makes searching easier at busy times.

Approved Caravan Holiday Homes

Approved caravan holiday homes are let as individual self-catering units and can be located on farms or holiday parks. All the facilities, including a bathroom and toilet, are contained within the caravan and all main services are provided. There are no star ratings, but all caravans are assessed annually to minimum standards.

Camping and Caravan Parks

Camping Park
These sites only have pitches available for tents.

Touring Park
If you are planning to travel with your own caravan, motor home or tent, then look for a Touring Park.

Holiday Park
If you want to hire a caravan holiday home for a short break or longer holiday, or are looking to buy your own holiday home, a Holiday Park is the right choice. They range from small, rural sites to larger parks with all the added extras, such as a pool.

Many parks will offer a combination of these categories.

Holiday Village
Holiday Villages usually comprise a variety of types of accommodation, with the majority in custom-built rooms, chalets for example. The option to book on a bed and breakfast, or dinner, bed and breakfast basis is normally available. A range of facilities, entertainment and activities are also provided which may, or may not, be included in the tariff.

Holiday Villages must meet a minimum entry requirement for both the provision and quality of facilities and services, including fixtures, fittings, furnishings, decor and any other extra facilities. Progressively higher levels of quality and customer care are provided at each star level.

Forest Holiday Village
A holiday village which is situated in a forest setting with conservation and sustainable tourism being a key feature. It will usually comprise of a variety of accommodation, often purpose built; and with a range of entertainment, activities and facilities available on site free of charge or at extra cost.

Hostel Accommodation

Hostel
Safe, budget-priced, short-term accommodation for individuals and groups. Visitors usually share a dormitory as well as lounge, bathroom and kitchen facilities, though higher star-rated hostels sometimes have en suite bedrooms and may offer meal services.

Group Hostel
Hostels that predominantly accept group bookings.

Activity Accommodation
Caters predominantly for groups and provides fully certified or licensed activities for visitors. May be self catering or fully serviced.

Backpacker
Similar to hostels, but tend to cater for younger, longer-term independent travellers rather than groups and families. Usually operate on a less rigid basis and offer 24-hour access to guests.

All of the above are awarded star ratings.

Bunkhouse
Bunkhouses offer a similar style of accommodation to hostels but usually with more limited services and facilities, often on a self-catering basis. Bunkhouses are not star rated but meet the same minimum requirements as hostels, where applicable.

Camping Barn
Camping Barns, often referred to as 'stone tents', provide very simple self-catering accommodation, and have the advantage of being roomy and dry. Camping Barns are not star rated and will be assessed as being fit for the purpose, meeting a specific minimum entry requirement.

Campus Accommodation

Campus Accommodation This includes educational establishments, such as universities and colleges with sleeping accommodation in halls of residence, or student village complexes available for individuals, families and groups.

Availability is mainly throughout the academic vacations (during the summer from June to September, Easter and Christmas), however, some universities provide accommodation all year. There is often a wide choice of recreational facilities, with most venues providing TV rooms, bars and restaurants, and a variety of sporting and special interest holidays.

Establishments meet a minimum requirement for both the provision of facilities and services, including fixtures, fittings, furnishings and decor. Progressively higher levels of quality and customer care are provided for each of the star ratings. Quite simply, the more stars, the higher the overall level of quality you can expect.

Accommodation
entries explained

Each accommodation entry contains detailed information to help you decide if it is right for you. This has been provided by proprietors and our aim is to ensure that it is as objective and factual as possible.

Accommodation entries contain detailed information to help you decide if it is right for you. This information has been provided by the proprietors themselves.

1   Listing under town or village with map reference

2   Quality rating plus Gold and Silver Awards where applicable

3   Prices
   Hotels – Per room for bed and breakfast (B&B) and per person for half board (HB)
   Guest accommodation – Per room for bed and breakfast (B&B) and per person for evening meal
   Self-catering – Per unit per week for low and high season
   Camping and caravan parks – Per pitch per night for touring pitches; per unit per week for caravan holiday homes

4   National Accessible Scheme rating

5   Establishment name and booking details

6   Indicates when the establishment is open

7   Travel directions

8   Special promotions or facilities

9   Payment accepted

10 At-a-glance facility symbols

① ② ③ ④ ⑤

HUNSTANTON, Norfolk Map ref 3B1   **HOTEL**

★★

B&B per room per night
s £45.00–£59.00
d £70.00–£99.00
HB per person per night
£55.00–£75.00

Caley Hall Hotel

Old Hunstanton Road, Old Hunstanton, Hunstanton PE36 6HH
t (01485) 533486   **f** (01485) 533348   **e** mail@caleyhallhotel.co.uk
w caleyhallhotel.co.uk

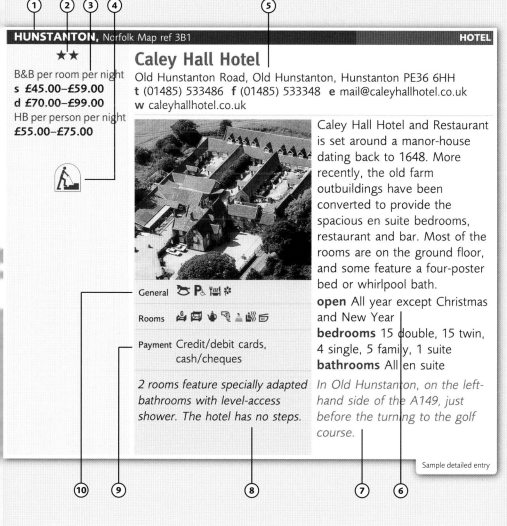

General 🐾 P♿ 🛏 ❋

Rooms 🖪 📺 🛁 🍵 ♨ 🖳 🗔

Payment Credit/debit cards,
cash/cheques

*2 rooms feature specially adapted
bathrooms with level-access
shower. The hotel has no steps.*

Caley Hall Hotel and Restaurant is set around a manor-house dating back to 1648. More recently, the old farm outbuildings have been converted to provide the spacious en suite bedrooms, restaurant and bar. Most of the rooms are on the ground floor, and some feature a four-poster bed or whirlpool bath.
open All year except Christmas and New Year
bedrooms 15 double, 15 twin, 4 single, 5 family, 1 suite
bathrooms All en suite

In Old Hunstanton, on the left-hand side of the A149, just before the turning to the golf course.

Sample detailed entry

⑩ ⑨ ⑧ ⑦ ⑥

A key to symbols can be found on the back-cover flap.
Keep it open for easy reference.

Map 1

A   B

Location
Maps

Every place name with a detailed entry in the regional accommodation sections of this VisitBritain guide has a map reference to help you locate it on the maps which follow. For example, to find Lewes, East Sussex, which has 'Map ref 2D3', turn to Map 2 and refer to grid square D3.

All place names with a detailed entry in the regional sections are shown in blue type on the maps. This enables you to find other places in your chosen area which may have suitable accommodation – the place index (at the back of this guide) gives page numbers.

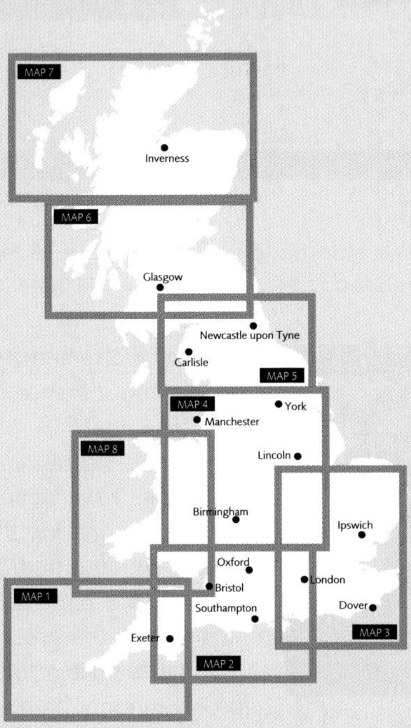

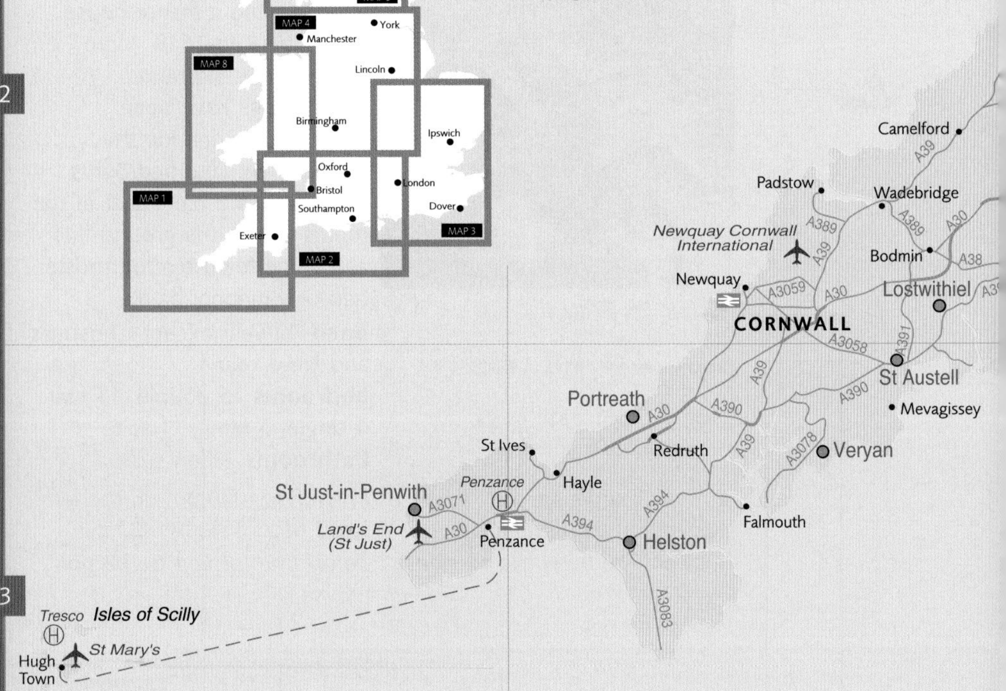

MAP 7

Inverness

MAP 6

Glasgow

Newcastle upon Tyne
Carlisle

MAP 5

MAP 4   York
Manchester

MAP 8

Lincoln

Birmingham

Ipswich

Oxford
Bristol   London
Southampton
Dover

MAP 1

Exeter

MAP 2

MAP 3

Camelford
A39

Padstow
Wadebridge
A389   A389   A30

Newquay Cornwall
International   A389
A38
Bodmin

Newquay   A3059   A30
Lostwithiel   A3

CORNWALL   A3058
A391

St Austell

Portreath   A30   A390
Mevagissey

St Ives
Redruth   A39   A3078   Veryan

St Just-in-Penwith   Penzance   Hayle
A3071   A394

Land's End   A30   A394   Falmouth
(St Just)   Penzance   Helston

A3063

Tresco   *Isles of Scilly*
St Mary's
Hugh
Town

Key to regions: South West England

Map 1

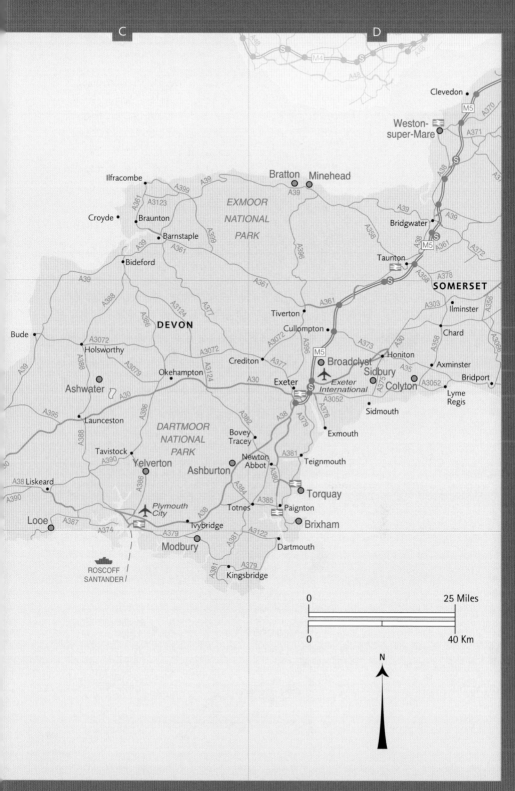

Map 2

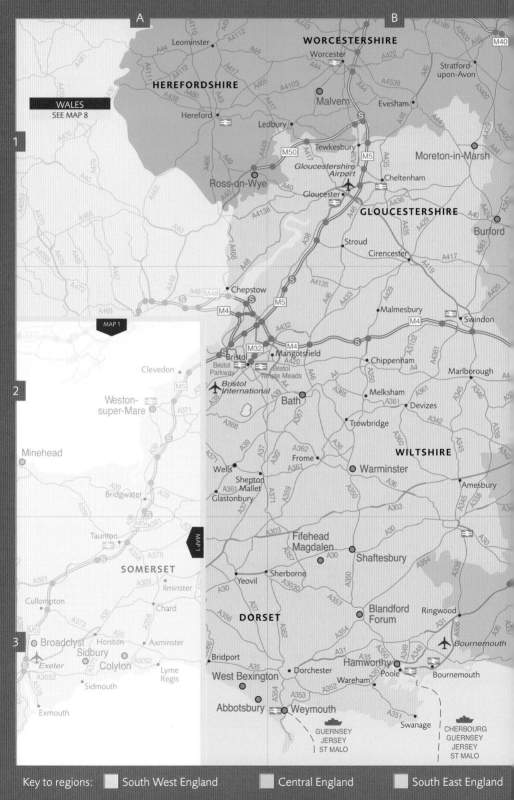

Key to regions: South West England • Central England • South East England

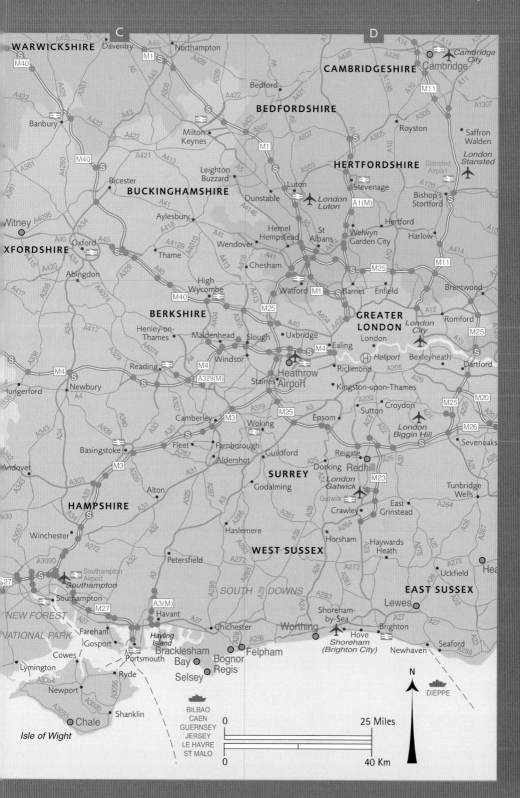

Map 2

Map 3

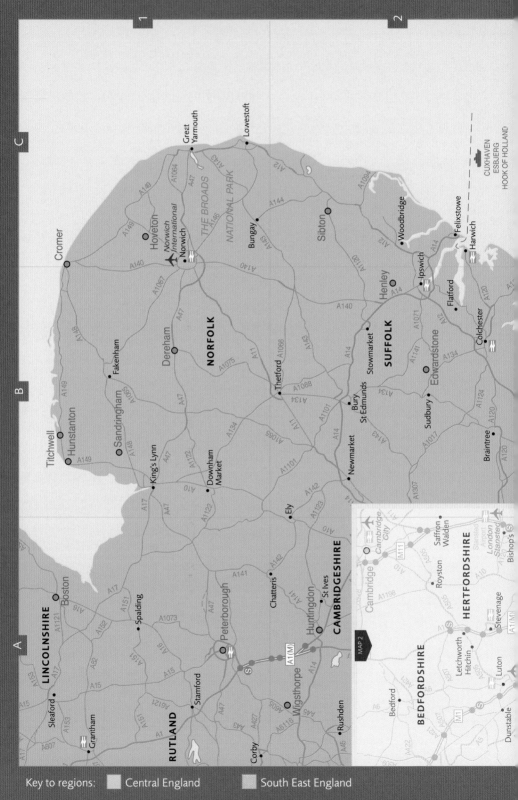

Key to regions: Central England   South East England

Map 3

Map 4

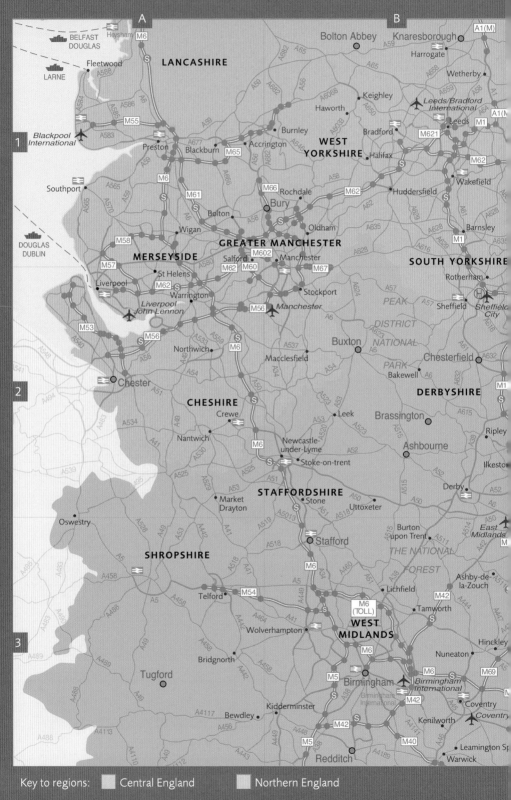

Key to regions: Central England | Northern England

Map 4

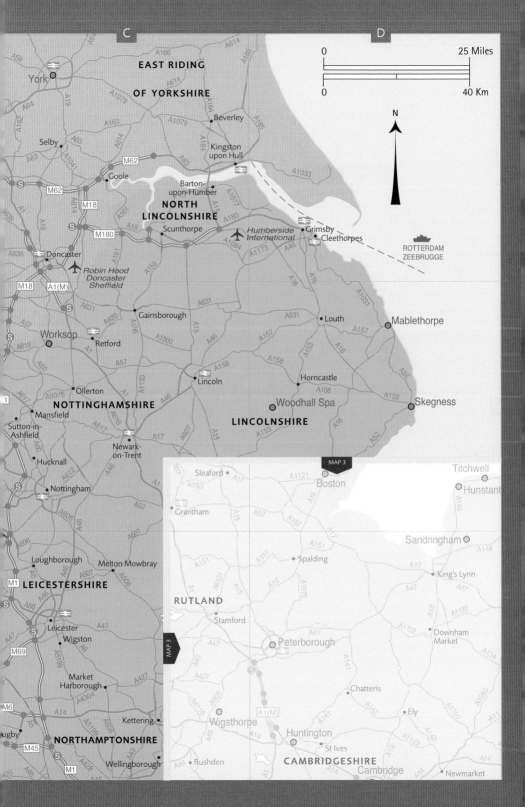

EAST RIDING OF YORKSHIRE

York

Selby

Beverley

Kingston upon Hull

Goole

Barton-upon-Humber

NORTH LINCOLNSHIRE

Scunthorpe

Grimsby
Cleethorpes

Humberside International

ROTTERDAM ZEEBRUGGE

Doncaster

Robin Hood Doncaster Sheffield

Gainsborough

Louth

Mablethorpe

Worksop

Retford

Lincoln

Horncastle

Skegness

Ollerton

Woodhall Spa

LINCOLNSHIRE

NOTTINGHAMSHIRE

Mansfield

Sutton-in-Ashfield

Hucknall

Newark-on-Trent

Nottingham

MAP 3

Sleaford

Boston

Titchwell

Hunstant

Grantham

Sandringham

Loughborough

Melton Mowbray

Spalding

King's Lynn

LEICESTERSHIRE

RUTLAND

Stamford

Peterborough

Downham Market

Leicester
Wigston

Market Harborough

Chatteris

Ely

Kettering

Wigsthorpe

Huntington

NORTHAMPTONSHIRE

St Ives

Cambridge

Newmarket

Wellingborough

Rushden

CAMBRIDGESHIRE

0 ——— 25 Miles
0 ——— 40 Km

N

All place names in blue have a detailed accommodation entry in this guide.

Map 5

A   B

1

SCOTLAND
SEE MAP 6

A74(M)

A74(M)

Berwick-
upon-
Tweed

Powburn

NORTHUMBERLAND

NATIONAL PARK

NORTHUMBERLAND

Bewcastle

Haydon
Bridge

Hexham

2

Carlisle

Carlisle

M6

CUMBRIA

Kirkoswald

Cornriggs

DURHAM

Workington

Penrith

Cockfield

Whitehaven

Newlands

Keswick

LAKE DISTRICT

NATIONAL PARK

Brough

M6

Ambleside

Windermere

Whinfell

Coniston

Kendal

Broughton
Mills

Oxenholme

3

YORKSHIRE DALES

NATIONAL PARK

Grange-
over-Sands

Barrow-
in-Furness

BELFAST
DOUGLAS

Morecambe

Lancaster

Heysham

M6

Map 5

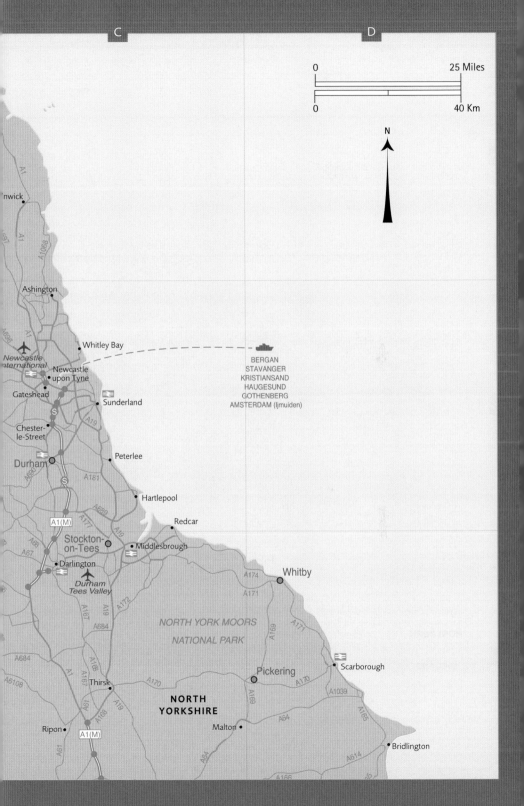

C   D

0   25 Miles

0   40 Km

N

nwick

Ashington

Whitley Bay

Newcastle International

Newcastle upon Tyne

Gateshead

Sunderland

S

Chester-le-Street

Durham

S

Peterlee

Hartlepool

Redcar

A1(M)

Stockton-on-Tees

Middlesbrough

Darlington

Durham Tees Valley

Whitby

NORTH YORK MOORS NATIONAL PARK

Scarborough

Pickering

Thirsk

NORTH YORKSHIRE

Ripon

A1(M)

Malton

Bridlington

BERGAN
STAVANGER
KRISTIANSAND
HAUGESUND
GOTHENBERG
AMSTERDAM (Ijmuiden)

Map 6

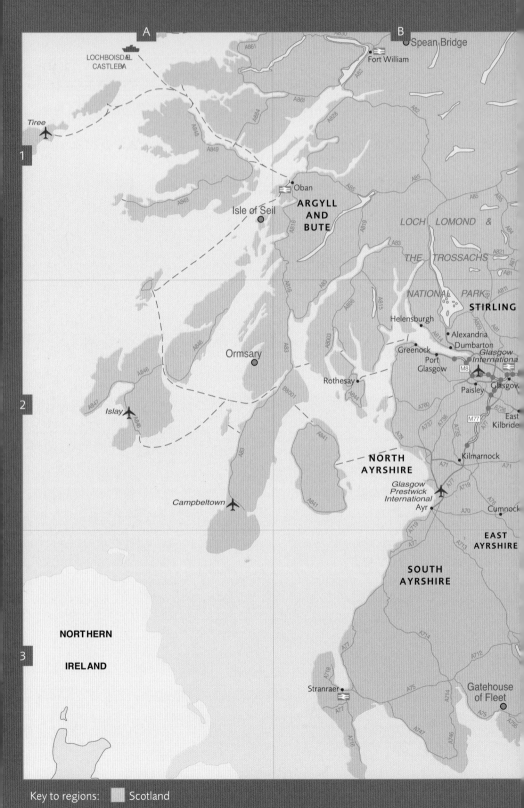

Key to regions: █ Scotland

Map 6

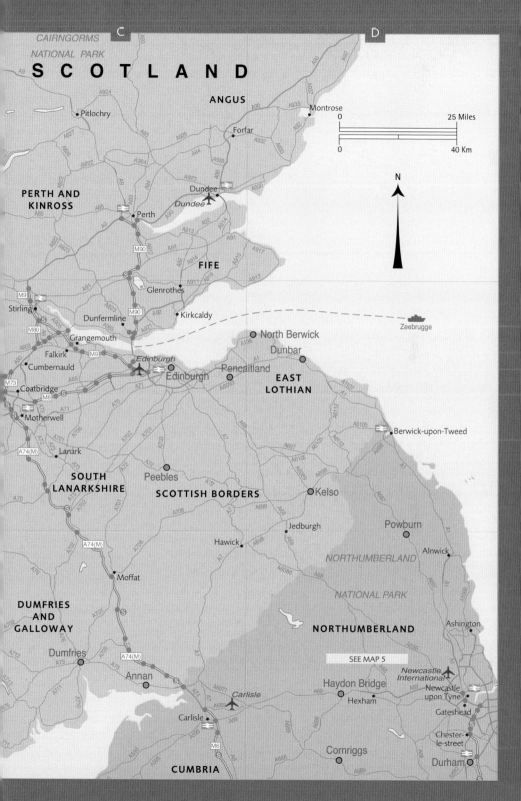

Map 7

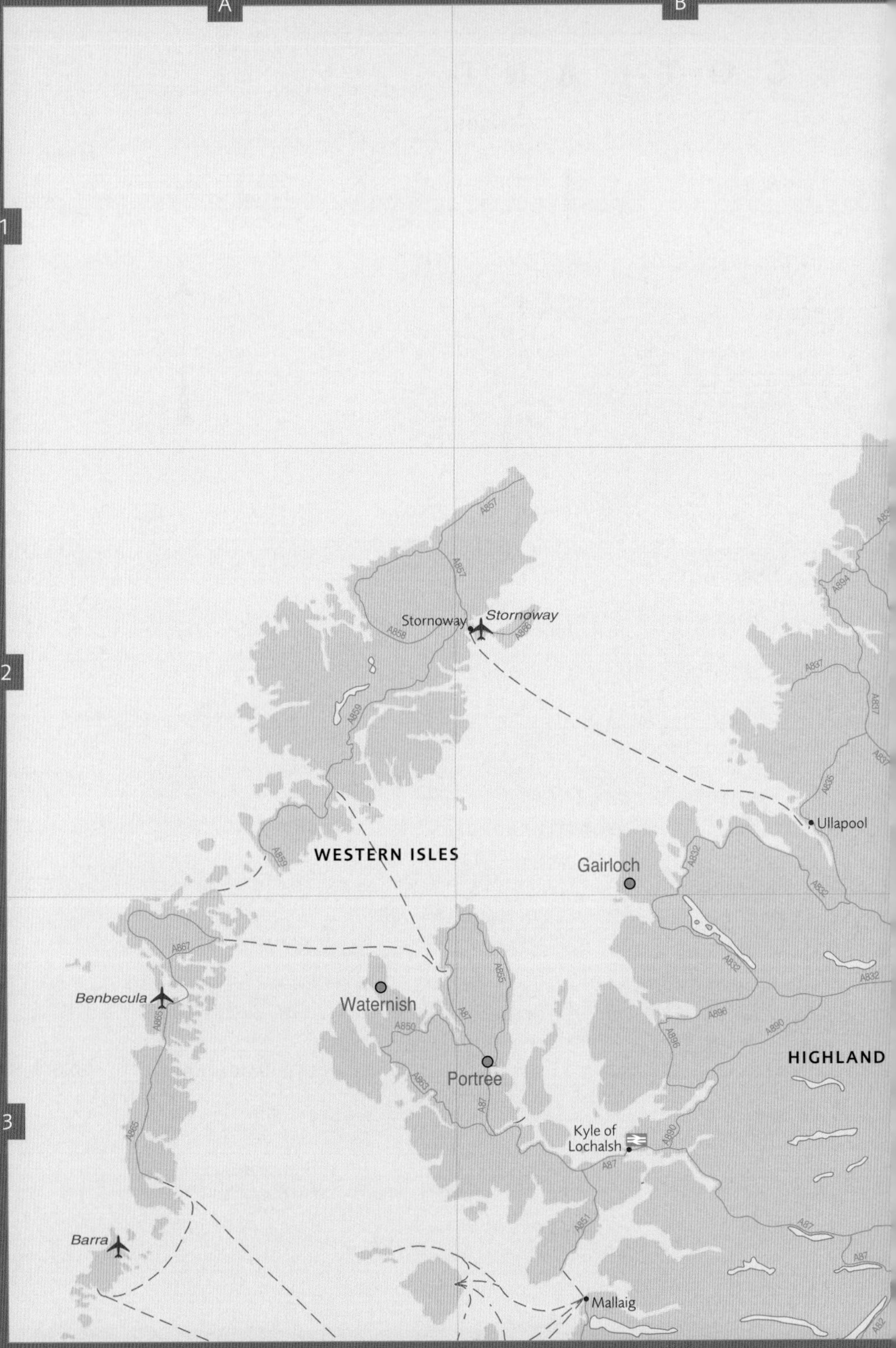

A
B
1
2
3
A857
Stornoway
Stornoway
A858
A866
A859
WESTERN ISLES
A867
Benbecula
A865
Barra
Waternish
A850
A855
A87
Portree
A863
Kyle of
Lochalsh
A851
Mallaig
Gairloch
A832
A835
A837
A894
Ullapool
A896
A890
HIGHLAND
A82

Key to regions: Scotland

Map 7

Shetland

Orkney

SCOTLAND

Papa
Westray
Westray
LERWICK
North Ronaldsay

ORKNEY

Sanday

Eday
Stronsay

Kirkwall
Kirkwall

Stromness

Hoy

N

0   25 Miles
0   40 Km

John o' Groats

Thurso

Wick
Wick

Unst

Fetlar

Scatsta
Whalsay

SHETLAND

Lerwick
Lerwick

Sumburgh

Fair
Isle

KIRKWALL
ABERDEEN

0   25 Miles
0   40 Km

Elgin
Fraserburgh

LERWICK

Nairn

Inverness
Inverness

Peterhead

MORAY

ABERDEENSHIRE

Aberdeen
Aberdeen

CAIRNGORMS
NATIONAL PARK
Ballater

Map 8

Key to regions: ▢ Wales

All place names in blue have a detailed accommodation entry in this guide.

Ford. A car for every trip.

If you or anyone you know receives the Higher Mobility Component of the Disability Living Allowance, it can be exchanged for a new Ford every three years on the Motability scheme. The car will be fully taxed, serviced and insured, and with a choice of models available with nil advance payment, getting to your destination will be just that little bit more enjoyable.

FordMobility | Feel the difference

www.ford.co.uk/mobility |

Disabled people are going places

Waterloo, Leeds, Glasgow, Leicester, Manchester, Hastings, Swansea, Colchester etc...

Isn't it time you caught up with them?

The Disabled Person's Railcard gives you a third off most rail tickets. The discount also applies to one adult companion travelling with you. Whether you're going for a day out or away for a longer holiday, the Disabled Person's Railcard makes perfect sense.

To find out if you qualify visit www.disabledpersons-railcard.co.uk or phone 0845 605 0525

 **National Rail**   **Disabled Person's Railcard**

SCENIC

The New Grand Scénic 5 Seat. With more boot space.

We've also packed it with new styling, an improved interior and the option of a 2.0 dCi diesel engine.
And it comes in two other models as well, the Grand Scénic 7 Seat and the original 5 Seat Scénic.
For details of how you can get any of the new Scénic range on the Motability scheme, visit

• Motability   **www.motability.renault.co.uk** or call **0800 387 626.**

Fuel consumption figures for the Grand Scénic 5 Seat 2.0 dCi 150 6 speed model in mpg (l/100km):
Urban 38.7 (7.3), Extra Urban 56.5 (5.0), Combined 48.7 (5.8). CO_2 emissions (g/km): 154.

Forests for All

Forestry Commission England welcomes visitors to our forests and woodlands. We manage hundreds of sites, many of which offer excellent access for people with disabilities to enjoy the varied landscapes, wildlife and recreational opportunities offered by England's forests.

There are thousands of kilometres of trails running throughout England's trees and woodlands, and many sites have trails on flatter ground for easy access (although some manual wheelchair users may need assistance on some sections).

However some of our woodlands due to their location and terrain have hilly, long or uneven paths that can be challenging for those with mobility issues. The Forestry Commission is working hard to open up more of our woodland landscape and making our sites more accessible to all.

Visitors can call 0845 FORESTS (0845 3673787) for advice on site accessibility.

Bedgebury, Kent
- New all-ability scenic walking routes promoting healthy living, including challenging health walks and calorie mapped trails.
- An all-terrain mobility buggy is available for hire if you fancy exploring off the beaten track.

Rosliston, The National Forest, Derbyshire
- Rosliston Forestry Centre provides motorised mobility scooters for people to borrow.
- There are also all-ability access forest lodges for disabled visitors who wish to stay the night.

Haldon, near Exeter in Devon, The Mamhead Sensory Trail
- Discover the breathtaking viewpoint at the Obelisk with its tactile interpretation board.
- There are plenty of resting places that have been enhanced with special interpretation features to stimulate your senses.

Forest of Dean, Gloucestershire
- Adapted cycles (including cycles for wheelchair users) are available for hire locally for the less-abled but still adventurous.
- A new facility from Forest Mobility 'Walking-on-Wheels' for hiring motorised scooters for anyone who would in the past have been restricted to short distance visits.

Dalby, North Yorkshire
- There are four all-ability trails with an electric buggy and two wheelchairs are available to hire from the Visitor Centre.

www.forestry.gov.uk/england

activewoods
naturally good for you

Forestry Commission England

The Camping and Caravanning Club

The friendly Club

Explore Britain through our sites...

routbeck Head Caravan Club Site

The Caravan Club.
Touring for all.

Low Manesty Caravan Club Site

The Caravan Club has around 200 sites throughout the UK. Over 140 of the sites have bathroom facilities for wheel chair users and a further 24 have extra handrails in amenity blocks.

70 Caravan Club Sites are graded under the Visit Britain National Accessible Scheme, each achieving M1 grading.

The Caravan Club is the first organisation of its kind to participate in this scheme and full details of the sites can be found in the 2008 Site Collection brochure.

THE
CARAVAN
CLUB

Morn Hill Caravan Club Site

Call today for your FREE 2008 Site Collection brochure on 0800 521 161 quoting RAD08 or visit www.caravanclub.co.uk

Dockray Meadow Caravan Club Site

Five UK Locations
Five Unique Experiences

Whatever your access needs, our staff will help you have a memorable day out. To find out more please call directly or visit **www.iwm.org.uk**

Imperial War Museum London: 020 7416 5320/5321
Churchill Museum and Cabinet War Rooms: 020 7930 6961
HMS *Belfast*: **020 7940 6300**
Imperial War Museum Duxford: 01223 835 000
Imperial War Museum North: 0161 836 4000

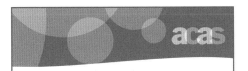

Acas answers over 900,000 calls a year on employment relations issues

Call **08457 47 47 47** for free and confidential advice about rights at work

08456 06 16 00 for minicom users

08456 00 34 44 for questions on managing equality in the workplace

www.acas.org.uk

BJK INSURANCE BROKERS LTD

If you are planning a holiday or trip you may need travel insurance. BJK are pleased to offer a range of travel insurance policies, enabling us to select the most suitable cover for each client.

From standard travel insurance to the more specialist travel policies covering hazardous pursuits, activity holidays and work abroad, for extended trips or 'Gap' years, for individuals, couples, families, groups, or even whole school trips.

We also have policies for persons aged up to age 85 & annual multi trip policies for persons aged up to 79.

Please contact Jennifer Franks for more information or a quotation
Tel: 01271 345005 or
jfranks@bjkinsurance.co.uk

BJK Insurance Brokers Ltd.
2nd Floor, Devonshire House, Riverside Road,
Pottington Business Park, Barnstaple, Devon , EX31 1EY

BJK Insurance Brokers Ltd. is Authorised and Regulated by the Financial Services Authority. The Financial Services Authority does not regulate all the forms of the products and services we provide.

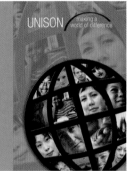

Official tourist board guide **Easy Access Britain**

Northern England

Lindisfarne Castle, Holy Island, Northumberland

Cheshire, County Durham, Cumbria, Greater Manchester, Lancashire, Merseyside, Northumberland, Tees Valley, Tyne and Wear, Yorkshire

The Lowry Gallery, Manchester

It's out of this **world...**

Windswept moors and breathtaking coastlines. Mirrored glass lakes and the magnificent cathedrals of York and Durham. The urban wonders of the Gateshead Millennium Bridge and Urbis in Manchester. Not forgetting all-year-round fun and games at Blackpool... **It's all just part of an ordinary day in England's proud and historic North.**

Built to impress

Northern England has more than its fair share of remarkable buildings. Alnwick Castle, magically transformed into a location for the renowned Harry Potter films, provides a memorable outing. While in the area, visit The Alnwick Garden with its unique water features – the aerial walkways and treehouse restaurant are accessible to everyone, including wheelchair users. Equally impressive is 900-year-old Durham cathedral which perches high above the city and the towering vaulted ceilings of York Minster, the largest medieval Gothic cathedral in Northern Europe. Built on simpler scales, the twin Anglo-Saxon monastery of Wearmouth-Jarrow, home to the Venerable Bede, is the UK's nomination for World Heritage Status in 2009.

Fountains Abbey, Britain's largest monastic ruin, and adjacent Studley Royal Water Garden, are must-sees. Art-lovers should plan a trip to Castle Howard where Canalettos, Holbeins and Gainsboroughs are just some of the art treasures on display. To view the work of William Morris, visit Liverpool's half-timbered Speke Hall. And if you're looking for a challenge The Forbidden Corner, Leyburn in Yorkshire, will live up to expectations as you get lost in the underground labyrinth of chambers and passages.

Roman Britain

Venture along Hadrian's Wall just as soldiers did nearly two millennia ago. The wall was a huge undertaking – 73 miles long and built in six years. Explore the many forts, milecastles and turrets that dot its length then bring their history lessons to life with a visit to Housesteads Fort, the most complete

Coniston, Cumbria

remaining outpost. The walled city of Chester is Britain's best-preserved Roman town – complete with partially excavated amphitheatre. The Dewa fortress – buried beneath the town – now lives on through the Dewa Roman Experience. If you feel inclined you can try on a suit of Roman armour and see, touch and smell just how it was!

Natural wonders

Wide-open spaces abound in the National Parks – Yorkshire alone has over 1,000 square miles to explore. Wander lonely as a cloud in the Lake District – home to William Wordsworth and Samuel Taylor Coleridge – and pay a visit to Mr McGregor's garden at the charming World of Beatrix Potter Attraction, Windermere. Can you sense mystical goings-on at Alderley Edge, Cheshire, linked to the legends of King Arthur? There's an accessible route that offers wonderful views from this Site of Special Scientific Interest. On the north-east coast take a boat to Holy Island to behold the treasured Lindisfarne Gospels. Don't forget the binoculars; the Farne Islands are home to hundreds of thousands of puffins and dewy-eyed grey seals.

Albert Dock, Liverpool

Inset pictures
Lancashire Hot Pot; the ruins of Fountains Abbey, North Yorkshire; town crier, Chester; spectacular views of NewcastleGateshead and the Tyne Bridge

Hands-on heritage

Meet people who once worked in cotton mills with a lifetime of stories to share with you at Quarry Bank Mill in Cheshire, and learn more about early industrialisation at the Armley Mills Leeds Industrial Museum. Get a taste of Victorian times at Saltaire World Heritage Site, a 'model' industrial village. Hear vivid tales at the National Coal Mining Museum in Wakefield, and let the youngsters try their skills at sweet making at the award-winning Beamish, The North of England Open Air Museum. Imagine once more the romantic age of steam on the Settle-Carlisle or East Lancashire Railway or gaze in wonder at the giant locomotives at the National Railway Museum in York and Locomotion in Shildon.

> From fearless Romans to John Lennon, there's an unbelievable range of attractions

City culture

Enjoy the renaissance of Newcastle and Gateshead, highlighted by the stunning architecture of the Gateshead Millennium Bridge. Check out new artists at the Baltic in Gateshead, the Centre for Contemporary Art, or listen to a favourite score at Opera North. Seven Stories, the Centre for Children's Books in Newcastle will touch your imagination and bring back childhood memories. Explore Liverpool, famed as the birthplace of The Beatles. You can follow in their footsteps, from the world-famous Cavern Club, to John Lennon's childhood home, Mendips, now in the care of the National Trust.

In Manchester head for Salford Quays and The Lowry, an inspirational waterfront centre for the visual arts and entertainment. The gallery scene embraces Manchester Art Gallery, the Cornerhouse and The Whitworth, and there's a choice of 50 free museums, including the Imperial War Museum North designed by Daniel Libeskind. Middlesbrough may not have attained city-status but the newly opened Middlesbrough Institute of Modern Art is a gallery of national importance, housing works by Emin, Hockney and Frink among others.

If you're young at heart head for Blackpool's Pleasure Beach or book ringside seats at the UK's best circus at the Blackpool Tower! Forget Sudoku, stimulate the brain cells at Rotherham's Magna, a science adventure centre where fun is unavoidable, or test out a fascinating world of hands-on exploration at Eureka! in Halifax.

Castle Howard, North Yorkshire

North East England

Find your Passion

World-famous for our friendliness and hospitality, come and share our passion for this wonderful region of coastline and castles, countryside and culture!

Want to experience our tranquil countryside and undiscovered coastline? Head for Kielder, where you can take a cruise on Europe's largest man-made lake, wander miles of forest paths and stay in a wheelchair-accessible forest village. Or take a boat trip from Seahouses, on the Northumberland Coast Area of Outstanding Natural Beauty, to see breeding puffins and grey seals on the Farne Islands.

Love your history? Come and marvel at Hadrian's Wall, still marking the northernmost limit of the Roman Empire after almost 2,000 years. You'll find amazing interactive exhibits and events at several of its forts, including Segedunum and Arbeia in North and South Tyneside respectively. You can board HMS Trincomalee, the oldest warship still afloat, at Hartlepool's Maritime Experience in Tees Valley. And at Beamish, The North of England Open Air Museum in Country Durham, you can travel back in time to 1825 and 1913 via an easy-access bus, to visit the town, farm, manor house and colliery village.

Main: Kielder Water and Forest Park, Northumberland
Above: Beamish, The North of England Open Air Museum, County Durham

Our cities are alive with world-class culture and fantastic shopping. Visit mima, Middlesbrough's Institute of Modern Art, or BALTIC, Centre for Contemporary Art, on NewcastleGateshead's Quayside, for vibrant and often highly provocative exhibitions. Nearby, The Sage Gateshead, an award-winning centre for music, offers breathtaking waterfront views and access to its café, restaurant and library whether you're attending a concert or not. Or why not treat yourself to some retail therapy at MetroCentre, Europe's largest shopping and leisure complex, or see beautiful glass being hand-made at the National Glass Centre, Sunderland?

Find out more, and book quality, accessible accommodation at **visitnortheastengland.com**. We look forward to welcoming you.

north east
england

Right: BALTIC and The Sage Gateshead on the NewcastleGateshead Quayside
Above right: Hartlepool's Maritime Experience, Tees Valley

Useful regional contacts

For information before you travel, check out the useful regional contacts below. Local Tourist Information Centres will also be able to give you information on accessible attractions and accommodation.

England's Northwest
t (01925) 400100
w visitenglandsnorthwest.com

One NorthEast Tourism Team
t 0870 160 1781
w visitnortheastengland.com

Yorkshire Tourist Board
t 0870 609 0000
w yorkshire.com

Publications

Access Guide to Blackpool
Available from Blackpool Tourism on (01253) 478222 or from visitblackpool.com.

Durham City Access for All
Available from Durham Tourist Information Centre.
Call (01938) 43720, email touristinfo@durhamcity.gov.uk or go to burrows.co.uk/durhamaccessguide.

Easy Going North York Moors
Available from the National Park Authority. Call (01845) 597426 or visit visitthemoors.co.uk.

Miles without Stiles
An online guide to 21 routes in the Lake District National Park for those with limited mobility. Available from lake-district.gov.uk.

Resources

Disability North
The Dene Centre, Castle Farm Road, Newcastle upon Tyne NE3 1PH
t (0191) 284 0480
e reception@disabilitynorth.org.uk
w disabilitynorth.org.uk
A charity offering advice on holidays in Newcastle-upon-Tyne.

Visit Chester
w visitchester.com
The official website of Chester tourism and a pilot site for a European access project.

Tourist Information Centres

When you arrive at your destination, visit a Tourist Information Centre for help with accommodation and information about local attractions and events, or email your request before you go.

Cheshire

Altrincham	20 Stamford New Road	(0161) 912 5931	tourist.information@trafford.gov.uk
Chester (Town Hall)	Northgate Street	(01244) 402111	tis@chestercc.gov.uk
Chester Visitor Centre	Vicars Lane	(01244) 402111	tis@chestercc.gov.uk
Congleton	High Street	(01260) 271095	tourism@congleton.gov.uk
Ellesmere Port	Kinsey Road	(0151) 356 7879	cheshireoaks-tic@hotmail.co.uk
Knutsford	Toft Road	(01565) 632611	ktic@macclesfield.gov.uk
Macclesfield	Town Hall	(01625) 504114	informationcentre@macclesfield.gov.uk
Nantwich	Church Walk	(01270) 610983	touristi@crewe-nantwich.gov.uk
Northwich	1 The Arcade	(01606) 353534	tourism@valeroyal.gov.uk
Warrington	Horsemarket Street	(01925) 428585	informationcentre@warrington.gov.uk
Wilmslow	Rectory Fields	(01625) 522275	i.hillaby@macclesfield.gov.uk

County Durham

Barnard Castle	Woodleigh, Flatts Road	(01833) 690909	tourism@teesdale.gov.uk
Bishop Auckland	Market Place	(01388) 604922	bishopauckland.tourisminfo@durham.gov.uk
Durham	2 Millennium Place	(0191) 384 3720	touristinfo@durhamcity.gov.uk
Middleton-in-Teesdale	10 Market Place	(01833) 641001	middletonplus@myzen.co.uk
Peterlee	4 Upper Yoden Way	(0191) 586 4450	touristinfo@peterlee.gov.uk
Stanhope	Durham Dales Centre	(01388) 527650	durham.dales.centre@durham.gov.uk

Cumbria

Alston Moor	Front Street	(01434) 382244	alston.tic@eden.gov.uk
Ambleside	Market Cross	(015394) 32582	amblesidetic@southlakeland.gov.uk
Appleby-in-Westmorland	Boroughgate	(017683) 51177	tic@applebytown.org.uk
Barrow-in-Furness	Duke Street	(01229) 894784	touristinfo@barrowbc.gov.uk
Bowness	Glebe Road	(015394) 42895	bownesstic@lake-district.gov.uk
Brampton*	Market Place	(016977) 3433	tourism@carlisle.gov.uk
Broughton in Furness	The Square	(01229) 716115	email@broughton-tic.fsnet.co.uk
Carlisle	Greenmarket	(01228) 625600	tourism@carlisle.gov.uk
Cockermouth	Market Street	(01900) 822634	email@cockermouth-tic.fsnet.co.uk
Coniston	Ruskin Avenue	(015394) 41533	mail@conistontic.org
Egremont	12 Main Street	(01946) 820693	email@egremont-tic.fsnet.co.uk

Grange-over-Sands	Main Street	(015395) 34026	grangetic@southlakeland.gov.uk
Kendal	Highgate	(01539) 725758	kendaltic@southlakeland.gov.uk
Keswick	Market Square	(017687) 72645	keswicktic@lake-district.gov.uk
Kirkby Lonsdale	24 Main Street	(015242) 71437	kltic@southlakeland.gov.uk
Kirkby Stephen	Market Street	(017683) 71199	ks.tic@eden.gov.uk
Maryport	Senhouse Street	(01900) 812101	maryporttic@allerdale.gov.uk
Millom*	Station Road	(01229) 774819	millomtic@copelandbc.gov.uk
Penrith	Middlegate	(01768) 867466	pen.tic@eden.gov.uk
Rheged	Redhills, Penrith	(01768) 860034	tic@rheged.com
Sedbergh	72 Main Street	(015396) 20125	tic@sedbergh.org.uk
Silloth-on-Solway	Liddell Street	(016973) 31944	sillothtic@allerdale.gov.uk
Southwaite	M6 Service Area	(016974) 73445	southwaitetic@visitscotland.com
Ullswater	Glenridding	(017684) 82414	ullswatertic@lake-district.gov.uk
Ulverston	County Square	(01229) 587120	ulverstontic@southlakeland.gov.uk
Whitehaven	Market Place	(01946) 598914	tic@copelandbc.gov.uk
Windermere	Victoria Street	(015394) 46499	windermeretic@southlakeland.gov.uk
Workington	21 Finkle Street	(01900) 606699	workingtontic@allerdale.gov.uk

Greater Manchester

Bolton	Le Mans Crescent	(01204) 334321	tourist.info@bolton.gov.uk
Bury	Market Street	(0161) 253 5111	touristinformation@bury.gov.uk
Manchester Visitor Information Centre	Lloyd Street	0871 222 8223	touristinformation@ marketing-manchester.co.uk
Oldham	12 Albion Street	(0161) 627 1024	ecs.tourist@oldham.gov.uk
Saddleworth	High Street, Uppermill	(01457) 870336	ecs.tourist@oldham.gov.uk
Salford	Salford Quays	(0161) 848 8601	tic@salford.gov.uk
Stockport	30 Market Place	(0161) 474 4444	tourist.information@stockport.gov.uk
Wigan	Trencherfield Mill	(01942) 825677	tic@wlct.org

Lancashire

Accrington	Blackburn Road	(01254) 380293	tourism@hyndburnbc.gov.uk
Ashton-under-Lyne	Wellington Road	(0161) 343 4343	tourist.information@mail.tameside.gov.uk
Barnoldswick	Fernlea Avenue	(01282) 666704	tourist.info@pendle.gov.uk
Blackburn	50-54 Church Street	(01254) 53277	visit@blackburn.gov.uk
Blackpool	1 Clifton Street	(01253) 478222	tourism@blackpool.gov.uk
Blackpool*	Central Promenade	(01253) 478222	tourism@blackpool.gov.uk
Burnley	Croft Street	(01282) 664421	tic@burnley.gov.uk
Cleveleys	Victoria Square	(01253) 853378	cleveleystic@wyrebc.gov.uk
Clitheroe	12-14 Market Place	(01200) 425566	tourism@ribblevalley.gov.uk
Fleetwood	The Esplanade	(01253) 773953	fleetwoodtic@wyrebc.gov.uk
Garstang	High Street	(01995) 602125	garstangtic@wyrebc.gov.uk
Lancaster	29 Castle Hill	(01524) 32878	lancastertic@lancaster.gov.uk
Lytham St Annes	67 St Annes Road West	(01253) 725610	touristinformation@fylde.gov.uk

Morecambe	Marine Road Central	(01524) 582808	morecambevic@lancaster.gov.uk
Pendle Heritage Centre	Park Hill	(01282) 661701	heritage.centre@pendle.gov.uk
Preston	Lancaster Road	(01772) 253731	tourism@preston.gov.uk
Rochdale	The Esplanade	(01706) 864928	tic@link4life.org

Merseyside

Liverpool	John Lennon Airport	(0151) 907 1057	08place@liverpool.gov.uk
Liverpool 08 Place	Whitechapel	(0151) 233 2008	08place@liverpool.gov.uk
St Helens	Chalon Way East	(01744) 755150	info@sthelenstic.com
Southport	112 Lord Street	(01704) 533333	info@visitsouthport.com

Northumberland

Adderstone	Adderstone Services	(01668) 213678	
Alnwick	2 The Shambles	(01665) 511333	alnwicktic@alnwick.gov.uk
Amble*	Queen Street Car Park	(01665) 712313	ambletic@alnwick.gov.uk
Bellingham	Main Street	(01434) 220616	bellinghamtic@btconnect.com
Berwick-upon-Tweed	106 Marygate	(01289) 330733	tourism@berwick-upon-tweed.gov.uk
Corbridge*	Hill Street	(01434) 632815	corbridgetic@btconnect.com
Craster*	Craster Car Park	(01665) 576007	crastertic@alnwick.gov.uk
Haltwhistle	Station Road	(01434) 322002	haltwhistletic@btconnect.com
Hexham	Wentworth Car Park	(01434) 652220	hexham.tic@tynedale.gov.uk
Morpeth	Bridge Street	(01670) 500700	tourism@castlemorpeth.gov.uk
Once Brewed*	Military Road	(01434) 344396	tic.oncebrewed@nnpa.org.uk
Otterburn	Otterburn Mill	(01830) 520093	tic@otterburnmill.co.uk
Rothbury*	Church Street	(01669) 620887	tic.rothbury@nnpa.org.uk
Seahouses*	Seafield Car Park	(01665) 720884	seahousestic@berwick-upon-tweed.gov.uk
Wooler*	12 Padgepool Place	(01668) 282123	woolertic@berwick-upon-tweed.gov.uk

Tees Valley

Darlington	13 Horsemarket	(01325) 388666	tic@darlington.gov.uk
Guisborough	Church Street	(01287) 633801	guisborough_tic@redcar-cleveland.gov.uk
Hartlepool	Church Square	(01429) 869706	hpooltic@hartlepool.gov.uk
Middlesbrough	99-101 Albert Road	(01642) 729700	middlesbrough_tic@middlesbrough.gov.uk
Redcar	West Terrace	(01642) 471921	redcar_tic@redcar-cleveland.gov.uk
Saltburn-by-the-Sea	3 Station Square	(01287) 622422	saltburn_tic@redcar-cleveland.gov.uk
Stockton-on-Tees	Church Road	(01642) 528130	touristinformation@stockton.gov.uk

Tyne and Wear

Gateshead (Central Library)	Prince Consort Road	(0191) 433 8400	tic@gateshead.gov.uk
Gateshead (Information Centre)	Gateshead Quays	(0191) 478 4222	tourism@gateshead.gov.uk
Newcastle International Airport		(0191) 214 4422	niatic@hotmail.com

Newcastle upon Tyne 8-9 Central Arcade (City centre)		(0191) 277 8000	tourist.info@newcastle.gov.uk
Newcastle upon Tyne Quayside (Guildhall)		(0191) 277 8000	tourist.info@newcastle.gov.uk
North Shields	Royal Quays Outlet Shopping	(0191) 200 5895	ticns@northtyneside.gov.uk
South Shields	Ocean Road	(0191) 454 6612	museum.tic@southtyneside.gov.uk
South Shields (Amphitheatre)*	Sea Road	(0191) 455 7411	foreshore.tic@southtyneside.gov.uk
Sunderland	50 Fawcett Street	(0191) 553 2000	tourist.info@sunderland.gov.uk
Whitley Bay	Park Road	(0191) 200 8535	ticwb@northtyneside.gov.uk

Yorkshire

Aysgarth Falls	Aysgarth Falls National Park Centre	(01969) 662910	aysgarth@ytbtic.co.uk
Barnsley	Central Library	(01226) 206757	barnsley@ytbtic.co.uk
Batley	Bradford Road	(01924) 426670	batley@ytbtic.co.uk
Beverley	34 Butcher Row	(01482) 867430	beverley.tic@eastriding.gov.uk
Bradford	City Hall	(01274) 433678	tourist.information@bradford.gov.uk
Bridlington	25 Prince Street	(01262) 673474	bridlington.tic@eastriding.gov.uk
Brigg	Market Place	(01652) 657053	brigg.tic@northlincs.gov.uk
Cleethorpes	42-43 Alexandra Road	(01472) 323111	cleetic@nelincs.gov.uk
Danby*	Lodge Lane	(01439) 772737	moorscentre@northyorkmoors-npa.gov.uk
Doncaster	38-40 High Street	(01302) 734309	tourist.information@doncaster.gov.uk
Filey*	John Street	(01723) 383636	tourismbureau@scarborough.gov.uk
Grassington	Hebden Road	(01756) 751690	grassington@ytbtic.co.uk
Guisborough	Church Street	(01287) 633801	guisborough_tic@redcar-cleveland.gov.uk
Halifax	Piece Hall	(01422) 368725	halifax@ytbtic.co.uk
Harrogate	Crescent Road	(01423) 537300	tic@harrogate.gov.uk
Hawes	Station Yard	(01969) 666210	hawes@ytbtic.co.uk
Haworth	2/4 West Lane	(01535) 642329	haworth@ytbtic.co.uk
Hebden Bridge	New Road	(01422) 843831	hebdenbridge@ytbtic.co.uk
Helmsley	Castlegate	(01439) 770173	helmsley@ytbtic.co.uk
Holmfirth	49-51 Huddersfield Road	(01484) 222444	holmfirth.tic@kirklees.gov.uk
Hornsea*	120 Newbegin	(01964) 536404	hornsea.tic@eastriding.gov.uk
Horton in Ribblesdale	Pen-y-ghent Cafe	(01729) 860333	horton@ytbtic.co.uk
Huddersfield	3 Albion Street	(01484) 223200	huddersfield.tic@kirklees.gov.uk
Hull	1 Paragon Street	(01482) 223559	tourist.information@hullcc.gov.uk
Humber Bridge	Ferriby Road	(01482) 640852	humberbridge.tic@eastriding.gov.uk
Ilkley	Station Road	(01943) 602319	ilkley@ytbtic.co.uk
Ingleton*	The Community Centre Car Park	(015242) 41049	ingleton@ytbtic.co.uk
Knaresborough	9 Castle Courtyard	08453 866886	kntic@harrogate.gov.uk

Leeds	The Arcade, City Station	(0113) 242 5242	tourinfo@leeds.gov.uk
Leeming Bar	The Great North Road	(01677) 424262	leeming@ytbtic.co.uk
Leyburn	4 Central Chambers	(01969) 623069	leyburn@ytbtic.co.uk
Malham		(01969) 652380	malham@ytbtic.co.uk
Malton	58 Market Place	(01653) 600048	maltontic@btconnect.com
Northallerton	Applegarth Car Park	(01609) 776864	northallerton@ytbtic.co.uk
Otley	Nelson Street	(01943) 462485	otleytic@leedslearning.net
Pateley Bridge*	18 High Street	(01423) 711147	pbtic@harrogate.gov.uk
Pickering	The Ropery	(01751) 473791	pickering@ytbtic.co.uk
Redcar	West Terrace	(01642) 471921	redcar_tic@redcar-cleveland.gov.uk
Reeth	The Green	(01748) 884059	reeth@ytbtic.co.uk
Richmond	Friary Gardens	(01748) 850252	richmond@ytbtic.co.uk
Ripon*	Minster Road	(01765) 604625	ripontic@harrogate.gov.uk
Rotherham Visitor Centre	40 Bridgegate	(01709) 835904	tic@rotherham.gov.uk
Saltburn-by-the-sea	Station Square	(01287) 622422	saltburn_tic@redcar-cleveland.gov.uk
Scarborough	Brunswick Centre	(01723) 383636	tourismbureau@scarborough.gov.uk
Scarborough (Harbourside)	Sandside	(01723) 383636	tourismbureau@scarborough.gov.uk
Scunthorpe	Carlton Street	(01724) 297354	brigg.tic@northlincs.gov.uk
Selby	52 Micklegate	(01757) 212181	selby@ytbtic.co.uk
Settle	Cheapside	(01729) 825192	settle@ytbtic.co.uk
Sheffield	Winter Garden	(0114) 221 1900	visitor@sheffield.gov.uk
Skipton	35 Coach Street	(01756) 792809	skipton@ytbtic.co.uk
Sutton Bank	Sutton Bank	(01845) 597426	suttonbank@ytbtic.co.uk
Thirsk	49 Market Place	(01845) 522755	thirsktic@hambleton.gov.uk
Todmorden	15 Burnley Road	(01706) 818181	todmorden@ytbtic.co.uk
Wakefield	9 The Bull Ring	0845 601 8353	tic@wakefield.gov.uk
Wetherby	17 Westgate	(01937) 582151	wetherbytic@leedslearning.net
Whitby	Langborne Road	(01723) 383637	tourismbureau@scarborough.gov.uk
Withernsea*	131 Queen Street	(01964) 615683	withernsea@ytbtic.gov.uk
York (De Grey Rooms)	Exhibition Square	(01904) 550099	tourism@yorkvic.co.uk
York (Railway Station)	Station Road	(01904) 550099	tourism@yorkvic.co.uk

* seasonal opening

ALNWICK, Northumberland — SELF CATERING

★★★–★★★★★★
SELF CATERING

Village Farm contact Mrs Crissy Stoker, Town Foot Farm, Shilbottle, Alnwick NE66 2HG **t** (01665) 575591 **f** (01665) 575591 **e** crissy@villagefarmcottages.co.uk **w** villagefarmcottages.co.uk

AMBLESIDE, Cumbria Map ref 5A3 — HOTEL

★★★
**HOTEL
SILVER AWARD**

B&B per room per night
**s £85.00–£135.00
d £135.00–£210.00**
HB per person per night
£95.00–£165.00

Rothay Manor

Rothay Bridge, Ambleside LA22 0EH **t** (015394) 33605
f (015394) 33607
e hotel@rothaymanor.co.uk **w** rothaymanor.co.uk

Access ☺

General ⛺ P♿ ✂ ♥ 🍴 ❀

Rooms 🛁 🛈 ♨ ⛏ 📺 🖨

Payment Credit/debit cards, cash/cheques

1 room and 1 suite adapted for wheelchair users; roll-in showers; shower chairs; dedicated wheelchair access; disabled parking.

Regency country-house hotel in its own landscaped gardens in the heart of the Lake District, renowned for the warm, comfortable, friendly atmosphere and excellent food and wine. Family owned and run for 40 years, the hotel makes an excellent base for sightseeing. Special interest holidays and mid-week breaks available. Closed 3 to 25 January.

bedrooms 6 double, 4 twin, 1 single, 5 family, 3 suites
bathrooms All en suite

From M6 jct 36 follow A591 to Ambleside. At Ambleside, turn left at traffic lights and left again 0.25 miles further on. Hotel on right.

AMBLESIDE, Cumbria — SELF CATERING

★★★★
SELF CATERING

The Larches contact Mrs Susan Jackson, Heart of the Lakes, Fisherbeck Mill, Old Lake Road, Ambleside LA22 0DH **t** (015394) 32321 **f** (015394) 33251 **e** info@heartofthelakes.co.uk

AMBLESIDE, Cumbria

See also entry on p90

ARMATHWAITE, Cumbria — CAMPING & CARAVANNING

★★★★
TOURING PARK

Englethwaite Hall Caravan Club Site Armathwaite, Carlisle CA4 9SY
t (01228) 560202
w caravanclub.co.uk

At-a-glance symbols are explained on the flap inside the back cover.

ARNSIDE, Cumbria — GUEST ACCOMMODATION

★★★★
GUEST ACCOMMODATION

Willowfield Hotel 53 The Promenade, Arnside LA5 0AD **t** (01524) 761354
e info@willowfield.uk.com **w** willowfield.uk.com

BAMBURGH, Northumberland — SELF CATERING

★★★★
SELF CATERING

Dukesfield Farm Holiday Cottages contact Mrs Maria Eliana Robinson,
EMR Properties, The Glebe, Radcliffe Road, Bamburgh NE69 7AE
t (01668) 214456 **f** (01668) 214354
e eric_j_robinson@compuserve.com **w** secretkingdom.com/dukes/field.htm

BARDON MILL, Northumberland — GUEST ACCOMMODATION

♦♦♦♦♦
GUEST ACCOMMODATION
GOLD AWARD

Montcoffer Bardon Mill, Hexham NE47 7HZ **t** (01434) 344138
e john-dehlia@talk21.com **w** montcoffer.co.uk

BARNARD CASTLE, County Durham — SELF CATERING

★★★★
SELF CATERING

Hauxwell Grange Cottages (The Stone Byre and Curlew Cottage)
contact Mrs Val Pearson,
Hauxwell Grange Cottages (The Stone Byre and Curlew Cottage), Hauxwell Grange,
Barnard Castle DL12 8QU **t** (01833) 695022 **f** (01833) 695022
e hauxwellvmp@supaworld.com **w** hauxwellgrangecottages.co.uk

BELFORD, Northumberland — SELF CATERING

★★★★
SELF CATERING

Elwick Farm Cottages contact Mrs Roslyn Reay, Elwick Farm Cottages, Elwick,
Belford NE70 7EL **t** (01668) 213242 **f** (01668) 213783
e w.r.reay@talk21.com **w** elwickcottages.co.uk

BERWICK-UPON-TWEED, Northumberland — GUEST ACCOMMODATION

★★★★
GUEST HOUSE

Meadow Hill Guest House Duns Road, Berwick-upon-Tweed TD15 1UB
t (01289) 306325 **f** (01289) 307466
e pammewing@onetel.com **w** meadow-hill.co.uk

BERWICK-UPON-TWEED, Northumberland — SELF CATERING

★★★–★★★★★
SELF CATERING

West Ord Holiday Cottages contact Mrs Carol Lang, West Ord Holiday Cottages,
West Ord Farm, Berwick-upon-Tweed TD15 2XQ
t (01289) 386631 **f** (01289) 386800
e stay@westord.co.uk **w** westord.co.uk

BERWICK-UPON-TWEED, Northumberland — CAMPING & CARAVANNING

★★★★
TOURING &
CAMPING PARK

Seaview Caravan Club Site Billendean Road, Berwick-upon-Tweed TD15 1QU
t (01289) 305198
w caravanclub.co.uk

BEVERLEY, East Riding of Yorkshire — GUEST ACCOMMODATION

★★★★
GUEST ACCOMMODATION

Rudstone Walk Country B&B South Cave, Nr Beverley HU15 2AH
t (01430) 422230 **f** (01430) 424552
e sylvia@rudstone-walk.co.uk **w** rudstone-walk.co.uk

BEVERLEY, East Riding of Yorkshire — SELF CATERING

★★–★★★★★
SELF CATERING

Rudstone Walk Country Accommodation contact Sylvia Spinks,
Rudstone Walk Country Accommodation, Brough HU15 2AH
t (01430) 422230 **f** (01430) 424552
e sylvia@rudstone-walk.co.uk **w** rudstone-walk.co.uk

BEWCASTLE, Cumbria

See entry on p90

BINGFIELD, Northumberland	SELF CATERING

★★★★★

SELF CATERING

The Hytte contact Mr & Mrs S R Gregory, The Hytte, Bingfield, Hexham NE46 4HR
t (01434) 672321 **f** (01434) 672321
e sgregory001@tiscali.co.uk **w** thehytte.com

BISPHAM, Lancashire	SELF CATERING

★★★★–★★★★★

SELF CATERING

Burbage Holiday Lodge **t** (01253) 356657
e enquires@burbageholidaylodge.co.uk **w** burbageholidaygroup.co.uk

BLACKPOOL, Lancashire	HOTEL

★★★★

HOTEL

Awaiting
NAS rating

Big Blue Hotel Ocean Boulevard, Pleasure Beach, Blackpool FY4 1ND
t 0845 367 3333 **f** (01253) 400046
e reservations@bigbluehotel.com **w** bigbluehotel.com

BLACKPOOL, Lancashire	HOTEL

★★

HOTEL

New Mayfair 673-677 New South Promenade, Blackpool FY4 1RN
t (01253) 347543 **f** (01253) 349678
e NewMayfair@arthritiscare.org.uk **w** newmayfairhotel.co.uk

BLACKPOOL, Lancashire	GUEST ACCOMMODATION

◆◆◆

GUEST ACCOMMODATION

Holmsdale Hotel 6-8 Pleasant Street, Blackpool FY1 2JA
t (01253) 621008 **f** 0870 133 1487
e office@holmsdalehotel-blackpool.com **w** holmsdalehotel-blackpool.com

BLACKPOOL, Lancashire	GUEST ACCOMMODATION

★★★★

GUEST ACCOMMODATION

Pembroke Hotel 11 King Edward Avenue, Blackpool FY2 9TD
t (01253) 351306 **f** (01253) 351306
e info@neartheprom.com **w** neartheprom.com

At-a-glance symbols are explained on the flap inside the back cover.

BOLTON ABBEY, North Yorkshire Map ref 4B1 — CAMPING & CARAVANNING

★★★★★
TOURING PARK

⊟ (57) £13.60–£25.60
⊟ (57) £13.60–£25.60
57 touring pitches

Strid Wood Caravan Club Site
Skipton BD23 6AN **t** (01756) 710433
w caravanclub.co.uk

One of the prettiest sites on the network, part of the Bolton Abbey estate, in an open glade surrounded by woodland and the glorious Yorkshire Dales. Within the boundaries of the estate are some 75 miles of footpaths through moors, woods and farmland. Open March to January.

General 🖵 P 🔌 🛍 🍴 ⓦⓟ 🕼 ☉ 🛢 🗄

Payment Credit/debit cards, cash/cheques

THE
CARAVAN
CLUB

BOSLEY, Cheshire — SELF CATERING

★★★
SELF CATERING

The Old Byre contact Mrs Dorothy Gilman, The Old Byre, Pye Ash Farm, Leek Road, Macclesfield SK11 0PN **t** (01260) 223293 **f** (01260) 223293
e d.gilman@hotmail.co.uk

BOSLEY, Cheshire — SELF CATERING

★★★
SELF CATERING

Strawberry Duck Holidays contact Mr Bruce Carter, Strawberry Duck Holidays, Bryher Cottage, Bullgate Lane, Macclesfield SK11 0PP
t (01260) 223591 **f** (01260) 223591

BOWES, County Durham — SELF CATERING

★★★★
SELF CATERING

Mellwaters Barn contact Mr Andrew Tavener, Mellwaters Barn, East Mellwaters Farm, Stainmore Road, Bowes, Barnard Castle DL12 9RH
t (01833) 628181 **f** (01833) 628020
e mellwatesbarn@aol.com **w** mellwatersbarn.co.uk

BOWNESS-ON-SOLWAY, Cumbria — GUEST ACCOMMODATION

★★
BED & BREAKFAST

The Old Chapel Meadow View, Bowness-on-Solway, Wigton CA7 5BL
t (01697) 351126
e oldchapelbowness@hotmail.com **w** oldchapelbownessonsolway.com

BRIDLINGTON, East Riding of Yorkshire — HOTEL

★★
HOTEL

The Bay View Hotel 52 South Marine Drive, Bridlington YO15 3JJ
t (01262) 674225 **f** (01262) 678070
e info@bay-view-hotel.com **w** bay-view-hotel.com

BRIDLINGTON, East Riding of Yorkshire — GUEST ACCOMMODATION

★★★★
GUEST ACCOMMODATION

Providence Place 11 North View Terrace, Bridlington YO15 2QP **t** (01262) 603840
e enquiries@providenceplace.info

BROUGHTON MILLS, Cumbria Map ref 5A3 — SELF CATERING

★★★★
SELF CATERING

Units **1**
Sleeps **1–6**

Low season per wk
Min £250.00
High season per wk
Max £895.00

Swallows Nest, Broughton-in-Furness

contact Janet Johnson, Hobkinground Farm, Broughton Mills,
Broughton-in-Furness LA20 6AU **t** (01229) 716338
e enquiries@hobkinground.co.uk **w** hobkinground.co.uk

Spacious, three-bedroomed
Lakeland cottage, furnished to a
high standard. Centrally heated,
open fire, exposed beams, well-
equipped kitchen. Level access,
ground-floor bedroom with en suite
wet room. Ample parking.
open All year
nearest shop 3 miles
nearest pub 0.5 miles

General 🛏 🎬 🔥 P ⚡ ◐ S
Unit 🛋 🎖 🔲 🔳 🔊 🔟 👜 🔧

Payment Cash/cheques

BURTON-IN-LONSDALE, North Yorkshire — SELF CATERING

★★★★
SELF CATERING

Brentwood Farm Cottages contact Anita Taylor, Brentwood Farm Cottages,
Barnoldswick Lane, Burton in Lonsdale LA6 3LZ **t** (01524) 262155 **f** (01524) 262155
e info@brentwoodfarmcottages.co.uk **w** brentwoodfarmcottages.co.uk

BURY, Greater Manchester Map ref 4B1 — CAMPING & CARAVANNING

★★★★★
TOURING PARK

🚐 (85) £13.60–£25.60
🚎 (85) £13.60–£25.60
85 touring pitches

THE
CARAVAN
CLUB

Burrs Country Park Caravan Club Site

Woodhill Road, Bury BL8 1BN **t** (0161) 761 0489
w caravanclub.co.uk

General P 🔌 🚻 📶 🐾 🔟

Payment Credit/debit cards,
cash/cheques

On an historic mill site, Burrs has
much to offer with relaxing river
and countryside walks,
contemporary art, and the East
Lancashire Steam Railway
passing by. The country park is
easily accessible, situated just
north of Bury town centre and is
handy for trips into Manchester.
open All year

*From A676 (signposted
Ramsbottom), follow signs for
Burrs Country Park.*

CARLISLE, Cumbria — GUEST ACCOMMODATION

★★★★★
GUEST HOUSE
GOLD AWARD

Bessiestown Catlowdy, Longtown, Carlisle CA6 5QP
t (01228) 577219 **f** (01228) 577019
e info@bessiestown.co.uk **w** bessiestown.co.uk

At-a-glance symbols are explained on the flap inside the back cover.

CATON, Lancashire — SELF CATERING

★★★★
SELF CATERING &
SERVICED APARTMENTS

Croft (The) – Ground Floor Apartment contact Mrs Sue Brierly-Hampton, Croft (The) - Ground Floor Apartment, 4 The Croft, Caton, Lancaster LA2 9QG
t (01524) 770725
e suebrierly@hotmail.com

CHESTER, Cheshire — HOTEL

★★★
HOTEL

Grosvenor Pulford Hotel Wrexham Road, Pulford, Chester CH4 9DG
t (01244) 570560 f (01244) 570809
e reservations@grosvenorpulfordhotel.co.uk w grosvenorpulfordhotel.co.uk

CHESTER, Cheshire Map ref 4A2 — CAMPING & CARAVANNING

★★★★★
TOURING &
CAMPING PARK

🚐 (100)
£14.30–£27.70
🚍 (100)
£14.30–£27.70
100 touring pitches

Awaiting
NAS rating

THE
CARAVAN
CLUB

Chester Fairoaks Caravan Club Site

Rake Lane, Little Stanney, Chester CH2 4HS t (0151) 355 1600
w caravanclub.co.uk

A very pleasant, open and level site with oak trees on the boundary, conveniently placed just off the M53 and close to the delightful walled city of Chester, gateway to North Wales. Take an open-top bus or walk around the walls to absorb the colourful atmosphere.

open All year

General P 🍴 🛁 🍽 WP 🐾 ☺ 📱🖥
☼

Leisure ⚠

Payment Credit/debit cards,
cash/cheques

From the M53 take jct 10 and join the A5117. Travel towards Queensferry, follow the brown signs. Turn left in Little Stanney at signpost Chorlton. Site 0.25 miles on left.

CHIPPING, Lancashire — HOTEL

★★★★
HOTEL

The Gibbon Bridge Hotel Chipping, Forest of Bowland, Preston PR3 2TQ
t (01995) 61456 f (01995) 61277
e reception@gibbon-bridge.co.uk w gibbon-bridge.co.uk

CLITHEROE, Lancashire — HOTEL

★★★
HOTEL

Mytton Fold Hotel and Golf Complex Whalley Road, Langho, Ribble Valley BB6 8AB t (01254) 240662 f (01254) 248119
e enquiries@myttonfold.co.uk w myttonfold.co.uk

CLITHEROE, Lancashire — SELF CATERING

★★★★
SELF CATERING

Higher Gills Farm contact Mrs Freda Pilkington, Higher Gills Farm, Whytha Lane, Rimington, Clitheroe BB7 4DA t (01200) 445370
e pilko@highergills.co.uk w highergills.co.uk

COCKFIELD, County Durham Map ref 5B3 — **SELF CATERING**

★★★★
SELF CATERING

Units **2**
Sleeps **4–5**

Low season per wk
Min £160.00
High season per wk
Max £340.00

Stonecroft and Swallows Nest, Bishop Auckland

contact Mrs Alison Tallentire, Low Lands Farm,
Bishop Auckland DL13 5AW **t** (01388) 718251 **f** (01388) 718251
e info@farmholidaysuk.com **w** farmholidaysuk.com

Winners County Durham Accessible Award 2002. Comfortable, cosy, accessible cottage. Level-entry shower, ground-floor rooms/bedrooms/bathrooms, all linen and towels provided, log fire, original beams, own garden, gas barbecue. Lots to see and do for everyone. Friendly owner-run farm. A truly relaxing holiday. A warm welcome awaits you.

open All year
nearest shop 1 mile
nearest pub 1 mile

Directions on request.

Access

General

Unit

Payment Cash/cheques

Adapted kitchen, level-entry shower with shower chair, raised toilet seat with handrails, ground-floor rooms/bedrooms/bathrooms, turning circles in every room.

CONGLETON, Cheshire — **GUEST ACCOMMODATION**

★★★★
GUEST ACCOMMODATION

Sandhole Farm Hulme Walfield, Congleton CW12 2JH
t (01260) 224419 **f** (01260) 224766
e veronica@sandholefarm.co.uk **w** sandholefarm.co.uk

CONISTON, Cumbria — **SELF CATERING**

★★★★
SELF CATERING

Red Dell Cottage contact Mr Philip Johnston, The Coppermines & Lakes Cottages, The Estate Office, The Bridge, Coniston LA21 8HJ
t (015394) 41765 **f** (015394) 41944
e info@coppermines.co.uk **w** coppermines.co.uk

Check it out

Information on accommodation listed in this guide has been supplied by proprietors. As changes may occur you should remember to check all relevant details at the time of booking.

At-a-glance symbols are explained on the flap inside the back cover.

CONISTON, Cumbria Map ref 5A3 **CAMPING & CARAVANNING**

★★★★
TOURING &
CAMPING PARK

 (280)
£12.10–£24.90
 (280)
£12.10–£24.90
280 touring pitches

Park Coppice Caravan Club Site

Park Gate, Coniston LA21 8LA **t** (015394) 41555
w caravanclub.co.uk

General 🔲 P 🔌 ⬚ 🛈 WP ℟ ☉ ⬚
🔲 ☼

Leisure /⊓\

Payment Credit/debit cards,
cash/cheques

THE
CARAVAN
CLUB

An imaginatively landscaped site in 63 acres of National Trust woodland, with pitches grouped in open glades. There's access from the bottom of the site across fields to Coniston Water, the proximity of which is a great bonus, for a short walk of 400 yards brings you to the lakeside launching point for dinghy sailing. Open March to November.

Follow A593, 1.5 miles south of Coniston village. Final approach from the north or south is narrow in places.

Gold and Silver Awards

VisitBritain's unique Gold and Silver Awards recognise exceptional quality in serviced accommodation.

Enjoy England assessors make recommendations for Gold and Silver Awards during assessments in recognition of levels of quality over and above that expected of a particular rating.

Look for the Gold and Silver Awards in the regional sections.

CORNRIGGS, County Durham Map ref 5B2 — SELF CATERING

★★★★★
SELF CATERING

Units **2**
Sleeps **2-6**
Low season per wk
£290.00-£385.00
High season per wk
£385.00-£545.00

Cornriggs Cottages, Bishop Auckland

contact Mrs Janet Elliot, Cornriggs Cottages, c/o Low Cornriggs Farm, Cornriggs, Cowshill, Bishop Auckland DL13 1AQ **t** (01388) 537600 **f** (01388) 537777
e enquiries@lowcornriggsfarm.fsnet.co.uk
w britnett.net/lowcornriggsfarm

Access   abc 🐾

General 🛋 ♿ P ✂ S

Unit ♿ 🛏 🖥 □ ■ 🖥 ℚ 🖥 ⚱ 🖫 🖬 🖳 🖱 ✳

Payment Credit/debit cards, cash/cheques, euros

Full weeks/short breaks. Discount for booking both cottages.

Peacefully located on a working farm in the heart of the Weardale but within easy reach of the Lakes, Northumberland and the North East. Large, detached, single-storey cottages, wheelchair-accessible (including shower). All rooms fitted to a high standard. Well fitted kitchen, cosy lounge, TV/DVD. Home cooking. Ample parking. Service pets only. Green Business Scheme Silver Award.
open All year
nearest shop 4 miles
nearest pub 1 mile

Situated midway between Alston and Stanhope on the A689.

CRASTER, Northumberland — SELF CATERING

★★★★
SELF CATERING

Craster Pine Lodges contact Mr & Mrs Robson, Craster Pine Lodges, c/o Rock Ville, 19 Heugh Road, Alnwick NE66 3TJ **t** (01665) 576286
e rockville@barkpots.co.uk **w** crasterpinelodges.co.uk

Don't forget www.

Web addresses throughout this guide are shown without the prefix www. Please include www. in the address line of your browser. If a web address does not follow this style it is shown in full.

At-a-glance symbols are explained on the flap inside the back cover.

DURHAM, County Durham Map ref 5C2 |

★★★★★
**TOURING &
CAMPING PARK**

(77) £22.40–£25.60
(77) £22.40–£25.60
77 touring pitches

Grange Caravan Club Site

Meadow Lane, Durham DH1 1TL **t** (0191) 384 4778
w caravanclub.co.uk

An open and level site, just off the A1(M) and within easy reach of the City of Durham with walks from the site into the city. Durham is only three miles away, dramatically set on its 70-foot rocky semi-island in a hairpin bend of the River Wear.

open All year

A1(M) jct 62, A690 towards Durham. Turn right after 50m. Signposted Maureen Terrace and brown caravan sign.

General 🚐 P 🚗 🚻 🔥 ⊙ 📶 🖥 ☼

Leisure 🎢

Payment Credit/debit cards, cash/cheques

THE
CARAVAN
CLUB

EASINGWOLD, North Yorkshire |

★★★★
FARMHOUSE

Thornton Lodge Farm Thornton Hill, York YO61 3QA
t (01347) 821306 **f** (01347) 821306
e sue.raper@btopenworld.com **w** thorntonlodgefarm.co.uk

EBBERSTON, North Yorkshire |

★★★–★★★★★
SELF CATERING

Cow Pasture Cottage Cow Pasture Cottage, 67 Main Street,
Scarborough YO13 9NR **t** (01723) 859285 **f** (01723) 859285
e ernie@jhodgson.fsnet.co.uk **w** studley-house.co.uk

ELLESMERE PORT, Cheshire |

★★★
HOTEL

Holiday Inn Ellesmere Port/Cheshire Oaks Lower Mersey Street,
Ellesmere Port CH65 2AL **t** (0151) 356 8111 **f** (0151) 356 8444
e clare.bebb@hiellesmereport.com

GAINFORD, County Durham |

★★★★–★★★★★
SELF CATERING

East Greystone Farm Cottages contact Mrs Sue Hodgson,
East Greystone Farm Cottages, East Greystone Farm, Main Road, Darlington DL2 3BL
t (01325) 730236 **f** (01325) 730236
e sue@holidayfarmcottages.co.uk **w** holidayfarmcottages.co.uk

---

GILLING WEST, North Yorkshire |

★★★★
TOURING PARK

Hargill House Caravan Club Site Richmond DL10 5LJ
t (01342) 336732 **f** (01342) 410258
e natalie.tiller@caravanclub.co.uk **w** caravanclub.co.uk

GRANGE-OVER-SANDS, Cumbria |

★★★
**HOTEL
SILVER AWARD**

Netherwood Hotel Lindale Road, Grange-over-Sands LA11 6ET
t (015395) 32552 **f** (015395) 34121
e enquiries@netherwood-hotel.co.uk **w** netherwood-hotel.co.uk

---

GRANGE-OVER-SANDS, Cumbria Map ref 5A3 — CAMPING & CARAVANNING

★★★★★
TOURING PARK

 (131)
£13.60–£25.60
(131)
£13.60–£25.60
131 touring pitches

THE
CARAVAN CLUB

Meathop Fell Caravan Club Site

Meathop, Grange-over-Sands LA11 6RB **t** (015395) 32912
w caravanclub.co.uk

General **P** ⊡ ☚ ☂ ⓦ ⌂ ☉ ☰ ☐
☼

Leisure **⚲**

Payment Credit/debit cards,
cash/cheques

Gentle and peaceful, this thoughtfully laid out site is divided into separate pitching areas which are punctuated by shrubs and grass. This is an ideal base from which to explore north Lancashire and the southern Lake District. Brockhole, the National Park Visitor Centre, is a good place to start your exploration. **open** All year

M6 jct 36, A590 to Barrow. After about 3.25 miles take slip road and follow A590 to Barrow. At 1st roundabout follow International Camping signs. Steep approach.

HARBOTTLE, Northumberland — GUEST ACCOMMODATION

★★★★
**BED & BREAKFAST
SILVER AWARD**

The Byre Vegetarian B&B Harbottle, Morpeth NE65 7DG
t (01669) 650476
e rosemary@the-byre.co.uk **w** the-byre.co.uk

HARMBY, North Yorkshire — CAMPING & CARAVANNING

★★★
**TOURING &
CAMPING PARK**

Lower Wensleydale Caravan Club Site Harmby, Leyburn DL8 5NU
t (01969) 623366
w caravanclub.co.uk

HARROGATE, North Yorkshire — SELF CATERING

★★★★
SELF CATERING

Brimham Rocks Cottages contact Jacqueline Martin, Brimham Rocks Cottages, High North Farm, Harrogate HG3 5EY
t (01765) 620284 **f** (01765) 620477
e brimhamrc@yahoo.co.uk **w** brimham.co.uk

HARWOOD DALE, North Yorkshire — GUEST ACCOMMODATION

★★★★
FARMHOUSE

The Grainary Scarborough YO13 0DT
t (01723) 870026 **f** (01723) 870026
e thesimpsons@grainary.co.uk **w** grainary.co.uk

At-a-glance symbols are explained on the flap inside the back cover.

HAYDON BRIDGE, Northumberland Map ref 5B2 — GUEST ACCOMMODATION

★★★★
BED & BREAKFAST

R&B per room per night
s £30.00
d £60.00
Evening meal per person
£15.00

Grindon Cartshed

Haydon Bridge, Hexham NE47 6NQ **t** (01434) 684273
e cartshed@grindon.force9.co.uk **w** grindon cartshed.co.uk

We extend a warm welcome and aim for excellence and quality. Cosy, comfortable bedrooms. Unrestricted views from lounge over Tyne Valley towards market town of Hexham. High quality, locally produced food. Licensed.
open All year
bedrooms 1 double, 2 twin
bathrooms All en suite

General ♿ P   ✂ ♥ ✕ ❄

Rooms ▢ ☕ ⌨ ⌇

Payment Credit/debit cards, cash/cheques

HEBDEN BRIDGE, West Yorkshire — CAMPING & CARAVANNING

★★★★★
TOURING PARK

Lower Clough Foot Caravan Club Site Cragg Vale, Hebden Bridge HX7 5RU
t (01422) 882531
w caravanclub.co.uk

HIGH CATTON, East Riding of Yorkshire — SELF CATERING

★★★★–★★★★★
SELF CATERING

The Courtyard contact Sheila Foster, High Catton Grange, High Catton,
York YO41 1EP **t** (01759) 371374 **f** (01759) 371374
e sheila.foster@btclick.com **w** yorkshirevisitor.com/thecourtyard

---

HOLMES CHAPEL, Cheshire — GUEST ACCOMMODATION

★★★★
BED & BREAKFAST
SILVER AWARD

Padgate Guest House Twemlow Lane, Cranage, Crewe CW4 8EX
t (01477) 534291 **f** (01477) 544726
e lynda@padgate.freeserve.co.uk
w http://wpadgateguesthouse.mysite.wanadoo-members.co.uk

ILKLEY, West Yorkshire — SELF CATERING

★★★★–★★★★★
SELF CATERING

Westwood Lodge, Ilkley Moor contact Tim & Paula Edwards,
Westwood Lodge, Ilkley Moor, Westwood Drive, Ilkley LS29 9JF
t (01943) 433430 **f** (01943) 433431
e welcome@westwoodlodge.co.uk **w** westwoodlodge.co.uk

INGLETON, County Durham — SELF CATERING

★★★★★
SELF CATERING

The Mill Granary contact Mr & Mrs Richard & Kate Hodgson, The Mill Granary,
c/o Middleton House, Darlington DL2 3HG **t** (01325) 730339
e info@millgranary.co.uk **w** millgranary.co.uk

INGLETON, North Yorkshire — GUEST ACCOMMODATION

★★★★
GUEST ACCOMMODATION

Riverside Lodge 24 Main Street, Carnforth LA6 3HJ
t (01524) 241359
e info@riversideingleton.co.uk **w** riversideingleton.co.uk

KENDAL, Cumbria Map ref 5B3 **SELF CATERING**

★★★
SELF CATERING

Units **1**
Sleeps **2–4**
Low season per wk
£250.00–£300.00
High season per wk
£300.00–£350.00

Barkinbeck Cottage, Kendal

contact Mrs Ann Hamilton, Barkinbeck Cottage, c/o Barkin House Barn, Gatebeck, Kendal LA8 0HX **t** (015395) 67122 **e** barkinhouse@yahoo.co.uk **w** barkinbeck.co.uk

Converted barn in peaceful, rural location. Ideal for visiting the Lakes and Yorkshire Dales. Level access throughout. Adapted bathroom. One double, one twin bedroom, open fire, panoramic views. Owner maintained.

open All year
nearest shop 5 miles
nearest pub 5 miles

General 12 P
Unit
Payment Cash/cheques

KENDAL, Cumbria Map ref 5B3 **CAMPING & CARAVANNING**

★★★★
TOURING PARK

(141)
£10.40–£22.40
(141)
£10.40–£22.40
141 touring pitches

Low Park Wood Caravan Club Site

Sedgwick, Kendal LA8 0JZ **t** (015395) 60186
w caravanclub.co.uk

General P
Leisure
Payment Credit/debit cards, cash/cheques

Midweek discount.

From the country lane approach running beside a tumbling river, to the glades where you pitch amidst the wild flowers, this site is heaven – so peaceful you'll not want to leave. Take your binoculars, as the bird life is varied and colourful, and if you're a wild flower enthusiast you'll find plenty to note. Open April to November.

Leave M6 at jct 36 and go onto A590 signed South Lakes. After approximately 3.25 miles leave via slip road (signed Milnthorpe, Barrow) at roundabout and follow caravan signs.

THE CARAVAN CLUB

KESWICK, Cumbria **HOTEL**

★★★
COUNTRY HOUSE HOTEL
SILVER AWARD

Derwentwater Hotel Portinscale, Keswick CA12 5RE
t (017687) 72538 **f** (017687) 71002
e info@derwentwater-hotel.co.uk **w** derwentwater-hotel.co.uk

KESWICK, Cumbria **SELF CATERING**

★★★★★
SELF CATERING

The Coach House & Derwent Cottage Mews contact Sue Newman, Derwent Cottage, Portinscale, Keswick CA12 5RF **t** (01768) 774838
w derwentcottage.co.uk

At-a-glance symbols are explained on the flap inside the back cover.

KIELDER, Northumberland — CAMPING & CARAVANNING

★★★★
**TOURING &
CAMPING PARK**

Kielder Water Caravan Club Site Leaplish Waterside Park, Falstone,
Hexham NE48 1AX
t (01434) 250278
w caravanclub.co.uk

KIELDER WATER, Northumberland — SELF CATERING

★★★★
SELF CATERING

Calvert Trust Kielder Calvert Trust Kielder, Falstone, Hexham NE48 1BS
t (01434) 250232 **f** (01434) 250015
e enquiries@calvert-kielder.com **w** calvert-trust.org.uk

KIRKBYMOORSIDE, North Yorkshire — GUEST ACCOMMODATION

★★★★
**GUEST HOUSE
SILVER AWARD**

The Cornmill Kirby Mills, Kirkbymoorside, York YO62 6NP
t (01751) 432000
e cornmill@kirbymills.demon.co.uk **w** kirbymills.demon.co.uk

KIRKBYMOORSIDE, North Yorkshire — SELF CATERING

★★★★
SELF CATERING

Low Hagg Holidays contact Mr J Lee, Low Hagg, Starfitts Lane,
Kirkbymoorside YO62 7JF **t** (01751) 430500
w longhaggfarm.com

KIRKOSWALD, Cumbria Map ref 5B2 — SELF CATERING

★★★★
SELF CATERING

Units **1**
Sleeps **2**
Low season per wk
£200.00–£340.00
High season per wk
£300.00–£480.00

Howscales, Penrith
contact Liz Webster, Howscales, Kirkoswald, Penrith CA10 1JG
t (01768) 898666 **f** (01768) 898710 **e** liz@howscales.co.uk **w** howscales.co.uk

Hazelrigg, a single-storey cottage,
has one large double, or twin by
arrangement, with an en suite
bathroom. Stunning garden and
views. Ample parking. Service dogs
welcome. Four other properties
available for carers/family.
open All year
nearest shop 1.5 miles
nearest pub 1.5 miles

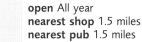

Access
General
Unit
Payment Credit/debit cards,
cash/cheques

visitBritain.com

Get in the know – log on for a wealth of
information and inspiration. All the latest
news on places to visit, events and quality-
assessed accommodation is literally at
your fingertips. Explore all that Britain has
to offer!

KNARESBOROUGH, North Yorkshire Map ref 4B1 — CAMPING & CARAVANNING

★★★★★
TOURING PARK

(65) £13.60–£25.60
(65) £13.60–£25.60
65 touring pitches

THE CARAVAN CLUB

Knaresborough Caravan Club Site

New Road, Scotton, Knaresborough HG5 9HH **t** (01342) 336732
w caravanclub.co.uk

General P

Leisure

Payment Credit/debit cards, cash/cheques

This site offers a gateway to the Yorkshire Dales and the many attractions of the north of England. The site is surrounded by mature trees and hedges and on fine days it is sunny yet well sheltered. Knaresborough is an historic market town with a town crier, ancient walkways, castle ruins and cobbled alleys. Open March to January.

Turn right off A59 onto B6165. After approximately 1.5 miles turn right immediately after petrol station into New Road. Site is on right-hand side after 50yds.

LAMPLUGH, Cumbria — CAMPING & CARAVANNING

★★★★
TOURING PARK

Dockray Meadow Caravan Club Site Lamplugh CA14 4SH
t (01946) 861357
w caravanclub.co.uk

LONGFRAMLINGTON, Northumberland — SELF CATERING

★★★–★★★★
SELF CATERING

Dene House Farm Cottages contact Mrs Vivien Mason,
Dene House Farm Cottages, Dene House, Longframlington, Morpeth NE65 8EE
t (01665) 570665 **f** (01665) 570549
w denehousefarm.com

LONGHORSLEY, Northumberland — SELF CATERING

★★★★–★★★★★
SELF CATERING

Beacon Hill Farm Holidays contact Mr Alun Moore, Beacon Hill Farm Holidays,
Beacon Hill House, Longhorsley, Morpeth NE65 8QW
t (01670) 780900 **f** (01670) 780901
e alun@beaconhill.co.uk **w** beaconhill.co.uk

LUCKER, Northumberland — SELF CATERING

★★★★–★★★★★
SELF CATERING

Lucker Hall Steading contact Mrs Jane Mallen, Lucker Hall Steading,
Alnwick Castle, Lucker Hall Steading, Alnwick NE70 7JQ
t (01668) 219941 **f** (01665) 510876
e jane@nehc.co.uk **w** alnwickcastlecottages.co.uk

LYTHAM ST ANNES, Lancashire — HOTEL

★★★
HOTEL

The Chadwick Hotel South Promenade, Lytham St Annes FY8 1NP
t (01253) 720061 **f** (01253) 714455
e sales@thechadwickhotel.com **w** thechadwickhotel.com

At-a-glance symbols are explained on the flap inside the back cover.

MALTON, North Yorkshire — SELF CATERING

★★★★
SELF CATERING

Rowgate Cottage contact Janet Clarkson, Rowgate Cottage, Rowgate Farm, Malton YO17 8LU **t** (01944) 758277 **f** (01944) 758277
e janet@rowgatecottage.fsnet.co.uk

MANCHESTER, Greater Manchester — GUEST ACCOMMODATION

★★★
GUEST ACCOMMODATION

Luther King House Brighton Grove, Wilmslow Road, Manchester M14 5JP
t (0161) 224 6404 **f** (0161) 248 9201
e reception@lkh.co.uk **w** lkh.co.uk

MORECAMBE, Lancashire — SELF CATERING

★★★
SELF CATERING

Eden Vale Luxury Holiday Flats contact Mr John Coombs,
Eden Vale Luxury Holiday Flats, 338 Marine Road Central, Morecambe LA4 5AB
t (01524) 415544

MORPETH, Northumberland — HOTEL

★★★★
COUNTRY HOUSE HOTEL
SILVER AWARD

Linden Hall Longhorsley, Morpeth NE65 8XF
t (01670) 500000 **f** (01670) 500001
e general.lindenhall@macdonald-hotels.co.uk
w macdonald-hotels.co.uk/lindenhall

MORPETH, Northumberland — HOTEL

★★★
HOTEL

Longhirst Hall Longhirst, Morpeth NE61 3LL
t (01670) 791348 **f** (01670) 791385
e enquiries@longhirst.co.uk **w** longhirst.co.uk

NEWBROUGH, Northumberland — GUEST ACCOMMODATION

★★★★
FARMHOUSE

Carr Edge Farm Newbrough, Hexham NE47 5EA
t (01434) 674788 **f** (01434) 674783
e stay@carredge.co.uk **w** carredge.co.uk

NEWLANDS, Cumbria Map ref 5A3 — CAMPING & CARAVANNING

★★★★
TOURING PARK

(60) £9.10–£20.20
(60) £9.10–£20.20
60 touring pitches

THE
CARAVAN
CLUB

Low Manesty Caravan Club Site

Manesty, Keswick CA12 5UG **t** (01768) 777275
w caravanclub.co.uk

Set in National Trust woodland, close to Derwentwater, this is a site to delight the eye and the heart with the lovely fells soaring up and the wild flowers and animals at your feet. There are numerous walks you can take direct from the site, just awaiting your walking boots. Open March to November.

From B5289 turn right over bridge. Site on right in 1 mile.

General **P** 🅰 🅗 🆆🅿
Payment Credit/debit cards, cash/cheques

NEWTON-IN-BOWLAND, Lancashire — SELF CATERING

★★★★
SELF CATERING

Stonefold Holiday Cottage contact Mrs Helen Blanc, Stonefold Farm, Slaidburn Road, Newton-in-Bowland BB7 3DL **t** 07966 582834
w stonefoldholidaycottage.co.uk

NORTHALLERTON, North Yorkshire — GUEST ACCOMMODATION

★★★★
FARMHOUSE

Lovesome Hill Farm Northallerton DL6 2PB
t (01609) 772311 **f** (01609) 774715
e pearsonlhf@care4free.net

PATELEY BRIDGE, North Yorkshire — SELF CATERING

★★★★
SELF CATERING &
SERVICED APARTMENTS

Helme Pasture, Old Spring Wood contact Mrs Rosemary Helme, Hartwith Bank, Summerbridge, Harrogate HG3 4DR
t (01423) 780279 **f** (01423) 780994
e helmepasture@btinternet.com **w** helmepasture.co.uk

PENRITH, Cumbria Map ref 5B2 — CAMPING & CARAVANNING

★★★★★
TOURING PARK

🚐(151)
£14.30–£27.70
🚏(151)
£14.30–£27.70
151 touring pitches

THE
CARAVAN
CLUB

Troutbeck Head Caravan Club Site

Troutbeck, Penrith CA11 0SS **t** (01768) 483521
w caravanclub.co.uk

General P 🚐 🜨 📶 🐾 ☉ 🛢 🗐 ☼

Leisure 🔍 🏔

Payment Credit/debit cards, cash/cheques

This site is set in classical north Lakeland countryside, near Ullswater and surrounded by the great outdoors. Fabulous for nature lovers and walkers alike, the site nestles in a valley alongside a babbling brook, below Great Mell Fell and with spectacular views of Blencathra to the west. Open March to January.

From north or south on M6, leave at jct 40 onto A66 signposted Keswick. In about 7.25 miles turn left onto A5091, signposted Dockray/Ullswater, site on right after 1.5 miles.

PICKERING, North Yorkshire — SELF CATERING

★★★★–★★★★★★
SELF CATERING

Beech Farm Cottages contact Mrs Pat Massara, Beech Farm Cottages, Wrelton YO18 8PG **t** (01751) 476612 **f** (01751) 475032
e holiday@beechfarm.com **w** beechfarm.com

PICKERING, North Yorkshire — SELF CATERING

★★★★
SELF CATERING

Eastgate Cottages contact Elaine Bedford, Eastgate Cottages, 117 Eastgate, Pickering YO18 7DW **t** (01751) 476653 **f** (01751) 471310
e info@northyorkshirecottages.co.uk **w** northyorkshirecottages.co.uk

At-a-glance symbols are explained on the flap inside the back cover.

PICKERING, North Yorkshire | SELF CATERING

★★★★
SELF CATERING

Easthill Farm House and Gardens contact Mrs Diane Stenton,
Easthill Farm House and Lodges, Wilton Road, Thornton Dale, Pickering YO18 7QP
t (01751) 474561
e info@easthill-farm-holidays.co.uk **w** easthill-farm-holidays.co.uk

---

PICKERING, North Yorkshire Map ref 5D3 | SELF CATERING

★★★★
SELF CATERING

Units **9**
Sleeps **2–8**

Low season per wk
£196.00–£395.00
High season per wk
£440.00–£1,050.00

Keld Head Farm Cottages, *Pickering*

contact Julian & Penny Fearn, Keld Head Farm Cottages, Keld Head,
Pickering YO18 8LL **t** (01751) 473974
e julian@keldheadcottages.com **w** keldheadcottages.com

Access abc

General 🐢 🏠 ♿ P ⚔ ⬤S

Unit ♿ 🛁 🖥️ S 📺 🔌 🍳 ☕🍽️ 🧺 ❄

Payment Credit/debit cards,
cash/cheques, euros

*Six single-storey easy-access
cottages. Senior citizen and two-
person discounts. Short breaks.
See virtual tour on website.*

On the edge of Pickering, in
open countryside overlooking
fields where sheep and cows
graze, sit nine beautiful, spacious,
character stone cottages,
tastefully furnished with the
emphasis on comfort and
relaxation. Award-winning level
access gardens with garden
house. Local shops, York, moors
and coast easily accessible.
Ample parking.

open All year
nearest shop < 0.5 miles
nearest pub 0.5 miles

*The cottages are on westerly
edge of Pickering at corner of
A170 and a road signposted
'Marton'. Turn into this road and
the entrance is on the right.*

PICKERING, North Yorkshire | SELF CATERING

★★★★
SELF CATERING

Let's Holiday contact John and Penny Wicks, Let's Holiday, Pickering YO18 8QA
t (01751) 475396
e holiday@letsholiday.com **w** letsholiday.com

visitBritain.com

Big city buzz or peaceful panoramas? Take a fresh look
at Britain and you may be surprised at what's right on
your doorstep. Explore the diversity online at
visitBritain.com

PICKERING, North Yorkshire Map ref 5D3 — SELF CATERING

★★★★
SELF CATERING

Units **4**
Sleeps **2–7**

Low season per wk
£350.00–£450.00
High season per wk
£450.00–£550.00

Rawcliffe House Farm, Pickering

contact Duncan & Jan Allsopp, Rawcliffe House Farm,
Pickering YO18 8JA **t** (01751) 473292
e stay@rawcliffehousefarm.co.uk **w** rawcliffehousefarm.co.uk

General 〰 🏠 ⚄ P ⚙ ◉ Ⓢ

Unit ♿ 🛁 📺 ⓢ 🖥 📺 🍵 ♨

Payment Credit/debit cards,
cash/cheques

*All on one level, spacious with a
twin bedroom and a large en
suite fitted with a roll-in shower.*

Situated in beautiful countryside within the North York Moors. This fully accessible cottage, with one twin bedroom, has its own patio with panoramic open views across the fields. Ideally situated to visit moors, coast, villages, stately homes, York, Heartbeat country or to ride the steam railway. Owners on site to give assistance.

open All year
nearest shop 6 miles
nearest pub 1.5 miles

POULTON-LE-FYLDE, Lancashire — SELF CATERING

★★★★
SELF CATERING

Hardhorn Breaks contact Mr Pawson, Hardhorn Breaks, High Bank Farm,
Fairfield Road, Hadhorn FY6 8DN **t** (01253) 890422
e anna@rosewood8.1.freeserve.co.uk **w** holidaycotts.co.uk

Discover Britain's heritage

Our travel map and guide is perfectly tailored to your needs. Discover the history and beauty of over 250 of Britain's best-known historic houses, castles, gardens and smaller manor houses. You can purchase Britain's Historic Houses and Gardens – Guide and Map from good bookshops and online at visitbritaindirect.com

At-a-glance symbols are explained on the flap inside the back cover.

POWBURN, Northumberland Map ref 5B1 — CAMPING & CARAVANNING

★★★★★
**TOURING &
CAMPING PARK**

(74) £10.40–£22.40
(74) £10.40–£22.40
74 touring pitches

River Breamish Caravan Club Site

Powburn, Alnwick NE66 4HY **t** (01665) 578320
w caravanclub.co.uk

The site is set amid the Cheviot Hills, with excellent walking and cycling in the immediate area. A footbridge in Branton (one mile away) takes you over the river to the delightful Breamish Valley. At the National Park Centre at Ingram, staff will help you plan your stay. Open March to November.

General 🚐 P 🔌 🚰 🏕 👜 ⊙ 🏧🖥

Turn off A1 onto A697, after about 20m turn left. Site on right.

Payment Credit/debit cards, cash/cheques

THE
**CARAVAN
CLUB**

PRESTON, East Riding of Yorkshire — GUEST ACCOMMODATION

★★★★
**FARMHOUSE
SILVER AWARD**

Little Weghill Farm Weghill Road, Hull HU12 8SX
t (01482) 897650 **f** (01482) 897650
e info@littleweghillfarm.co.uk **w** littleweghillfarm.co.uk

QUEBEC, County Durham — SELF CATERING

★★★★
SELF CATERING

Clydesdale Cottage contact Mrs June Whitfield, Clydesdale Cottage, Hamsteels Hall, Hamsteels Lane, Durham DH7 9RS
t (01207) 520388 **f** (01207) 520388
e june@hamsteelshall.co.uk **w** hamsteelshall.co.uk

RIBCHESTER, Lancashire — GUEST ACCOMMODATION

★★★★★
GUEST ACCOMMODATION

Riverside Barn Riverside, Ribchester, Preston PR3 3XS **t** (01254) 878095
e andy@riversidebarn.co.uk **w** riversidebarn.co.uk

RICCALL, North Yorkshire — SELF CATERING

★★★★
SELF CATERING

Pound Cottage contact Peggy Swann, South Newlands Farm, Selby Road, York YO19 6QR **t** (01757) 248203
e southnewlandsfarm@yahoo.co.uk **w** southnewlands.co.uk

ROTHBURY, Northumberland — CAMPING & CARAVANNING

★★★
TOURING PARK

Nunnykirk Caravan Club Site Nunnykirk, Morpeth NE61 4PZ
t (01669) 620762
w caravanclub.co.uk

RUNSWICK BAY, North Yorkshire — GUEST ACCOMMODATION

★★★★
**INN
SILVER AWARD**

Ellerby Hotel Ryeland Lane, Saltburn-by-the-Sea TS13 5LP
t (01947) 840342 **f** (01947) 841221
e david@ellerbyhotel.co.uk **w** ellerbyhotel.co.uk

SCARBOROUGH, North Yorkshire — GUEST ACCOMMODATION

★★★
GUEST ACCOMMODATION

Scarborough Travel and Holiday Lodge 33 Valley Road, Scarborough YO11 2LX
t (01723) 363537 **f** (01723) 501239
e enquiries@scarborough-lodge.co.uk **w** scarborough-lodge.co.uk

SEDBERGH, Cumbria — SELF CATERING

★★★–★★★★★
SELF CATERING

Cobble Country Holidays contact Mrs R Elizabeth Close,
Cobble Country Holidays, 59 Main Street, Sedbergh LA10 5AB
t (015396) 21000 **f** (015396) 21710
e cobblesedbergh@yahoo.co.uk **w** cobblecountry.co.uk

SELBY, North Yorkshire — SELF CATERING

★★★★
SELF CATERING

Lund Farm Cottages contact Mr & Mrs Chris & Helen Middleton,
Lund Farm Cottages, Lund Farm, Gateforth, Selby YO8 9LE
t (01757) 228775 **f** (01757) 228775
e chris.middleton@farmline.com **w** lundfarm.co.uk

SEWERBY, East Riding of Yorkshire — SELF CATERING

★★★★–★★★★★★
SELF CATERING

Field House Farm Cottages contact Angela & John Foster,
Field House Farm Cottages, Jewison Lane, Bridlington YO16 6YG
t (01262) 674932 **f** (01262) 608688
e john.foster@farmline.com **w** fieldhousefarmcottages.co.uk

SILVERDALE, Lancashire — SELF CATERING

★★★★
SELF CATERING

The Stables at Silverdale contact Mrs Cathy Ranford, The Stables at Silverdale,
The Stables, Lindeth Road LA5 0TT **t** (01524) 702121 **f** (01524) 702226
e stables@lindethhouse.co.uk **w** lindethhouse.co.uk

SKELWITH FOLD, Cumbria — SELF CATERING

★★★★★
SELF CATERING

Crop Howe contact Mrs Susan Jackson, Hart of the Lakes, Old Lake Road,
Ambleside LA22 0DH **t** (015394) 33251 **f** (015394) 33110

SLEDMERE, East Riding of Yorkshire — SELF CATERING

★★★★
SELF CATERING

Life Hill Farm Cottage contact Fay Grace, Life Hill Farm, Sledmere,
Driffield YO25 3EY **t** (01377) 236224
e info@lifehillfarm.co.uk **w** lifehillfarm.co.uk

SNEATON, North Yorkshire — CAMPING & CARAVANNING

★★★★
TOURING PARK

Low Moor Caravan Club Site Sneaton, Whitby YO22 5JE **t** (01947) 810505
w caravanclub.co.uk

STAPE, North Yorkshire — GUEST ACCOMMODATION

★★★★
FARMHOUSE
SILVER AWARD

Rawcliffe House Farm Pickering YO18 8JA **t** (01751) 473292 **f** (01751) 477020
e stay@rawcliffehousefarm.co.uk **w** rawcliffehousefarm.co.uk

STAVELEY, Cumbria — SELF CATERING

★★★
SELF CATERING

Avondale contact Helen Hughes, Avondale, 2 Lynstead, Thornbarrow Road,
Windermere LA23 2DG **t** (015394) 45713
e enquiries@avondale.uk.net **w** avondale.uk.net

At-a-glance symbols are explained on the flap inside the back cover.

STOCKTON-ON-TEES, Tees Valley Map ref 5C3 | **CAMPING & CARAVANNING**

★★★★★
TOURING PARK

(115)
£10.40–£22.40
(115)
£10.40–£22.40
115 touring pitches

White Water Caravan Club Park

Tees Barrage, Stockton-on-Tees TS18 2QW **t** (01642) 634880
w caravanclub.co.uk

General ⏚ **P** 🚗 🖰 🛍 🆆 🝢 ☉ 🚽
🔲 ☼

Leisure 🔍 ⚠

Payment Credit/debit cards,
cash/cheques

CARAVAN CLUB

This pleasantly landscaped site is adjacent to the largest white water canoeing and rafting course built to international standard in Britain. The centre provides facilities including a sheltered viewing balcony, a drying and changing room, canoe storage area, shop and cafe. Nearby Teesside Park is a shoppers' paradise with restaurants, multi-screen cinema complex and bowling alley.
open All year

Come off the A66 Teesside Park. Follow Teesdale sign, go over Tees Barrage Bridge, turn right. Site 200yds on the left.

THORPE BASSETT, North Yorkshire | **SELF CATERING**

★★★★
SELF CATERING

The Old Post Office contact Sandra Simpson, S Simpson Cottages,
The Old Post Office, Malton YO17 8LU **t** (01944) 758047 **f** (01944) 758047
e ssimpsoncottages@aol.com **w** ssimpsoncottages.co.uk

THRELKELD, Cumbria | **GUEST ACCOMMODATION**

★★★★
**GUEST HOUSE
SILVER AWARD**

Scales Farm Country Guest House Scales, Threlkeld, Keswick CA12 4SY
t (017687) 79660 **f** (017687) 79510
e scales@scalesfarm.com **w** scalesfarm.com

THURSTASTON, Merseyside | **CAMPING & CARAVANNING**

★★★★
**TOURING &
CAMPING PARK**

Wirral Country Park Caravan Club Site Station Road, Wirral CH61 0HN
t (0151) 648 5228
w caravanclub.co.uk

WARRINGTON, Cheshire | **GUEST ACCOMMODATION**

★★★
GUEST ACCOMMODATION

Tall Trees Lodge Tarporley Road, Lower Whitley, Warrington WA4 4EZ
t (01928) 790824 & (01928) 715117 **f** (01928) 791330
e booking@talltreeslodge.co.uk **w** talltreeslodge.co.uk

WHINFELL, Cumbria Map ref 5B3 — SELF CATERING

★★★
SELF CATERING

Units **2**
Sleeps **6–9**

Low season per wk
£300.00–£450.00
High season per wk
£450.00–£750.00

Topthorn Holiday Cottages, Nr Kendal

contact Mrs Diane Barnes, Topthorn Holiday Cottages, Topthorn, Whinfell, Nr Kendal LA8 9EG **t** (01539) 824252 **f** (01539) 824386
e info.barnes@btconnect.com **w** topthorn.com

Cobblestone Cottage has been built with special facilities for the less mobile. Wheelchair-friendly. Doorways one metre wide. One downstairs queen-sized bedroom. Downstairs wet room with Doc M Pack.
open All year
nearest shop 4 miles
nearest pub 4 miles

Access

General

Unit

Payment Credit/debit cards, cash/cheques

WHITBY, North Yorkshire — SELF CATERING

★★★ – ★★★★★
SELF CATERING

Captain Cook's Haven contact Anne Barrowman, Captain Cook's Haven, Larpool Lane, Whitby YO22 4NE **t** (01947) 893573 **f** (01947) 893573
w whitbyholidayhomes.co.uk

WHITBY, North Yorkshire Map ref 5D3 — SELF CATERING

★★★
SELF CATERING

Units **1**
Sleeps **1–5**

Low season per wk
Max £300.00
High season per wk
Max £520.00

Groves Dyke Holiday Cottage, Whitby

t (01947) 810220
e relax@grovesdyke.co.uk **w** grovesdyke.co.uk

Access

General

Unit

Payment Cash/cheques

Half-price special offer for late bookings made within 4 weeks of arrival date.

Comfortable, secluded, modernised semi-detached house. Warm and helpful welcome from the owner, next door. Full gas central heating included. Picture windows, conservatory/deck, patio, large sunny garden, woodland wildlife. Step-free sitting room, kitchen/dining room and shower room/toilet. Upstairs bathroom and three bedrooms (double, twin, single).
open All year
nearest shop 0.5 miles
nearest pub 0.5 miles

On the A169 Pickering to Whitby Road, leave Sleights, cross the river Esk and immediately left onto a private road, then right in 100m.

At-a-glance symbols are explained on the flap inside the back cover.

WHIXLEY, North Yorkshire — GUEST ACCOMMODATION

★★★
GUEST ACCOMMODATION

Little Orchard High Street, Whixley, York YO26 8AW
t (01423) 330615

WIGAN, Greater Manchester — HOTEL

★★★
HOTEL

Quality Hotel – Wigan Riverway, Wigan WN1 3SS
t (01942) 826888 f (01942) 825800
e enquiries@hotels-wigan.com w hotels-wigan.com

WINDERMERE, Cumbria — HOTEL

★★★
HOTEL

Burnside Hotel Kendal Road, Bowness-on-Windermere, Bowness LA23 3EP
t 0870 046 8640 f 0870 046 8621
e stay@burnsidehotel.com w burnsidehotel.com

WINDERMERE, Cumbria — HOTEL

★★★
COUNTRY HOUSE HOTEL
GOLD AWARD

Linthwaite House Hotel Crook Road, Bowness-on-Windermere,
Windermere LA23 3JA t (015394) 88600 f (015394) 88601
e stay@linthwaite.com w linthwaite.com

WINDERMERE, Cumbria — SELF CATERING

★★★–★★★★★
SELF CATERING

Deloraine contact Mrs Fanstone, Deloraine, Helm Road,
Bowness-on-Windermere LA23 2HS t (015394) 45557 f 0870 051 7981
e info@deloraine.demon.co.uk w deloraine.demon.co.uk

WINDERMERE, Cumbria Map ref 5A3 — CAMPING & CARAVANNING

★★★
TOURING PARK

🚐(66) £13.60–£25.60
🚛(66) £13.60–£25.60
66 touring pitches

Braithwaite Fold Caravan Club Site

Glebe Road, Bowness-on-Windermere, Windermere LA23 3GZ
t (015394) 42177
e enquiries@caravanclub.co.uk w caravanclub.co.uk

General 🔌P🏕️🚻🚿📶☉📱🔋☀️

Payment Credit/debit cards,
cash/cheques

An attractively laid out site, close to the shores of Windermere and within easy walking distance of the town. Windermere has an excellent sailing centre from which to enjoy sailing, windsurfing and canoeing – you can hire equipment and take instruction. And then there are always the fells – don't forget your walking boots. Open March to November.

From Bowness follow signpost for Bowness Bay; in 300yds turn right into Glebe Road. Site on right.

WINSFORD, Cheshire — GUEST ACCOMMODATION

★★★
GUEST HOUSE

The Winsford Lodge 85-87 Station Road, Winsford CW7 3DE
t (01606) 862008 **f** (01606) 591822
e winsfordlodge@aol.com **w** winsfordlodge.co.uk

WINSTON, County Durham — SELF CATERING

★★★★
SELF CATERING

The Cottage at Alwent Mill contact Mrs Libby Hampson,
The Cottage at Alwent Mill, Alwent Mill, Staindrop Road, Winston DL2 3QH
t (01325) 730479
e libby@alwentmill.co.uk

WOOLER, Northumberland — SELF CATERING

★★★★
SELF CATERING

Crookhouse contact Mrs Lynne Holden, Crookhouse, Kirknewton,
Wooler NE71 6TN **t** (01668) 216113
e stay@crookhousecottages.co.uk **w** crookhouse.co.uk

WOOLER, Northumberland — SELF CATERING

★★★★
SELF CATERING

Fenton Hill Farm Cottages contact Mrs Margaret Logan,
Fenton Hill Farm Cottages, Fenton Hill Farm, Wooler NE71 6JJ
t (01668) 216228 **f** (01668) 216169
e stay@fentonhillfarm.co.uk **w** fentonhillfarm.co.uk

YAPHAM, East Riding of Yorkshire — SELF CATERING

★★★★ – ★★★★★★★
SELF CATERING

Wolds View Holiday Cottages contact Margaret Woodliffe,
Wolds View Holiday Cottages, Mill Farm, York YO42 1PH
t (01759) 302172 **f** (01759) 302172
e info@woldsview.co.uk

YORK, North Yorkshire — HOTEL

★★★
HOTEL

Best Western Monkbar Hotel St Maurices Road, York YO31 7JA
t (01904) 638086 **f** (01904) 629195
e sales@monkbarhotel.co.uk **w** monkbarhotel.co.uk

YORK, North Yorkshire — HOTEL

★★★
HOTEL
GOLD AWARD

The Grange Hotel 1 Clifton, York YO30 6AA
t (01904) 644744 **f** (01904) 612453
e info@grangehotel.co.uk **w** grangehotel.co.uk

YORK, North Yorkshire — HOTEL

QA HOTEL

Hilton York 1 Tower Street, York YO1 9WD **t** (01904) 648111 **f** (01904) 610317
e reservations.york@hilton.com **w** hilton.co.uk/york

YORK, North Yorkshire — GUEST ACCOMMODATION

★★★
GUEST ACCOMMODATION

Groves Hotel St Peters Grove, York YO30 6AQ
t (01904) 559777 **f** (01904) 645832
e admin@ecsyork.co.uk **w** ecsyork.co.uk

YORK, North Yorkshire — SELF CATERING

★★★
SELF CATERING

Classique Select Holiday Accommodation contact Mr Rodney Inns, 21 Larchfield,
Stockton Lane, York YO31 1JS **t** (01904) 421339 **f** (01904) 421339
e rodela_2194_inns@hotmail.com **w** classique-york.co.uk

At-a-glance symbols are explained on the flap inside the back cover.

YORK, North Yorkshire — SELF CATERING

★★★–★★★★★
SELF CATERING

Stakesby Holiday Flats contact Anthony Bryce, Stakesby Holiday Flats, 4 St George's Place, York YO24 1DR **t** (01904) 611634
e ant@stakesby.co.uk **w** stakesby.co.uk

YORK, North Yorkshire — SELF CATERING

★★★★
SELF CATERING

York Lakeside Lodges contact Mr Manasir, York Lakeside Lodges Ltd, Moor Lane, York YO24 2QU **t** (01904) 702346 **f** (01904) 701631
e neil@yorklakesidelodges.co.uk **w** yorklakesidelodges.co.uk

YORK, North Yorkshire — CAMPING & CARAVANNING

★★★★★
TOURING PARK

Beechwood Grange Caravan Club Site Malton Road, York YO32 9TH
t (01904) 424637 **f** (01342) 410258
e natalie.tiller@caravanclub.co.uk **w** caravanclub.co.uk

YORK, North Yorkshire Map ref 4C1 — CAMPING & CARAVANNING

★★★★★
TOURING &
CAMPING PARK

(102)
£14.30–£27.70
(102)
£14.30–£27.70
102 touring pitches

THE
CARAVAN
CLUB

Rowntree Park Caravan Club Site

Terry Avenue, York YO23 1JQ **t** (01904) 658997
w caravanclub.co.uk

General 〔symbols〕
☼

Payment Credit/debit cards, cash/cheques

A very popular site, level and on the banks of the Ouse, within easy walking distance of the beautiful and historic city of York, and a good base to explore Yorkshire. York is a feast – there's so much to see you'll find the days slipping past before you go anywhere else.
open All year

Turn off A64 onto A19 signposted York centre. 2 miles join one-way system. Keep left over bridge. Left after 200yds at ICC site. Right onto Terry Avenue. Site on right 0.25 miles.

Key to symbols

Symbols at the end of each entry help you pick out the services and facilities which are most important for your stay. A key to the symbols can be found inside the back-cover flap. Keep this open for easy reference.

NATIONAL ACCESSIBLE SCHEME RATINGS ONLY

The following establishments hold a National Accessible Scheme rating as shown in their entry, but do not participate in VisitBritain's Enjoy England quality assessment scheme. However, to participate in the National Accessible Scheme accommodation must meet a minimum level of quality. In addition to being assessed under the National Accessible Scheme the entries listed below may hold a quality rating from another organisation.

AMBLESIDE, Cumbria Map ref 5A3   SELF CATERING

Units **1**	
Sleeps **1–7**	

Low season per wk
Min £220.00
High season per wk
Max £450.00

Awaiting
NAS rating

Nationwide Bungalow, Ambleside

contact Gail Lewis, PO Box 36, Cowbridge CF71 7GB   **t** 08456 584478
f (01446) 775060   **e** selfcatering@johngrooms.org.uk   **w** groomsholidays.org.uk

Holiday bungalow, specially adapted for disabled people, close to Lake Windermere. Accommodation for up to seven people in three bedrooms. Level throughout. Roll-in shower. Hoist and shower-chair available.
open All year
nearest shop 1 mile
nearest pub 1 mile

Access   abc 

General

Unit

Payment Credit/debit cards, cash/cheques, euros

BEWCASTLE, Cumbria Map ref 5B2   SELF CATERING

Units **2**	
Sleeps **2–6**	

Low season per wk
£198.00–£398.00
High season per wk
£298.00–£598.00

Bailey Mill, Newcastleton

contact Pamela Copeland, Bailey Mill Trekking Centre, Bailey, Newcastleton TD9 0TR   **t** (01697) 748617   **e** pam@baileymill.fsnet.co.uk
w baileycottages-riding-racing.com

Self-catering courtyard apartments (short breaks available or bed and breakfast). Situated on beautiful Scottish/Cumbria borders. Ideal touring centre. Return to relax in our jacuzzi or sauna before enjoying a drink and/or meal in our cosy bar.
open All year
nearest shop 7 miles
nearest pub < 0.5 miles

General

Unit

Payment Credit/debit cards, cash/cheques

Accessible index

If you have specific accessible requirements, the Accessible index at the back of the guide lists accommodation under different categories for mobility, hearing and visual impairment.

    At-a-glance symbols are explained on the flap inside the back cover.

Country ways

The Countryside Rights of Way Act gives people new rights to walk on areas of open countryside and registered common land.

To find out where you can go and what you can do, as well as information about taking your dog to the countryside, go online at countrysideaccess.gov.uk.

And when you're out and about...

Always follow the Country Code
- Be safe – plan ahead and follow any signs
- Leave gates and property as you find them
- Protect plants and animals, and take your litter home
- Keep dogs under close control
- Consider other people

with wheelchair boarding **RAMPS**, a **SPACIOUS** dedicated area for two wheelchairs, a tip-up **COMPANION SEAT** adjacent to each wheelchair space, wheelchair boarding door **CLEARLY INDICATED**, laptop **SOCKETS** and **FOLD-AWAY** tables, **IMPROVED** access to 20% of seats, **CLEARER,** visible and audible announcements, **EASIER** access to toilet facilities...

...our new trains make life
EASIER FOR EVERYONE.

Book now at **www.tpexpress.co.uk** or for assisted travel bookings call **0800 107 2149**

Inspirational.
Aspirational. Accessible

The moment you arrive at The Trafford Centre you'll see it's a centre designed with accessibility in mind, with 54 parking spaces reserved for disabled drivers immediately next to the entrance.

Once inside, getting around the 230 stores and 55 restaurants, cafes and bars couldn't be easier with free battery-operated scooters or manual wheelchairs, public areas, lifts and toilet blocks designed for wheelchair use, free lenses for the visually impaired and lots of red-coated assistants ready to help.

With so many accessibility features it's hardly surprising we were awarded the Queen Elizabeth Foundation EASE Award for Ease of Access, Services and Employment for disabled people.

For more information please call Customer Services on 0161 749 1510 or our Shopmobility office on 0161 7478046, or go to our website at www.traffordcentre.co.uk

The Trafford Centre ®
always ahead

Access the world

...with disabled facilities from Manchester Airport

Here at Manchester Airport, accessibility is a priority.
Wheelchair users will find special spaces in our car parks,
those with hearing difficulties will appreciate our
minicom system, whilst our Braille signage provides a
helpful touch too. And whenever you need to speak
to someone in person, our Customer Service Advisors
and Information Desk staff are there to assist.
Business or pleasure, there's no easier way to get away.

www.manchesterairport.co.uk

Manchester Airport, Manchester M90 1QX
Tel +44 (0) 161 489 3000

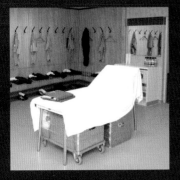

Not what you would expect from a Museum and Tour!

...everything you would expect from UNITED.

For more information or to book:
call: **0870 442 1994**
email: **tours@manutd.co.uk**
or visit: **www.manutd.com**

Breath will be taken

Finalist
The Gulbenkian Prize 2007
for museums and galleries

WESTON PARK MUSEUM FEATURES:

- Objects to Touch
- Displays Including Sound and Film
- Braille Signage
- Large Text in Displays
- Accessible Ramps
- Accessible Toilets and Baby Change
- Guided Tours Available

Western Bank, Sheffield S10 2TP.
Tel: 0114 278 2600
www.sheffieldgalleries.org.uk

Open Every Day Admission Free

 **Weston Park Museum**

SHEFFIELD GALLERIES & MUSEUMS TRUST

Lancashire's Country Parks

Lancashire's Country Parks are beautiful but sometimes challenging places. Access can be difficult due to the gradients and the rough nature of the terrain. To make sites more accessible Lancashire County Council provide Tramper all terrain electric vehicles to borrow free of charge.

Beacon Fell is the best introduction to using these vehicles. A first time user will be given a one to one induction by one of our Rangers. Once the user and the Ranger are happy that the control of the tramper has been mastered the user is free to explore at their leisure.

The result is a true countryside experience including rough paths and steep gradients. Users often come back tired and sometimes muddy, but they come back happy!

Trampers will be available at Beacon Fell and Wycoller Country Parks and can be used on a number of our guided walks.

Comments from users

"the Tramper will enable me to return to this wonderful place and be part of the able-bodied world – my deepest thanks."

"for someone who was a keen walker prior to my disability this has been a great experience, thank you."

"never thought I would do Beacon Fell again, just shows how wrong you can be."

Discover a great day out at the North East's most popular free museum

Discovery museum

Blandford Square
Newcastle upon Tyne
Tel: (0191) 232 6789
Textphone: 18001 0191 232 6789
www.twmuseums.org.uk/discovery

TYNE & WEAR museums

Sunderland Museum & Winter Gardens

SUNDERLAND
MUSEUM & WINTER GARDENS

Free entry

Burdon Road, Sunderland

Tel: (0191) 553 2323
Textphone: 18001 0191 553 2323
Fax: (0191) 553 7828

www.twmuseums.org.uk/sunderland

Open: Monday to Saturday 10am-5pm
& Sunday 2pm-5pm

RENAISSANCE
NORTH EAST
museums for
changing lives

Sunderland
City Council

TYNE & WEAR museums

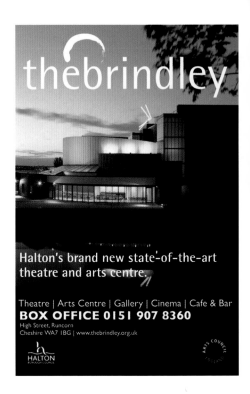
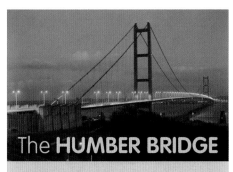

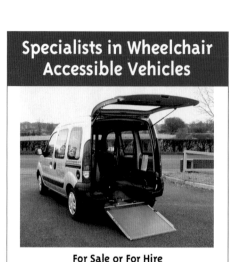

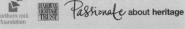

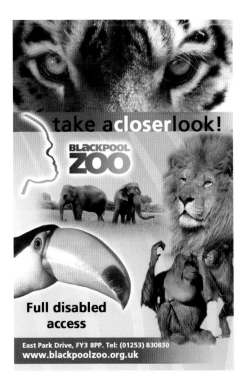

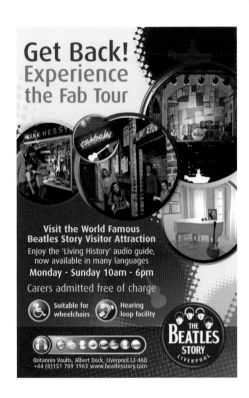

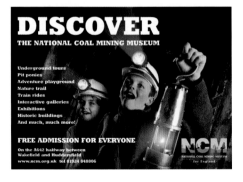

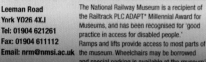

Central England

Thurne Dyke Wind Pump on the Norfolk Broads

Bedfordshire, Cambridgeshire, Derbyshire, Essex, Herefordshire, Hertfordshire, Leicestershire, Lincolnshire, Norfolk, Northamptonshire, Nottinghamshire, Rutland, Shropshire, Staffordshire, Suffolk, Warwickshire, West Midlands, Worcestershire

Cavendish, Suffolk

Central **attraction**

Artistic connections and inspiring landscapes, industrial heritage brought to life, thrilling spectator sports – it's all on a plate in Central England. Pack a picnic and explore the Pennines or the Malvern Hills, drift along one of the many canals that criss-cross the region or spot oyster catchers in one of the coastal nature reserves.

Creative masterpieces

With such a rich mix of industry, history, culture and raw natural beauty it's not surprising Central England inspired so much creative energy. Spot a solitary cottage near Flatford Mill in the Stour Valley, the location of The Hay Wain, a masterpiece by local boy John Constable. On the streets of Stratford-upon-Avon, you just can't avoid references to the town's greatest son, William Shakespeare. Book a seat at the Swan Theatre – home of the Royal Shakespeare Company. Take a factory tour at Wedgwood Visitor Centre, Stoke-on-Trent, and then browse the shops for a memorable souvenir.

Craftsmen hand-painting at the Royal Worcester factory, Worcestershire

Find out what shaped DH Lawrence's early life at his birthplace in Eastwood, near Nottingham. See at first hand the decadence of Lord Byron in gothic Newstead Abbey and, on a musical note, Benjamin Britten's Aldeburgh Festival at Snape Maltings, Suffolk, is the place for classical concerts in a rural setting. On Aldeburgh's beach, you can't miss a huge sculpture, The Scallop, dedicated to the composer. For more music, visit Audley End House and Garden to enjoy a summer evening concert.

Action and adventure

Head for the National Space Centre, Leicester, where you can test your ability to survive a little more with a voyage on the interactive Human Spaceflight. Pick up a Thrill Hopper ticket that gives you great value access to top theme park attractions: Drayton Manor Theme Park, Alton Towers and Waterworld. Take a walk on the wild side in Woburn Safari Park, hunt for the Lost World Tribe in the Lost World

Maze at the Dinosaur Adventure Park near Norwich or let the kids hit the assault course at Conkers, Swadlincote, in the heart of the National Forest. More of a spectator? Thrill to the sight of high-octane drag racing at Santa Pod or book early for the British Grand Prix at Silverstone. Hold on to your horse and back a winner at Newmarket, the historic home of British horseracing.

Create your own adventures crossing in and out of Wales on Offa's Dyke Path or tackle part of the Heart of England Way. There's 270 miles of the Pennine Way, stretching from the Peak District

The Pennine Way, Edale, Derbyshire

Inset pictures
Audley End, Essex; motor racing at Silverstone, Northamptonshire; Kenilworth Castle, Warwickshire; the National Space Centre at Leicester

The Iron Bridge - spanning the Severn Gorge at Ironbridge, Shropshire

Artist, architect, scientist, historian or aviator – whatever your interests, there's an attraction to suit

all the way to the Scottish Borders, to dip into or explore the long-distance paths that reach East Anglia's numerous sandy beaches. In the west of the region follow the Wye Valley through breaktaking scenery, including outstanding views from Symonds Yat.

Spotlight on the past

Spend time in the historic cities of Shrewsbury and Worcester – noted for uneven Tudor half-timbered architecture. Reach for your camera as you pass through Much Wenlock, one of the beautiful black and white villages of Shropshire. Castles and grand homes dot the landscape – Kenilworth Castle and Warwick Castle are favourites. For Elizabethan architecture at its most impressive, Hardwick Hall and Chatsworth are hard to beat. Step back into the area's proud industrial past at the Ironbridge Gorge Museums – at Enginuity let the kids switch on their imaginations in the interactive design and technology centre. Have a chat with the working craftsmen at The Black Country Living Museum. Trace the history of fighter planes at the Imperial War Museum Duxford in Cambridgeshire, Europe's premier aviation museum, or visit the new National Cold War Exhibition at RAF Museum Cosford.

Time and tides

Picnic, flask and binoculars at the ready for mile upon mile of sandy and shingle beaches running from Essex to Lincolnshire. Undeniably beautiful is the National Nature Reserve at Holkham, Norfolk, where creeks, sand dunes, pinewoods, pastures and marshes have merged. Down along the coast at RSPB Minsmere, Suffolk, peer from a hide to see just a few of the wading birds and waterfowl. Seek out the havens of Frinton-on-Sea, Covehithe and Anderby Creek and the coast's numerous quaint fishing villages. For bustling seaside resorts, try Felixstowe, Southend-on-Sea and Great Yarmouth. Try out a hammock, avoid the rats and beware of the cannon fire in Below Decks, an interactive recreation of HMS Victory, at the Norfolk Nelson Museum in Great Yarmouth.

Duxford, Cambridgeshire

Moving inland, explore the rivers and dykes in the Fens – spread over Cambridgeshire, Lincolnshire, Norfolk and Rutland. At Fenscape, the interactive Fens discovery centre in Spalding, learn about the unique past of the inhospitable marshland. For lazy days spent with friends and family, what could be more calming than the reed-fringed waterways of the Norfolk Broads?

Useful regional contacts

For information before you travel, check out the useful regional contacts below. Local Tourist Information Centres will also be able to give you information on accessible attractions and accommodation.

East Midlands Tourism
w discovereastmidlands.com

East of England Tourism
t (01284) 727470
w visiteastofengland.com

Marketing Birmingham
t (0121) 202 5115
w visitbirmingham.com

Black Country Tourism
w blackcountrytourism.co.uk

Visit Coventry & Warwickshire
t (024) 7622 7264
w visitcoventryand
warwickshire.co.uk

Visit Herefordshire
t (01432) 260621
w visitherefordshire.co.uk

Shakespeare Country
t 0870 160 7930
w shakespeare-country.co.uk

Shropshire Tourism
t (01743) 462462
w shropshiretourism.info

Destination Staffordshire
t 0870 500 4444
w enjoystaffordshire.com

Destination Worcestershire
t (01905) 728787
w visitworcestershire.org

Publications

Access for All
A free guide to the Peak District produced by the National Park Authority. Call (01629) 816200.

Access in Ludlow
A publication by South Shropshire Access Group. Available from the Tourist Information Centre. Call (01584) 875053 or visit ludlow.org.uk.

Access to Bedford
A range of leaflets from Bedford Council and Access Group. Call (01234) 215226 or visit bedford.gov.uk.

Staffordshire Access for Everyone
An information pack for visitors produced by Staffordshire Tourism. Call (01785) 277397 or email tourism@staffordshire.gov.uk.

Resources

Disabled Holiday Information
PO Box 185, Oswestry SY10 1AF
e info@disabledholidayinfo.org.uk
w disabledholidayinfo.org.uk
Provides information about holidays for people with disabilities and produces a range of wheelchair user's guides on attractions, accessible sites and trails, and activities in Shropshire. The publications are available by post or may be downloaded from the website.

stratford-upon-avon.co.uk
A website which includes information on accessible tourism facilities in Stratford-upon-Avon.

Tourist Information Centres

When you arrive at your destination, visit a Tourist Information Centre for help with accommodation and information about local attractions and events, or email your request before you go.

Bedfordshire

Bedford	St Paul's Square	(01234) 215226	touristinfo@bedford.gov.uk
Luton	St George's Square	(01582) 401579	tourist.information@luton.gov.uk

Cambridgeshire

Cambridge	Wheeler Street	0871 226 8006	info@visitcambridge.org
Ely	29 St Mary's Street	(01353) 662062	tic@eastcambs.gov.uk
Peterborough	3-5 Minster Precincts	(01733) 452336	tic@peterborough.gov.uk
St Neots	8 New Street	(01480) 388788	stneots.tic@huntsdc.gov.uk
Wisbech	2-3 Bridge Street	(01945) 583263	tourism@fenland.gov.uk

Derbyshire

Ashbourne	13 Market Place	(01335) 343666	ashbourneinfo@derbyshiredales.gov.uk
Bakewell	Bridge Street	(01629) 816558	bakewell@peakdistrict.gov.uk
Buxton	The Crescent	(01298) 25106	tourism@highpeak.gov.uk
Castleton Visitor Centre	Buxton Road	(01433) 620679	castleton@peakdistrict.gov.uk
Chesterfield	Rykneld Square	(01246) 345777	tourism@chesterfield.gov.uk
Derby City	Market Place	(01332) 255802	tourism@derby.gov.uk
Glossop	Victoria Street	(01457) 855920	info@glossoptouristcentre.co.uk
Matlock	Crown Square	(01629) 583388	matlockinfo@derbyshiredales.gov.uk
Matlock Bath*	The Pavillion	(01629) 55082	matlockbathinfo@derbyshiredales.gov.uk
Ripley	Market Place	(01773) 841488	touristinformation@ambervalley.gov.uk
Swadlincote	Sharpe's Pottery	(01283) 222848	tic@sharpespotterymuseum.org.uk

Essex

Braintree	Market Square	(01376) 550066	tic@braintree.gov.uk
Brentwood	44 High Street	(01277) 200300	
Clacton-on-Sea	Station Road	(01255) 686633	clactontic@tendringdc.gov.uk
Colchester	1 Queen Street	(01206) 282920	vic@colchester.gov.uk
Harwich Connexions	Iconfield Park	(01255) 506139	tic@harwichticconnexions.co.uk
Maldon	Coach Lane	(01621) 856503	tic@maldon.gov.uk
Saffron Walden	1 Market Place	(01799) 510444	tourism@uttlesford.gov.uk
Sandy	5 Shannon Court	(01767) 682728	tourism@sandytowncouncil.gov.uk
Southend-on-Sea	Western Esplanade	(01702) 215120	vic@southend.gov.uk
Waltham Abbey	2-4 Highbridge Street	(01992) 652295	tic@walthamabbey-tic.gov.uk

Herefordshire

Hereford	1 King Street	(01432) 268430	tic-hereford@herefordshire.gov.uk

Ledbury	3 The Homend	(01531) 636147	tic-ledbury@herefordshire.gov.uk
Leominster	1 Corn Square	(01568) 616460	
Queenswood*	Dinmore Hill	(01568) 797842	
Ross-on-Wye	Edde Cross Street	(01989) 562768	tic-ross@herefordshire.gov.uk

Hertfordshire

Birchanger Green	Welcome Break Service Area	(01279) 508656	
Bishop's Stortford	Windhill	(01279) 655831	tic@bishopsstortford.org
Hertford	10 Market Place	(01992) 584322	tic@hertford.gov.uk
Letchworth Garden City	33-35 Station Road	(01462) 487868	tic@letchworth.com
St Albans	Market Place	(01727) 864511	tic@stalbans.gov.uk

Leicestershire

Ashby-de-la-Zouch	North Street	(01530) 411767	ashby@nwleicestershire.gov.uk
Hinckley	Lancaster Road	(01455) 635106	hinckleytic@leics.gov.uk
Leicester City	7/9 Every Street	0906 294 1113**	info@goleicestershire.com
Loughborough	Market Place	(01509) 218113	loughborough@goleicestershire.com
Market Harborough	Adam & Eve Street	(01858) 821270	harborough@goleicestershire.com

Lincolnshire

Boston	Market Place	(01205) 356656	ticboston@boston.gov.uk
Brigg	Market Place	(01652) 657053	brigg.tic@norhtlincs.gov.uk
Grantham	St Peter's Hill	(01476) 406166	granthamtic@southkesteven.gov.uk
Horncastle	14 Bull Ring	(01507) 526636	horncastleinfo@e-lindsey.gov.uk
Lincoln Castle Hill	9 Castle Hill	(01522) 873213	tourism@lincoln.gov.uk
Lincoln Corn Hill	21 Cornhill	(01522) 873256	tourism@lincoln.gov.uk
Louth	The Market Hall	(01507) 609289	louthinfo@e-lindsey.gov.uk
Mablethorpe	High Street	(01507) 474939	mablethorpeinfo@e-lindsey.gov.uk
Scunthorpe	Central Library, Carlton Street	(01724) 297354	brigg.tic@norhtlincs.gov.uk
Skegness	Grand Parade	(01754) 899887	skegnessinfo@e-lindsey.gov.uk
Sleaford	Carre Street	(01529) 414294	tic@n-kesteven.gov.uk
Spalding	Market Place	(01775) 725468	tic@sholland.gov.uk
Stamford	27 St Mary's Street	(01780) 755611	stamfordtic@southkesteven.gov.uk
Woodhall Spa*	Iddesleigh Road	(01526) 353775	woodhallspainfo@e-lindsey.gov.uk

Norfolk

Aylsham	Norwich Road	(01263) 733903	aylsham.tic@broadland.gov.uk
Burnham Deepdale	Deepdale Farm	(01485) 210256	info@deepdalefarm.co.uk
Cromer	Prince of Wales Road	0871 200 3071	cromertic@north-norfolk.gov.uk
Diss	Mere Street	(01379) 650523	dtic@s-norfolk.gov.uk
Downham Market	78 Priory Road	(01366) 383287	downham-market.tic@west-norfolk.gov.uk
Great Yarmouth	25 Marine Parade	(01493) 846345	tourism@great-yarmouth.gov.uk
Holt*	3 Pound House	0871 200 3071	holttic@north-norfolk.gov.uk
Hoveton*	Station Road	(01603) 782281	hovetoninfo@broads-authority.gov.uk
Hunstanton	The Green	(01485) 532610	hunstanton.tic@west-norfolk.gov.uk
King's Lynn	Purfleet Quay	(01553) 763044	kings-lynn.tic@west-norfolk.gov.uk

Norwich	Millennium Plain	(01603) 727927	tourism@norwich.gov.uk
Sheringham*	Station Approach	0871 200 3071	sheringhamtic@north-norfolk.gov.uk
Swaffham*	Market Place	(01760) 722255	
Thetford	4 White Hart Street	(01842) 820689	info@thetfordtourism.co.uk
Wells-next-the-Sea*	Staithe Street	0871 200 3071	wellstic@north-norfolk.gov.uk
Wymondham	Market Place	(01953) 604721	wymondhamtic@btconnect.com

Northamptonshire

Brackley	2 Bridge Street	(01280) 700111	tic@southnorthants.gov.uk
Kettering	Sheep Street	(01536) 410266	tic@kettering.gov.uk
Northampton	St Giles Square	(01604) 838800	northampton.tic@ explorenorthamptonshire.co.uk
Oundle	14 West Street	(01832) 274333	oundle@east-northamptonshire.gov.uk

Nottinghamshire

Newark	Castlegate	(01636) 655765	gilstrap@nsdc.info
Nottingham	1-4 Smithy Row	0844 477 5678	tourist.information@nottinghamcity.gov.uk
Ollerton	Sherwood Heath	(01623) 824545	sherwoodheath@nsdc.info
Retford	40 Grove Street	(01777) 860780	retford.tourist@bassetlaw.gov.uk
Worksop	Memorial Avenue	(01909) 501148	worksop.tourist@bassetlaw.gov.uk

Rutland

| Oakham | Catmose Street | (01572) 758441 | museum@rutland.gov.uk |
| Rutland Water* | Sykes Lane | (01572) 653026 | tic@anglianwater.co.uk |

Shropshire

Bridgnorth	Listley Street	(01746) 763257	bridgnorth.tourism@shropshire-cc.gov.uk
Church Stretton	Church Street	(01694) 723133	churchstretton.scf@shropshire-cc.gov.uk
Ellesmere, Shropshire*	Mereside	(01691) 622981	ellesmere.tourism@shropshire-cc.gov.uk
Ironbridge	The Toll House	(01952) 884391	tic@ironbridge.org.uk
Ludlow	Castle Street	(01584) 875053	ludlow.tourism@shropshire-cc.gov.uk
Market Drayton	49 Cheshire Street	(01630) 653114	marketdrayton.scf@shropshire-cc.gov.uk
Much Wenlock*	High Street	(01952) 727679	muchwenlock.tourism@shropshire-cc.gov.uk
Oswestry (Mile End)	Mile End	(01691) 662488	tic@oswestry-bc.gov.uk
Oswestry Town (Heritage Centre)	2 Church Terrace	(01691) 662753	ot@oswestry-welshborders.org.uk
Shrewsbury	The Square	(01743) 281200	visitorinfo@shrewsbury.gov.uk
Telford	The Telford Centre	(01952) 238008	tourist-info@telfordshopping.co.uk
Whitchurch	12 St Mary's Street	(01948) 664577	whitchurch.heritage@ukonline.co.uk

Staffordshire

Burton upon Trent	Coors Visitor Centre	(01283) 508111	tic@eaststaffsbc.gov.uk
Leek	1 Market Place	(01538) 483741	tourism.services@staffsmoorlands.gov.uk
Lichfield	Castle Dyke	(01543) 412112	info@visitlichfield.com
Newcastle-under-Lyme	Ironmarket	(01782) 297313	tic.newcastle@staffordshire.gov.uk
Stafford	Market Street	(01785) 619619	tic@staffordbc.gov.uk
Stoke-on-Trent	Victoria Hall	(01782) 236000	stoke.tic@stoke.gov.uk

Tamworth	29 Market Street	(01827) 709581	tic@tamworth.gov.uk

Suffolk

Aldeburgh	152 High Street	(01728) 453637	atic@suffolkcoastal.gov.uk
Beccles*	Fen Lane	(01502) 713196	becclesinfo@broads-authority.gov.uk
Bury St Edmunds	6 Angel Hill	(01284) 764667	tic@stedsbc.gov.uk
Felixstowe	91 Undercliff Road West	(01394) 276770	ftic@suffolkcoastal.gov.uk
Flatford	Flatford Lane	(01206) 299460	flatfordvic@babergh.gov.uk
Ipswich	St Stephens Lane	(01473) 258070	tourist@ipswich.gov.uk
Lavenham	Lady Street	(01787) 248207	lavenhamtic@babergh.gov.uk
Lowestoft	Royal Plain	(01502) 533600	touristinfo@waveney.gov.uk
Newmarket	Palace Street	(01638) 667200	tic.newmarket@forest-heath.gov.uk
Southwold	69 High Street	(01502) 724729	southwold.tic@waveney.gov.uk
Stowmarket	Museum of East Anglican Life	(01449) 676800	tic@midsuffolk.gov.uk
Sudbury	Market Hill	(01787) 881320	sudburytic@babergh.gov.uk
Woodbridge	Station Buildings	(01394) 382240	wtic@suffolkcoastal.gov.uk

Warwickshire

Coventry Airport	Coventry Airport South	(024) 7622 7264	tic@cvone.co.uk
Coventry Cathedral	Cathedral Ruins	(024) 7622 7264	tic@cvone.co.uk
Coventry Ricoh Arena	Phoenix Way	0870 111 6397	tic@cvone.co.uk
Coventry Transport Museum	Hales Street	(024) 7622 7264	tic@cvone.co.uk
Kenilworth	11 Smalley Place	(01926) 748900	kenilworthlibrary@warwickshire.gov.uk
Leamington Spa	The Parade	0870 160 7930	info@shakespeare-country.co.uk
Nuneaton	Church Street	(024) 7634 7006	nuneatonlibrary@warwickshire.gov.uk
Rugby	Little Elborow Street	(01788) 533217	visitor.centre@rugby.gov.uk
Stratford-upon-Avon	Bridgefoot	0870 160 7930	info@shakespeare-country.co.uk
Warwick	Jury Street	(01926) 492212	touristinfo@warwick-uk.co.uk

West Midlands

Birmingham Rotunda	150 New Street	0870 225 0127	callcentre@marketingbirmingham.com
Coventry	4 Priory Row	(024) 7622 7264	tic@cvone.co.uk
Merry Hill	Merry Hill	(01384) 487900	
Solihull	Homer Road	(0121) 704 6130	ckelly@solihull.gov.uk
Wolverhampton	18 Queen Square	(01902) 556110	wolverhampton.tic@dial.pipex.com

Worcestershire

Bewdley	Load Street	(01299) 404740	bewdleytic@wyreforestdc.gov.uk
Bromsgrove	26 Birmingham Road	(01527) 831809	tic@bromsgrove.gov.uk
Droitwich Spa	Victoria Square	(01905) 774312	heritage@droitwichspa.gov.uk
Evesham	Abbey Gate	(01386) 446944	tic@almonry.ndo.co.uk
Malvern	21 Church Street	(01684) 892289	malvern.tic@malvernhills.gov.uk
Redditch	Alcester Street	(01527) 60806	info.centre@redditchbc.gov.uk
Upton-upon-Severn	4 High Street	(01684) 594200	upton.tic@malvernhills.gov.uk
Worcester	High Street	(01905) 726311	touristinfo@cityofworcester.gov.uk

* seasonal opening ** calls to this number are charged at a premium rate

ABBERLEY, Worcestershire — SELF CATERING

★★★
SELF CATERING

Old Yates Cottages contact Mr & Mrs Richard & Sarah Goodman,
Old Yates Cottages, Stockton Road, Abberley, Worcester WR6 6AT
t (01299) 896500 **f** (01299) 896065
e oldyates@aol.com **w** oldyatescottages.co.uk

ALDEBURGH, Suffolk — HOTEL

★★★
HOTEL
SILVER AWARD

Brudenell Hotel The Parade, Aldeburgh IP15 5BU
t (01728) 452071 **f** (01728) 454082
e info@brudenellhotel.co.uk **w** brudenellhotel.co.uk

ALFORD, Lincolnshire — HOTEL

★★★
SMALL HOTEL

Half Moon Hotel and Restaurant 25-28 West Street, Alford LN13 9DG
t (01507) 463477 **f** (01507) 462916
e halfmoonalford25@aol.com **w** halfmoonhotelalford.com

ASHBOURNE, Derbyshire — GUEST ACCOMMODATION

★★★★
BED & BREAKFAST

Mona Villas Bed and Breakfast 1 Mona Villas, Church Lane Mayfield,
Ashbourne DE6 2JS **t** (01335) 343773 **f** (01335) 343773
e info@mona-villas.fsnet.co.uk **w** mona-villas.fsnet.co.uk

ASHBOURNE, Derbyshire Map ref 4B2 — SELF CATERING

★★★★–★★★★★★
SELF CATERING

Units **2**
Sleeps **2–6**
Low season per wk
£342.00–£498.00
High season per wk
£509.00–£895.00

Ancestral Barn, Ashbourne

contact Mrs Sue Fowler, Ancestral Barn, Church Farm,
Stanshope, Nr Alstonefield, Ashbourne DE6 2AD **t** (01335) 310243
f (01335) 310243
e sue@fowler89.fsnet.co.uk **w** dovedalecottages.co.uk

Ancestral barn with splendid canopy beds, all en suite bathrooms. Sleeps six (two king-size and one twin). Downstairs bedroom, with king-size bed, is fully accessible. Full of old-world charm and character. Also idyllic country cottage, cosy and warm. Both nestling in a truly peaceful setting on an organic farm near Dovedale.

open All year
nearest shop 3 miles
nearest pub 1 mile

General ⛺ ▥ ♨ P ✂ ▣

Unit ♨ ▥ ▣ ▣ ▢ ▢ ▢ ▥ ▱
▢ ▢ ✿

Payment Cash/cheques

Fabulous canopy bed downstairs in king-size bedroom with walk-in shower and seat for the mobile disabled. A real touch of luxury.

From M1 jct 25, on the A515 Ashbourne/Buxton road. Opposite Newton Chalets take left-hand turning, at river turn left, go through Milldale and up valley to Watt Russell pub. Turn left then 1st left to Stanshope, immediately after hall turn left.

ASHBOURNE, Derbyshire | CAMPING & CARAVANNING

★★★★
TOURING PARK

Blackwall Plantation Caravan Club Site Kirk Ireton, Ashbourne DE6 3JL
t (01335) 370903 **f** (01335) 372152
w caravanclub.co.uk

ASHDON, Essex | SELF CATERING

★★★
SELF CATERING

Hill Farm Holiday Cottages contact Mrs Annette Bel, Radwinter Road,
Ashdon CM10 2ET **t** (01799) 584881
e hillfarm-holiday-cottages@hotmail.co.uk **w** hillfarm-holiday-cottages.co.uk

BAKEWELL, Derbyshire | CAMPING & CARAVANNING

★★★★★
TOURING PARK

Chatsworth Park Caravan Club Site Chatsworth, Bakewell DE45 1PN
t (01246) 582226 **f** (01246) 583762
w caravanclub.co.uk

BARTON TURF, Norfolk | SELF CATERING

★★★★
SELF CATERING

The Piggeries contact Mrs Debra Watson, Home Farm Barn, Water Lane,
Little Plumstead, Norwich NR13 5EX
t (01603) 712030

BASILDON, Essex | HOTEL

★★
HOTEL

Campanile Hotel A127 Southend Arterial Road, Pipps Hill, Basildon SS14 3AE
t (01268) 530810 **f** (01268) 286710
e basildon@campanile-hotels.com **w** campanile.com

BEESTON, Norfolk | SELF CATERING

★★★
SELF CATERING

Holmdene Farm contact Mrs Gaye Davidson, Syers Lane, Beeston PE32 2NJ
t (01328) 701284
e holmdenefarm@farmersweekly.net **w** northnorfolk.co.uk/holmdenefarm

BELCHFORD, Lincolnshire | SELF CATERING

★★★★–★★★★★★
SELF CATERING

Poachers Hideaway contact Mrs Sally Tuxworth, Flintwood Farm, Belchford,
Horncastle LN9 6QN **t** (01507) 533555 **f** (01507) 534264
e andrewtuxworth@poachershideaway.com

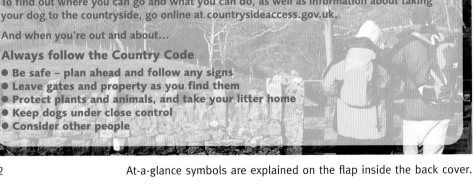

Country ways

The Countryside Rights of Way Act gives people new rights to walk on areas of open countryside and registered common land.

To find out where you can go and what you can do, as well as information about taking your dog to the countryside, go online at countrysideaccess.gov.uk.

And when you're out and about...

Always follow the Country Code

- Be safe – plan ahead and follow any signs
- Leave gates and property as you find them
- Protect plants and animals, and take your litter home
- Keep dogs under close control
- Consider other people

At-a-glance symbols are explained on the flap inside the back cover.

BIRMINGHAM, West Midlands Map ref 4B3

★★★★★
TOURING PARK

(99) £13.60–£25.60
(99) £13.60–£25.60
99 touring pitches

Chapel Lane Caravan Park

Chapel Lane, Wythall, Birmingham B47 6JX **t** (01564) 826483
w caravanclub.co.uk

Surprisingly rural, in the shadow of an old chapel and with a pleasant open aspect, yet convenient for the motorways (M1, M6 and M42), Birmingham and the National Exhibition Centre. The Transport Museum is adjacent to the site and Becketts Farm Shop with restaurant is just a ten-minute walk away.

open All year

From M1 jct 23a, jct 3 off M42 then A435 to Birmingham. After 1 mile at roundabout take 1st exit, Middle Lane. Turn right at church then immediately right into site.

General 🔲 P 📷 🔄 🎁 🆆🅿 📶 ☺ 📖
🔘 ☼

Leisure 🅰

Payment Credit/debit cards, cash/cheques

THE
**CARAVAN
CLUB**

BLACKSHAW MOOR, Staffordshire

★★★★★
TOURING PARK

Blackshaw Moor Caravan Club Site Blackshaw Moor, Leek ST13 8TW
t (01538) 300203
w caravanclub.co.uk

BLAKENEY, Norfolk

★★
HOTEL

The Pheasant Hotel Coast Road, Kelling, Holt NR25 7EG
t (01263) 588382 **f** (01263) 588101
e enquiries@pheasanthotelnorfolk.co.uk **w** pheasanthotelnorfolk.co.uk

BLYTON, Lincolnshire

★★★
BED & BREAKFAST

Blyton (Sunnyside) Ponds Sunnyside Farm, Station Road, Blyton,
Gainsborough DN21 3LE **t** (01427) 628240
e blytonponds@msn.com **w** blytonponds.co.uk

BOSTON, Lincolnshire Map ref 3A1 | SELF CATERING

★★★★–★★★★★★
SELF CATERING

Units **8**
Sleeps **1–5**

Low season per wk
£290.00–£320.00
High season per wk
£395.00–£450.00

Elms Farm Cottages, Boston

contact Carol Emerson, Elms Farm Cottages, The Elms, Hubberts Bridge, Boston PE20 3QP **t** (01205) 290840 & 07887 652021 **f** (01205) 290840
e carol@elmsfarmcottages.co.uk **w** elmsfarmcottages.co.uk

Award-winning barn conversion of high-quality cottages, some with wood-burning stoves. En suite facilities, private patio with picnic bench. All cottages are accessible, four with shower rooms especially suitable for wheelchair users. Grass field with wildflower meadow for guests to enjoy. Communal laundry and built-in barbecue.

open All year
nearest shop 2 miles
nearest pub < 0.5 miles

On A1121 (on western side of Boston), 250m from Hubberts Bridge crossroads.

Access abc ✗

General ⌂ 🏢 ♿ P ✂ ▣ Ⓢ

Unit ♨ 🏢 ▣ 📺 ▣ ▣ ♨ ♨ 🏠 ⬛ 🗄
🍽 👝 ❄

Payment Credit/debit cards, cash/cheques

Gold and Silver Awards

VisitBritain's unique Gold and Silver Awards recognise exceptional quality in serviced accommodation.

Enjoy England assessors make recommendations for Gold and Silver Awards during assessments in recognition of levels of quality over and above that expected of a particular rating.

Look for the Gold and Silver Awards in the regional sections.

At-a-glance symbols are explained on the flap inside the back cover.

BRASSINGTON, Derbyshire Map ref 4B2 — SELF CATERING

★★★★
SELF CATERING

Units **1**
Sleeps **2-4**

Low season per wk
£330.00-£500.00
High season per wk
£580.00-£780.00

Hoe Grange Holidays, Matlock

contact Felicity Brown, Hoe Grange, Matlock DE4 4HP
t (01629) 540262 **f** (01629) 540262
e info@hoegrangeholidays.co.uk **w** hoegrangeholidays.co.uk

Secluded self-catering log cabin furnished to a high standard with spacious outdoor decking; a real home away from home. Near Dovedale, Chatsworth and Carsington Water. Level access throughout. One double and one large twin bedroom with space for mobile hoist and fully adapted en suite shower. Ample parking. Service dogs welcome.

open All year
nearest shop 3 miles
nearest pub 2 miles

Access abc 🐾

General

Unit

Payment Credit/debit cards, cash/cheques

From Ashbourne take A515 for Buxton. Turn right onto B5056 towards Bakewell. Hoe Grange is on left, 5 miles from this junction, past turn for Parwich.

Mobile shower chair/bath boards included. 10% discount – Jan/Feb. Additional cabin for larger groups/families. Short breaks.

BROMYARD, Herefordshire — CAMPING & CARAVANNING

★★★★
TOURING PARK

Bromyard Downs Brockhampton, Bringsty, Worcester WR6 5TE
t (01885) 482607
w caravanclub.co.uk

BURGH ON BAIN, Lincolnshire — SELF CATERING

★★★★
SELF CATERING

Bainfield Lodge contact Mr & Mrs D Walker, Bainfield House, Main Road, Burgh-on-Bain, Market Rasen LN8 6JY
t (01507) 313540
e dennis.walker1@btinternet.com

BUTTERTON, Staffordshire — SELF CATERING

★★★★★
SELF CATERING

Swainsley Farm contact Mr & Mrs Chris Snook, Swainsley Farm, Butterton, Leek ST13 7SS **t** (01298) 84530 **f** (01298) 84530
e info@swainsleyfarm.co.uk **w** swainsleyfarm.co.uk

CAMPING & CARAVANNING

★★★★★
TOURING &
CAMPING PARK

(117)
£12.10–£24.90
(117)
£12.10–£24.90
117 touring pitches

CARAVAN
CLUB

Grin Low Caravan Club Site

Grin Low Road, Ladmanlow, Buxton SK17 6UJ **t** (01298) 77735
w caravanclub.co.uk

Hidden away on the valley floor, Grin Low is conveniently placed for just about everything going on in and around the Peak District, but particularly for the civilised little town of Buxton with its colourful Pavilion Gardens and the Opera House which offers a wide range of events. Open March to November.

From Buxton turn left off A53 Buxton to Leek road. Within 1.5 miles at Grin Low signpost, 300yds turn left into the site approach road; site entrance 0.25 miles away.

General ⌨ P 🔌 🛁 🚻 WP 📶 ☺ 💷 🔘 ☼

Leisure /🎢\

Payment Credit/debit cards, cash/cheques

CAMPING & CARAVANNING

★★★★★
TOURING &
CAMPING PARK

(60) £12.10–£24.90
(60) £12.10–£24.90
60 touring pitches

CARAVAN
CLUB

Cherry Hinton Caravan Club Site

Lime Kiln Road, Cherry Hinton, Cambridge CB1 8NQ **t** (01223) 244088
w caravanclub.co.uk

Set in old quarry workings and within a site of special scientific interest, this site has been imaginatively landscaped to create the impression of being in the heart of the countryside while only a ten-minute bus journey on the 'park & ride' (0.5 miles from site) to the city centre.

open All year

M11 jct 9 onto A11. After 7 miles slip road signposted Fulbourn and Tevisham. In Fulbourn continue to roundabout signposted Cambridge. At traffic lights turn left. Left again into Lime Kiln Road.

General ⌨ P 🔌 🛁 🚻 WP 📶 ☺ 💷 🔘 ☼

Payment Credit/debit cards, cash/cheques

At-a-glance symbols are explained on the flap inside the back cover.

CASTLETON, Derbyshire — CAMPING & CARAVANNING

★★★★★
TOURING &
CAMPING PARK

Losehill Caravan Club Site Castleton, Hope Valley S33 8WB
t (01433) 620636
w caravanclub.co.uk

CHADDESLEY CORBETT, Worcestershire — HOTEL

★★★
HOTEL
GOLD AWARD

Brockencote Hall Chaddesley Corbett, Nr Kidderminster DY10 4PY
t (01562) 777876 **f** (01562) 777872
e info@brockencotehall.com **w** brockencotehall.com

CHELMSFORD, Essex — HOTEL

★★
SMALL HOTEL

Boswell House Hotel 118 Springfield Road, Chelmsford CM2 6LF
t (01245) 287587 **f** (01245) 287587
e boswell118@aol.com **w** boswellhousehotel.co.uk

CHESTERFIELD, Derbyshire Map ref 4B2 — HOTEL

★★
SMALL HOTEL
SILVER AWARD

B&B per room per night
s £45.00–£55.00
d £68.00–£75.00
HB per person per night
£59.50–£70.50

Abbeydale Hotel

Cross Street, Chesterfield S40 4TD **t** (01246) 277849 **f** (01246) 558223
e Abbeydale1ef@aol.com **w** abbeydalehotel.co.uk

The Abbeydale Hotel is located in a quiet part of town, but still only five minutes' walk from Chesterfield town centre. A home away from home.
open All year except Christmas
bedrooms 7 double, 1 twin, 3 single, 1 family
bathrooms All en suite

Access
General
Rooms
Payment Credit/debit cards, cash/cheques

CHURCH STRETTON, Shropshire — SELF CATERING

★★★–★★★★★
SELF CATERING

Botvyle Farm Holiday Cottages contact Mrs Gill Bebbington, Botvyle Farm, All Stretton, Church Stretton SY6 7JN **t** (01694) 722869 **f** (01694) 722869
e enquiries@botvylefarm.co.uk **w** botvylefarm.co.uk

CLACTON-ON-SEA, Essex

See entry on p148

CLARE, Suffolk — GUEST ACCOMMODATION

★★★★
BED & BREAKFAST
SILVER AWARD

Fiddlesticks Pinkuah Lane, Pentlow Ridge, Pentlow, Sudbury CO10 7JW
t (01787) 280154 **f** (01787) 280154
e sarah@fiddlesticks.biz **w** tiscover.co.uk

CLEETHORPES, North East Lincolnshire — GUEST ACCOMMODATION

★★★★
GUEST HOUSE

Tudor Terrace Guest House 11 Bradford Avenue, Cleethorpes DN35 0BB
t (01472) 600800 **f** (01472) 501395
e enquiries.tudorterrace@ntlworld.com **w** tudorterrace.co.uk

COLSTERWORTH, Lincolnshire — SELF CATERING

★★★
SELF CATERING

Farrier Cottage contact Mrs Kathleen Clay, The Stables, Stainby Road, Colsterworth, Grantham NG33 5JB **t** (01476) 861057
e kathlen@btopenworld.com **w** stablesbandb.co.uk

COTTON, Suffolk — SELF CATERING

★★★★
SELF CATERING

Coda Cottages contact Mrs Kate Sida-Nicholls, Poplar Farm, Dandy Corner, Cotton, Stowmarket IP14 4QX **t** (01449) 780076 **f** (01449) 780280
e codacottages@dandycorner.co.uk **w** codacottages.co.uk

COVENHAM ST BARTHOLOMEW, Lincolnshire — SELF CATERING

★★★★
SELF CATERING

Westfield Mews & Lodges contact Mrs J Cream, Westfield Mews & Lodges, Westfield House, Louth LN11 0PB
t (01507) 363217

CRATFIELD, Suffolk — SELF CATERING

★★★★
SELF CATERING

Holly Tree Farm Barns contact Ms Rachel Boddy, Holly Tree Farm, Bell Green, Cratfield, Halesworth IP19 0DN **t** (01986) 798062
e hollytreebarns@lycos.co.uk **w** hollytreebarns.co.uk

CRATFIELD, Suffolk — SELF CATERING

★★★★
SELF CATERING

School Farm Cottages contact Mrs Claire Sillett, School Farm, Church Road, Cratfield, Halesworth IP19 0BU **t** (01986) 798844
e schoolfarmcotts@aol.com **w** schoolfarmcottages.com

CRAVEN ARMS, Shropshire — SELF CATERING

★★★★
SELF CATERING

Strefford Hall Self Catering – Robins & Swallows Nest
contact Mrs Caroline Morgan, Strefford Hall, Strefford, Craven Arms SY7 8DE
t (01588) 672383
w streffordhall.co.uk

CRAVEN ARMS, Shropshire — SELF CATERING

★★★★
SELF CATERING

Upper Onibury Cottages contact Mrs Hickman, Upper Onibury, Craven Arms SY7 9AW **t** (01584) 856206 **f** (01584) 856236
e info@shropshirecottages.com **w** shropshirecottages.com

CRESSBROOK, Derbyshire — GUEST ACCOMMODATION

★★★★
GUEST ACCOMMODATION

Cressbrook Hall Cressbrook, Buxton SK17 8SY **t** (01298) 871289 **f** (01298) 871845
e stay@cressbrookhall.co.uk **w** cressbrookhall.co.uk

Awaiting a rating

If you are considering accommodation that is awaiting a National Accessible Scheme rating, please confirm with the proprietor what facilities you can expect before booking.

At-a-glance symbols are explained on the flap inside the back cover.

CROMER, Norfolk Map ref 3C1   GUEST ACCOMMODATION

★★★★★
BED & BREAKFAST

B&B per room per night
d £140.00–£150.00

Incleborough House Luxury Bed and Breakfast

East Runton, Cromer NR27 9PG **t** (01263) 515939 **f** (01263) 510022
e enquiries@incleboroughhouse.co.uk **w** incleboroughhouse.co.uk

Built in 1687 for a wealthy landowner, Incleborough House has over the centuries lost much of its land but none of its character and grandeur. It still remains a stunning Grade II Listed country house which simply oozes charm, splendour and elegance and is only 300 metres from the beach.

open All year
bedrooms 2 double, 1 twin/double
bathrooms All en suite

Access ☺ 🛄 abc 🐾

General ☗ 14 P& ✂ ✗ 🍴 ❄

Rooms 🛏 ⌨ 🖵 🖳 ☕ 🍵 ♨ 📺 🖻

Payment Credit/debit cards, cash/cheques

Special offers for midweek breaks, see our website or ring 01263 515939 for details. Honeymoon, birthday and anniversary stays.

Take A149 from Sheringham towards Cromer. At East Runton turn right into Felbrigg Road, 200 metres and Incleborough House is on your left.

DARSHAM, Suffolk   SELF CATERING

★★★★
SELF CATERING

Granary and The Mallards contact Mrs S Bloomfield, Priory Farm, Darsham IP17 3QD **t** (01728) 668459
e suebloomfield@btconnect.com **w** holidaysatprioryfarm.co.uk

---

DERBY, Derbyshire   CAMPING & CARAVANNING

★★★
TOURING PARK

Elvaston Castle Caravan Club Site Elvaston Castle Country Park, Borrowash Road, Derby DE72 3EP **t** (01332) 573735
w caravanclub.co.uk

Town, country or coast

The entertainment, shopping and innovative attractions of the big cities, the magnificent vistas of the countryside or the relaxing and refreshing coast – this guide will help you find what you're looking for!

DEREHAM, Norfolk Map ref 3B1 — GUEST ACCOMMODATION

Greenbanks and Three Palms Leisure Pool

★★★★
GUEST ACCOMMODATION

B&B per room per night
s £80.00–£90.00
d £100.00–£120.00
Evening meal per person
£18.00–£27.00

Swaffham Road, Wendling, Dereham NR19 2AB t (01362) 687742
e jenny@greenbankshotel.co.uk w greenbankshotel.co.uk

Elegant 18thC luxury hotel. Excellent restaurant, heated indoor swimming pool with full access. Five ground-floor suites for wheelchair users, built-in shower rooms. Quality food adapted for all special diets. Numerous awards.
open All year except Christmas
bedrooms 3 double, 2 twin, 1 single, 3 family
bathrooms All en suite

Access ☺ abc .: ⚹
General ☎ P♿ ♿ ✂ ♛ ✕ ♨ ✿
Leisure ⚲ ♨
Rooms ♨ ♚ ♨ ♨ ♨ ♨

Payment Credit/debit cards, cash/cheques, euros

DILHAM, Norfolk — SELF CATERING

★★★★
SELF CATERING

Dairy Farm Cottages contact Mr James Paterson, Rumford Ltd, Rumford Limited, Dilham, North Walsham NR28 9PZ t (01692) 536883 f (01692) 536723
e japdilman@gmail.com w dairyfarmcottages.co.uk

DISS, Norfolk — SELF CATERING

★★★★
SELF CATERING

Norfolk Cottages Malthouse contact Ms Mary Mannion, Norfolk Cottages Booking Office, Diss IP22 4ER t (01379) 651177 f (01379) 651170
e bookings@norfolkcottages.net w norfolkcottages.net

DONINGTON, Lincolnshire — GUEST ACCOMMODATION

★★★★
GUEST ACCOMMODATION

Browntoft House Browntoft Lane, Donington PE11 4TQ
t (01775) 822091
e finchedward@hotmail.com w browntofthouse.co.uk

EAST HARLING, Norfolk — SELF CATERING

★★★★
SELF CATERING

Berwick Cottage contact Mrs Miriam Toosey, The Lin Berwick Trust, Upper East Street, Sudbury CO10 1UB t (01787) 372343 f (01787) 372343
e info@thelinberwicktrust.org.uk w thelinberwicktrust.org.uk

Check the maps

Colour maps at the front pinpoint all the places you will find accommodation entries in the regional sections. Pick your location and then refer to the place index at the back to find the page number.

At-a-glance symbols are explained on the flap inside the back cover.

EDWARDSTONE, Suffolk Map ref 3B2 — SELF CATERING

★★★★
SELF CATERING

Units **2**
Sleeps **2–6**
Low season per wk
Min £300.00
High season per wk
Max £675.00

Sherbourne Farm Lodge Cottages, Sudbury

contact Mrs Anne Suckling, Sherbourne House Farm, Edwardstone, Sudbury CO10 5PD **t** (01787) 210885
e enquiries@sherbournelodgecottages.co.uk **w** sherbournelodgecottages.co.uk

Family farm location. Stunning barn conversions in idyllic setting. Two-bedroomed twin/double, kitchen/living area, wet room. Village shops, pubs nearby. Enjoy our special Wildlife-Watch evening – an unforgettable experience!
open All year
nearest shop < 0.5 miles
nearest pub < 0.5 miles

Payment Cash/cheques

EWYAS HAROLD, Herefordshire — SELF CATERING

★★★★
SELF CATERING

Old King Street Farm contact Mr Robert Dewar, Old King Street Farm, Hereford HR2 0HB **t** (01981) 240208
e info@oldkingstreetfarm.co.uk **w** oldkingstreetfarm.co.uk

FINESHADE, Northamptonshire — CAMPING & CARAVANNING

★★★★
TOURING PARK

Top Lodge Caravan Club Site Fineshade, Duddington, Corby NN17 3BB
t (01780) 444617
w caravanclub.co.uk

FOXLEY, Norfolk — SELF CATERING

★★–★★★★★
SELF CATERING

Moor Farm Stable Cottages contact Mr Paul Davis, Moor Farm, Foxley, Dereham NR20 4QP **t** (01362) 688523 **f** (01362) 688523
e mail@moorfarmstablecottages.co.uk **w** moorfarmstablecottages.co.uk

GOULCEBY, Lincolnshire — SELF CATERING

★★★★
SELF CATERING

Bay Tree Cottage
t (01507) 343230
e goulcebypost@ukonline.co.uk **w** goulcebypost.co.uk

GREAT YARMOUTH, Norfolk — CAMPING & CARAVANNING

★★★★
TOURING PARK

Great Yarmouth Caravan Club Site Great Yarmouth Racecourse, Jellicoe Road, Great Yarmouth NR30 4AU **t** (01493) 855223
w caravanclub.co.uk

HADLEIGH, Suffolk — SELF CATERING

★★★★
SELF CATERING

Wattisham Hall Holiday Cottages contact Jeremy and Jo Squirrell, Wattisham Hall, Wattisham, Ipswich IP7 7JX **t** (01449) 740240 **f** (01449) 744535
e enquiries@wattishamhall.co.uk **w** wattishamhall.co.uk

HAGWORTHINGHAM, Lincolnshire — SELF CATERING

★★★★
SELF CATERING

Kingfisher Lodge t (01205) 870210 & 07970 128531
e info@meridianretreats.co.uk **w** meridianretreats.co.uk

HALLOW, Worcestershire — SELF CATERING

★★★★
SELF CATERING

The New Cottage contact Mrs Doreen Jeeves, Bridles End House, Greenhill Lane, Worcester WR2 6LG **t** (01905) 640953 **f** (01905) 640953
e jeeves@thenewcottage.co.uk **w** thenewcottage.co.uk

HALSTEAD, Essex — GUEST ACCOMMODATION

★★★
INN

The White Hart 15 High Street, Halstead CO9 2AA
t (01787) 475657
w innpubs.co.uk

HAPPISBURGH, Norfolk — SELF CATERING

★★★★
SELF CATERING

Boundary Stables contact Julian Burns, Boundary Stables, Boundary Cottage, Grub Street, Norwich NR12 0RX **t** (01692) 650171
e julianburns@onetel.net **w** boundarystables.co.uk

HARTINGTON, Derbyshire — SELF CATERING

★★★–★★★★★
SELF CATERING

Old House Farm Cottages contact Mrs Sue Flower, Old House Farm Cottages, Old House Farm, Newhaven, Buxton SK17 0DY **t** (01629) 636268 **f** (01629) 636268
e s.flower1@virgin.net **w** oldhousefarm.com

HENLEY, Suffolk Map ref 3B2 — SELF CATERING

★★★★
SELF CATERING

Units **5**
Sleeps **1–6**

Low season per wk
£255.00–£275.00
High season per wk
£425.00–£595.00

Damerons Farm Holidays, Henley

contact Wayne & Sue Leggett
t (01473) 832454 & 07881 824083 **e** info@dameronsfarmholidays.co.uk
w dameronsfarmholidays.co.uk

Three cottages (Level 1 access) sleeping between one and six people, and The Old Dairy (Level 3 access) sleeping two, plus sofa bed. Beautiful countryside setting.
open All year
nearest shop 3 miles
nearest pub 1.5 miles

Access

General 🛏 🎬 ♿ P ✄ Ⓢ

Unit ♿ 🍳 📺 ☎ ⊠ 🖥 📷 ♨ 🚭 📟 💷 🍴 ❄

Payment Credit/debit cards, cash/cheques

HEREFORD, Herefordshire — SELF CATERING

★★★★
SELF CATERING

Anvil Cottage, Apple Bough and Cider Press contact Mrs Jennie Layton, Grafton Villa Farmhouse, Grafton, Hereford HR2 8ED
t (01432) 268689 **f** (01432) 268689
e jennielayton@ereal.net **w** graftonvilla.co.uk

HERTFORD, Hertfordshire — SELF CATERING

★★★★
SELF CATERING

Petasfield Cottages contact Miss Helen Clark, Petasfield Stables, Mangrove Lane, Hertford SG13 8QQ **t** (01992) 504201
e helen@petasfieldcottages.co.uk **w** petasfieldcottages.co.uk

HOLBEACH, Lincolnshire — GUEST ACCOMMODATION

★★★★
BED & BREAKFAST

Ecklinville B&B 34 Fen Road, Holbeach, Spalding PE12 8QA
t (01406) 423625 **f** (01406) 423625
e info@poachersden.com **w** poachersden.com

At-a-glance symbols are explained on the flap inside the back cover.

HOLBEACH, Lincolnshire — SELF CATERING

★ ★ ★
SELF CATERING

Poachers Den
t (01406) 423625
e info@poachersden.com w poachersden.com

HOLBECK, Nottinghamshire — GUEST ACCOMMODATION

★ ★ ★ ★ ★
BED & BREAKFAST
GOLD AWARD

Browns The Old Orchard Cottage, Holbeck S80 3NF
t (01909) 720659 f (01909) 720659
e browns@holbeck.fsnet.co.uk w brownsholbeck.co.uk

HOLT, Norfolk — SELF CATERING

★ ★ ★ – ★ ★ ★ ★ ★
SELF CATERING

Wood Farm Cottages contact Mrs Diana Jacob, Wood Farm Cottages, Edgefield,
Holt NR24 2AQ t (01263) 587347 f (01263) 587347
e info@wood-farm.com w wood-farm.com

HORHAM, Suffolk — SELF CATERING

★ ★ ★
SELF CATERING

Alpha Cottages Alpha Cottages, Lodge Farm, Horham, Eye IP21 5DX
t (01379) 384424 f (01379) 384424

HORNCASTLE, Lincolnshire — HOTEL

★ ★ ★
HOTEL

Best Western Admiral Rodney Hotel North Street, Horncastle, Lincoln LN9 5DX
t (01507) 523131 f (01507) 523104
e reception@admiralrodney.com w admiralrodney.com

HORNING, Norfolk — SELF CATERING

★ ★ ★ – ★ ★ ★ ★ ★
SELF CATERING

King Line Cottages contact Mr Robert King, King Line Cottages,
Horning NR12 8LZ t (01692) 630297
e kingline@norfolk-broads.co.uk w norfolk-broads.co.uk

HORSINGTON, Lincolnshire — SELF CATERING

★ ★ ★
SELF CATERING

Wayside Cottage contact Mr & Mrs Ian & Jane Williamson, 72 Mill Lane,
Horsington, Woodhall Spa LN10 6QZ t (01526) 353101
e will@williamsoni.freeserve.co.uk w skegness.net/woodhallspa.htm

HOVETON, Norfolk

See entry on p148

Quality assessment

Our commitment to quality involves
wide-ranging accommodation assessment.
Ratings and awards were correct at the time
of going to press but may change following
a new assessment. Please check at the time
of booking.

HUNSTANTON, Norfolk Map ref 3B1　　　　　　　　　　　　　　　　**HOTEL**

★★★
HOTEL

B&B per room per night
s £49.00–£99.00
d £70.00–£150.00
HB per person per night
£55.00–£95.00

Caley Hall Hotel

Old Hunstanton Road, Old Hunstanton, Hunstanton PE36 6HH
t (01485) 533486 **f** (01485) 533348
e mail@caleyhallhotel.co.uk **w** caleyhallhotel.co.uk

General ☞ P. ♟ ¶ ⁓ ✿

Rooms 🛏 🖼 🖵 ♨ ⤵ ☎ 🛋 🗄

Payment Credit/debit cards,
cash/cheques

*2 rooms feature specially adapted
bathrooms with level-access
shower. The hotel has no steps.*

Caley Hall Hotel and Restaurant
is set around a manor house
dating back to 1648. More
recently, the old farm
outbuildings have been
converted to provide the
spacious en suite bedrooms,
restaurant and bar. Most of the
rooms are on the ground floor,
and some feature a four-poster
bed or whirlpool bath.
open All year except Christmas
and New Year
bedrooms 15 double, 15 twin,
4 single, 5 family, 1 suite
bathrooms All en suite

*In Old Hunstanton, on the left-
hand side of the A149, just
before the turning to the golf
course.*

HUNSTANTON, Norfolk　　　　　　　　　　　　　　　　　　　　　**SELF CATERING**

★★★★
SELF CATERING

Foxgloves Cottage contact Terry & Lesley Heade, Foxgloves Cottage,
29 Avenue Road, Hunstanton PE36 5BW **t** (01485) 532460
e deepdenehouse@btopenworld.com **w** smoothhound.co.uk/hotels/deepdene.html

HUNTINGDON, Cambridgeshire Map ref 3A2 — CAMPING & CARAVANNING

★★★★
TOURING PARK

£14.50–£25.60
£14.50–£25.60

Houghton Mill Caravan Club Site
Mill Street, Houghton, Huntingdon PE28 2AZ t (01480) 466716
w caravanclub.co.uk

The site, owned by the National Trust, is on the banks of the River Great Ouse with spectacular views across the river to the Trust's Houghton Mill, the last working watermill on this river. Milling demonstrations are held every Sunday during the season and visitors can purchase the flour. Open March to October.

General 🚐 P 🚙 🕁 🛆 🛝 ☺ 🗑

From Mill Street, past church on right, site entrance immediately on left before last house.

Payment Credit/debit cards, cash/cheques

THE
CARAVAN
CLUB

ILAM, Staffordshire — SELF CATERING

★★★★
SELF CATERING

Beechenhill Farm Cottages contact Mrs Sue Prince, Beechenhill Farm, Ilam, Ashbourne DE6 2BD t (01335) 310274 f (01335) 310467
e beechenhill@btinternet.com w beechenhill.co.uk

IPSWICH, Suffolk — HOTEL

★★★
HOTEL

Courtyard by Marriott Ipswich The Havens, Ransomes Europark, Ipswich IP3 9SJ
t (01473) 272244 f (01473) 272484
e res.ipscourtyard@kewgreen.co.uk w marriotthotels.com

KNIGHTCOTE, Warwickshire — SELF CATERING

★★★★★
SELF CATERING

Arbor Holiday & Knightcote Farm Cottages
contact Mr & Mrs Craig & Fiona Walker, The Bake House, Knightcote, Southam CV47 2EF t (01295) 770637 f (01295) 770135
e fionawalker@farmcottages.com w farmcottages.com

LEDBURY, Herefordshire — SELF CATERING

★★★–★★★★★
SELF CATERING

The Old Kennels Farm contact Mrs J.K. Wilce, The Old Kennels Farm, Bromyard Road, Ledbury HR8 1LG t (01531) 635024 f (01531) 635241
e wilceoldkennelsfarm@btinternet.com w oldkennelsfarm.co.uk

LEEK, Staffordshire — SELF CATERING

★★★
SELF CATERING

Lark's Rise contact Mrs Laura Melland, New House Farm, Bottomhouse, Leek ST13 7PA t (01538) 304350 f (01538) 304350
e newhousefarm@btinternet.com w staffordshiremoorlandsfarmholidays.co.uk

LEVERTON, Lincolnshire — SELF CATERING

★★★★
SELF CATERING

Crewyard Cottages
t (01205) 871389
e gina@gina31.wanadoo.co.uk w crewyardholidaycottages-boston.co.uk

LINCOLN, Lincolnshire — SELF CATERING

★★★★
SELF CATERING

Cliff Farm Cottage
t (01522) 730475
e info@cliff-farm-cottage.co.uk w cliff-farm-cottage.co.uk

LITTLE DEWCHURCH, Herefordshire — SELF CATERING

★★★★
SELF CATERING

The Granary contact Ms Karen Tibbetts, The Granary, Henclose Farm,
Little Dewchurch, Hereford HR2 6PP t (01432) 840826 f (01432) 840826

LITTLE SNORING, Norfolk — SELF CATERING

★★★★
SELF CATERING

Jex Farm Barns contact Mr Stephen Harvey, Jex Farm, Little Snoring,
Fakenham NR21 0JJ t (01328) 878257 & 07979 495760 f (01328) 878257
e farmerstephen@jexfarm.wanadoo.co.uk w jefarm.co.uk

LITTLE TARRINGTON, Herefordshire — SELF CATERING

★★★★
SELF CATERING

Stock's Cottage contact Mrs Angela Stock, Stock's Cottage, Little Tarrington,
Hereford HR1 4JA t (01432) 890243 f (01432) 890243
e stay@stockscottage.co.uk w stockscottage.co.uk

LITTLE TARRINGTON, Herefordshire — CAMPING & CARAVANNING

★★★★★
TOURING &
CAMPING PARK

The Millpond Little Tarrington, Hereford HR1 4JA
t (01432) 890243 f (01432) 890243
e enquiries@millpond.co.uk w millpond.co.uk

LOWESTOFT, Suffolk — HOTEL

★★★
HOTEL

Hotel Victoria Kirkley Cliff, Lowestoft NR33 0BZ
t (01502) 574433 f (01502) 501529
e info@hotelvictoria.freeserve.co.uk w hotelvictoria.freeserve.co.uk

LUDLOW, Shropshire — SELF CATERING

★★★★
SELF CATERING

Goosefoot Barn Cottages contact Mrs Sally Loft, Goosefoot Barn Cottages,
Pinstones, Diddlebury, Craven Arms SY7 9LB t (01584) 861326
e sally@goosefoot.freeserve.co.uk w goosefootbarn.co.uk

LUDLOW, Shropshire — SELF CATERING

★★★
SELF CATERING

Mocktree Barns Holiday Cottages contact Mr & Mrs Clive & Cynthia Prior,
Leintwardine, Ludlow SY7 0LY t (01547) 540441
e mocktreebarns@care4free.net w mocktreeholidays.co.uk

LUDLOW, Shropshire — SELF CATERING

★★★★
SELF CATERING

Sutton Court Farm Cottages contact Mrs Jane Cronin, Sutton Court Farm,
Little Sutton, Stanton Lacy, Ludlow SY8 2AJ t (01584) 861305 f (01584) 861441
e enquiries@suttoncourtfarm.co.uk w suttoncourtfarm.co.uk

Place index

If you know where you want to stay, the index at the
back of the guide will give you the page number which
lists accommodation in your chosen town, city or village.
Check out the other useful indexes too.

At-a-glance symbols are explained on the flap inside the back cover.

MABLETHORPE, Lincolnshire Map ref 4D2 — SELF CATERING

★★★★
SELF CATERING

Units **5**
Sleeps **4–6**

Low season per wk
£260.00–£350.00
High season per wk
£500.00–£700.00

Grange Cottages, Maltby le Marsh, Alford
contact Ann Graves, Grange Cottages, Main Road, Alford LN13 0JP
t (01507) 450267 **f** (01507) 450180 **w** grange-cottages.co.uk

Established 25 years. Set in secluded grounds of 12 acres. Private lakes. Everything you need for a relaxing break. Home from home. Ground-floor bedrooms. Great for children. Pets welcome.
open All year
nearest shop < 0.5 miles
nearest pub < 0.5 miles

General 🛋 P ⚡ ▣

Unit ▥ ▦ ▤ ▨ ▧ ▥ ✳

Payment Cash/cheques

MALVERN, Worcestershire Map ref 2B1 — SELF CATERING

★★★★–★★★★★★
SELF CATERING

Units **8**
Sleeps **2–12**

Low season per wk
£195.00–£995.00
High season per wk
£589.00–£3,669.00

Hidelow House Cottages, Worcester
contact Mr & Mrs Stuart & Pauline Diplock, Hidelow House Cottages, Hidelow House, Acton Green, Acton Beauchamp, Worcester WR6 5AH **t** (01886) 884547 **f** (01886) 884658
e easyaccess@hidelow.co.uk **w** hidelow.co.uk

Access abc 🐾 🏠

General 🛋 ▥ ♿ P ⚡ ▣ Ⓢ

Unit ♿ ▥ ▤ ▦ ▨ ▣ ▥
▧ ▦ ▥ ▨ ▧ ✳

Payment Credit/debit cards, cash/cheques, euros

Range of aids-to-living available, including profiling bed, hoist, mattress, shower-chairs etc. Qualified carers available; profile of local accessible places to visit. Home-cooked frozen meals.

Worry-free, award-winning holiday accommodation with second-to-none care, service and specialist facilities for disabled guests, carers and pets. Homely, level-access, spacious, single-storey cottages. Roll-in shower rooms, wheelchair-friendly kitchens, accessible landscaped gardens and stunning views across rural Herefordshire. Fully accessible shop, visitors' information room with free broadband and payphone, laundry and drying room.
open All year
nearest shop < 0.5 miles
nearest pub 3 miles

M5 jct 7. A4103 Worcester to Hereford. Turn right at B4220, signposted Bromyard. Hidelow House is 2 miles from this junction on left.

MATLOCK, Derbyshire · SELF CATERING

★★★★
SELF CATERING

Darwin Forest Country Park Darwin Forest Country Park, Darley Moor, Two Dales DE4 5LN t (01629) 732428 f (01629) 735015
e admin@pinelodgeholidays.co.uk w pinelodgeholidays.co.uk/darwin_forest.ihtml

MICHAELCHURCH ESCLEY, Herefordshire · SELF CATERING

★★★★
SELF CATERING

Holt Farm contact Mr Nick Pash, Hideaways, Chapel House, Luke Street, Berwick St John, Berwick St John SP7 0HQ t (01747) 828000
e enq@hideaways.co.uk w hideaways.co.uk

MILDENHALL, Suffolk · CAMPING & CARAVANNING

★★★★
TOURING PARK

Round Plantation Caravan Club Site Brandon Road, Mildenhall, Bury St Edmunds IP28 7JE t (01638) 713089
w caravanclub.co.uk

NAYLAND, Suffolk · SELF CATERING

★★★★–★★★★★★
SELF CATERING

Gladwins Farm contact Mr R Dossor, Gladwins Farm, Harpers Hill, Colchester CO6 4NU t (01206) 262261 f (01206) 263001
e gladwinsfarm@aol.com w gladwinsfarm.co.uk

NORWICH, Norfolk · SELF CATERING

★★★–★★★★★
SELF CATERING

Spixworth Hall Cottages contact Mrs Sheelah Cook, Spixworth Hall Cottages, Buxton Road, Spixworth, Norwich NR10 3PR t (01603) 898190 f (01603) 897176
e hallcottages@btinternet.com w hallcottages.co.uk

OLD BRAMPTON, Derbyshire · SELF CATERING

★★★★
SELF CATERING

Chestnut Cottage and Willow Cottage contact Mr & Mrs Jeffery & Patrica Green, Priestfield Grange, Hollins, Old Brampton, Chesterfield S42 7JH
t (01246) 566159

OUNDLE, Northamptonshire · SELF CATERING

★★★–★★★★★
SELF CATERING

Oundle Cottage Breaks contact Mr & Mrs Simmonds, Oundle Cottage Breaks, Market Place, Oundle, Peterborough PE8 4BE t (01832) 275508
e richard@simmondsatoundle.co.uk w oundlecottagebreaks.co.uk

At-a-glance symbols are explained on the flap inside the back cover.

PETERBOROUGH, Cambridgeshire Map ref 3A1   **CAMPING & CARAVANNING**

★★★★★
HOLIDAY PARK

(252)
£12.10–£24.90
(252)
£12.10–£24.90
252 touring pitches

Ferry Meadows Caravan Club Site
Ham Lane, Peterborough PE2 5UU   **t** (01733) 233526
w caravanclub.co.uk

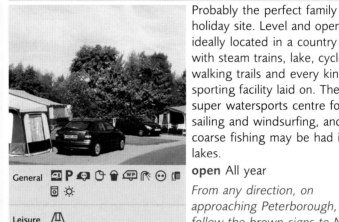

Probably the perfect family holiday site. Level and open, and ideally located in a country park with steam trains, lake, cycle and walking trails and every kind of sporting facility laid on. There's a super watersports centre for sailing and windsurfing, and coarse fishing may be had in the lakes.

General (icons)

Leisure (icons)

Payment Credit/debit cards, cash/cheques

open All year

From any direction, on approaching Peterborough, follow the brown signs to Nene Park and Ferry Meadows.

THE **CARAVAN CLUB**

PRESTHOPE, Shropshire   **CAMPING & CARAVANNING**

★★★
TOURING & CAMPING PARK

Presthope Caravan Club Site Stretton Road, Much Wenlock TF13 6DQ
t (01746) 785234
e enquiries@caravanclub.co.uk
w caravanclub.co.uk

REDDITCH, Worcestershire Map ref 4B3   **GUEST ACCOMMODATION**

★★★
INN

B&B per room per night
s £45.00–£55.00
d £50.00–£55.00
Evening meal per person
£5.00–£8.00

White Hart Inn
157 Evesham Road, Redditch B97 5EJ   **t** (01527) 545442
e enquiries@whitehartredditch.co.uk

Ten en suite bedrooms, disabled facilities, conference and wedding facilities. Local to NEC, Birmingham, Worcester and Stratford. Large free car park.
open All year
bedrooms 2 double, 7 twin, 1 family
bathrooms All en suite

General (icons)

Rooms (icons)

Payment Credit/debit cards, cash/cheques

Awaiting a rating

If you are considering accommodation that is awaiting a National Accessible Scheme rating, please confirm with the proprietor what facilities you can expect before booking.

ROSS-ON-WYE, Herefordshire Map ref 2A1 — GUEST ACCOMMODATION

★★★★
GUEST ACCOMMODATION

B&B per room per night
s £45.00–£48.00
d £59.00–£90.00
Evening meal per person
£17.50–£21.50

Portland House Guest House

Whitchurch, Ross-on-Wye HR9 6DB **t** (01600) 890757
e info@portlandguesthouse.co.uk **w** portlandguesthouse.co.uk

Uniquely placed in the Wye Valley between Monmouth and Ross-on-Wye. Portland House has wide and open areas for wheelchair users. The gorgeous Lloyd Suite has a double bed and a single bed, plus easy chairs, and a small conservatory overlooks the garden. A special place to relax.

open All year except Christmas and New Year
bedrooms 2 double, 1 twin, 2 family, 1 suite
bathrooms All en suite

Leave Monmouth on A40 towards Ross-on-Wye. Approx 3 miles sign on left Whitchurch/ Symonds Yat West. Past BP garage. Turn in at Crown Hotel. Portland House faces you.

Access ☺ abc

General 🛏 🅿 ✂ 🍽 ✕ 🎱 ✱

Rooms 🖥 📺 📻 💧 🔌 ♨ 📖

Payment Credit/debit cards, cash/cheques, euros

Shop, restaurant and pub within 60 yds. Feb and Mar: 4 nights for the price of 3.

RUNCTON HOLME, Norfolk — SELF CATERING

★★★★
SELF CATERING

Thorpland Manor Barns contact Mrs Mary Caley, Downham Road, Runcton Holme, King's Lynn PE33 0AD **t** (01553) 810409 **f** (01553) 811831
e w.p.caley@tesco.net **w** thorplandmanorbarns.co.uk

ST OWENS CROSS, Herefordshire — SELF CATERING

★★★★★
SELF CATERING

Trevase Granary contact Mrs Liz Pursey, Trevase Granary, Trevase Farm, St Owens Cross HR2 8ND **t** (01989) 730210 **f** (01989) 730210
e stay@trevasecottages.co.uk **w** trevasecottages.co.uk

Don't forget www.

Web addresses throughout this guide are shown without the prefix www. Please include www. in the address line of your browser. If a web address does not follow this style it is shown in full.

SANDRINGHAM, Norfolk Map ref 3B1 — HOTEL

★★
HOTEL
SILVER AWARD

Park House Hotel

Sandringham PE35 6EH t (01485) 543000 f (01485) 540663
e parkinfo@lc-uk.org w parkhousehotel.org.uk

B&B per room per night
s £104.00–£164.00
d £174.00–£302.00
HB per person per night
£102.00–£166.00

Access ☺ 🛎 abc .: 🦮 🅰

General 🐴 P♿ ♿ ♻ 🍴 🛗 ✳

Leisure 🏊

Rooms 📠 🕯 ♨ 💺 🗄

Payment Credit/debit cards

*Reduced rates during Jan and
Feb.*

A country-house hotel with a
difference. Located on the Royal
Sandringham Estate, the hotel is
adapted for people with mobility
difficulties and is fully
wheelchair-accessible. Care is on
hand if required and charged for
accordingly. Optional
entertainment and excursions are
always available.
open All year
bedrooms 8 twin, 8 single
bathrooms All en suite

SANDRINGHAM, Norfolk Map ref 3B1 — CAMPING & CARAVANNING

★★★★★
TOURING PARK

The Sandringham Estate Caravan Club Site

Glucksburgh Woods, Sandringham PE35 6EZ t (01553) 631614
w caravanclub.co.uk

🚐(136)
£14.30–£27.70
🚏(136)
£14.30–£27.70
136 touring pitches

General 🚐 P 🚙 🚽 🚰 🆒 📶 ☺ 📠
        🗄 ☼

Leisure ⛰

Payment Credit/debit cards,
         cash/cheques

THE
CARAVAN
CLUB

Set in the heart of the Royal
Estate and redeveloped to a very
high standard, this is one of the
Club's most prestigious sites. Of
the many popular walks, try the
one from the site to Sandringham
House, the famous residence of
the Royal Family. Open March to
January.

*Take A149 from King's Lynn
(signposted Hunstanton). After
approx 2 miles turn right onto
B1439 (signposted West
Newton). Site on left after
0.5 miles.*

SANDY, Bedfordshire — SELF CATERING

★★★★
SELF CATERING

Acorn Cottage contact Mrs Margaret Codd, Highfield Farm, Great North Road, Sandy SG19 2AQ **t** (01767) 682332 **f** (01767) 692503
e margaret@highfield-farm.co.uk **w** highfield-farm.co.uk

SHREWSBURY, Shropshire — GUEST ACCOMMODATION

★★★★
BED & BREAKFAST
GOLD AWARD

Lyth Hill House 28 Old Coppice, Lyth Hill, Shrewsbury SY3 0BP
t (01743) 874660
e bnb@lythhillhouse.com **w** lythhillhouse.com

SHREWSBURY, Shropshire — SELF CATERING

★★★★
SELF CATERING

Newton Meadows Holiday Cottages contact Mr & Mrs Simcox, Wem Road, Harmer Hill, Shrewsbury SY2 3DZ **t** (01939) 290346 **f** (01939) 290346
e e.simcox@btopenworld.com **w** newtonmeadows.co.uk

SIBTON, Suffolk Map ref 3C2 — SELF CATERING

★★★★
SELF CATERING

Units **4**
Sleeps **2–4**
Low season per wk
£250.00–£320.00
High season per wk
£340.00–£475.00

Bluebell, Bonny, Buttercup & Bertie, Saxmundham

contact Mrs Margaret Gray, Park Farm, Sibton, Saxmundham IP17 2LZ
t (01728) 668324
e mail@sibtonparkfarm.co.uk **w** sibtonparkfarm.co.uk

General 🛇🎠🏃P✂ 🔲S

Unit ♿🛁▥ ▣🖫🗨🏠🏚🗝
🖾🗲❄

Payment Credit/debit cards, cash/cheques

Single-storey cottages, all beautifully appointed, equipped to a very high standard with everything you might need for your stay. Zip-and-link beds throughout. Games room. Stroll around our fields and see the barn owls and kingfishers or visit the pretty villages nearby. The sea is only seven miles away. Christmas and New Year breaks.
open All year
nearest shop 1.5 miles
nearest pub 1.5 miles

On A1120, 1.5 miles west of junction with A12 at Yoxford.

visitBritain.com

Get in the know – log on for a wealth of information and inspiration. All the latest news on places to visit, events and quality-assessed accommodation is literally at your fingertips. Explore all that Britain has to offer!

At-a-glance symbols are explained on the flap inside the back cover.

SKEGNESS, Lincolnshire Map ref 4D2 — GUEST ACCOMMODATION

★★★
GUEST ACCOMMODATION

B&B per room per night
s £30.00–£42.00
d £60.00–£82.00
Evening meal per person
£12.00–£19.00

Chatsworth

16 North Parade, Skegness PE25 2UB **t** (01754) 764177 **f** (01754) 761173
e info@chatsworthskegness.co.uk **w** chatsworthskegness.co.uk

Centrally situated on the main seafront promenade close to many attractions with two wheelchair-accessible seaview premier rooms. Acclaimed for our best of traditional British cooking.
open All year
bedrooms 14 double, 15 twin, 10 single, 1 family
bathrooms All en suite

Access abc ⬚

General 🐕 ♿ 🍷 ✕ 🎱 🖼 ❀

Rooms 🅂 🛁 📺

Payment Credit/debit cards, cash/cheques, euros

SKEGNESS, Lincolnshire — GUEST ACCOMMODATION

★★★★
GUEST ACCOMMODATION
♿

Fountaindale Hotel 69 Sandbeck Avenue, Skegness PE25 3JS **t** (01754) 762731
e info@fountaindale-hotel.co.uk **w** fountaindale-hotel.co.uk

SKEGNESS, Lincolnshire — GUEST ACCOMMODATION

★★★
GUEST HOUSE

Sandgate Hotel 44 Drummond Road, Skegness PE25 3EB **t** (01754) 762667
e info@sandgate-hotel.co.uk **w** sandgate-hotel.co.uk

SKEGNESS, Lincolnshire — SELF CATERING

★★★★
SELF CATERING

Ingoldale Park contact Mrs Cathryn Whitehead, Ingoldale Park, Roman Bank, Ingoldmells, Skegness PE25 1LL **t** (01754) 872335 **f** (01754) 873887
e ingoldalepark@btopenworld.com

SOUTHWOLD, Suffolk — GUEST ACCOMMODATION

♦♦♦♦
GUEST ACCOMMODATION
♿

Newlands Country House 72 Halesworth Road, Southwold IP18 6NS
t (01502) 722164 **f** (01502) 725363
e info@newlandsofsouthwold.co.uk **w** tiscover.co.uk

STAFFORD, Staffordshire

See entry on p149

SWAFFHAM, Norfolk — CAMPING & CARAVANNING

★★★★
TOURING PARK

The Covert Caravan Club Site High Ash, Hilborough, Thetford IP26 5BZ
t (01842) 878356
w caravanclub.co.uk

TELFORD, Shropshire — GUEST ACCOMMODATION

★★★★
GUEST ACCOMMODATION
SILVER AWARD
♿

Old Rectory Stirchley Village, Telford TF3 1DY
t (01952) 596308 **f** (01952) 596308
e hazelmiller@waitrose.com **w** stmem.com/theoldrectory

TELFORD, Shropshire — SELF CATERING

★★★
SELF CATERING

Church Farm Self Catering (Rowton) contact Mrs Virginia Evans, Church Farm Cottages, Rowton, Wellington, Telford TF6 6QY **t** (01952) 770381
e churchfarm49@beeb.net **w** virtual-shropshire.co.uk/churchfarm

TITCHWELL, Norfolk Map ref 3B1 — HOTEL

★★
**HOTEL
GOLD AWARD**

Titchwell Manor Hotel

Titchwell Manor, Near Brancaster, Titchwell PE31 8BB   t (01485) 210221
f (01485) 210104   e margaret@titchwellmanor.com   w titchwellmanor.com

B&B per room per night
**s £50.00–£200.00
d £100.00–£200.00**
HB per person per night
£60.00–£150.00

Located on the North Norfolk coast. Several bedrooms have views to the golden beaches and RSPB reserve. 16 contemporary style bedrooms are situated on the ground floor for easy access. Two AA rosette restaurant serving locally produced food.
open All year
bedrooms 20 double, 6 twin
bathrooms All en suite

Access ☺ 🛄 🐾

General 🪑 P♿ ♿🍴❄

Rooms 📺🖥📶🍵♨📻📺

Payment Credit/debit cards, cash/cheques, euros

TUGFORD, Shropshire Map ref 4A3 — GUEST ACCOMMODATION

★★★★
FARMHOUSE

Tugford Farm B&B

Tugford Farm, Craven Arms SY7 9HS   t (01584) 841259
e williamstugford@supanet.com   w tugford.com

B&B per room per night
**s £45.00–£47.00
d £70.00–£74.00**
Evening meal per person
£12.00

Quality rural accommodation deep in the Corvedale Valley on a traditional working farm. Spacious en suite room. Hearty breakfast served in our beamed farmhouse dining room. Free Wi-Fi internet connection.
open All year except Christmas and New Year
bedrooms 1 twin
bathrooms All en suite

General 🪑✗🍴

Rooms 📺🖥📶🍵♨📻📺

Payment Cash/cheques

WALTON-ON-THE-NAZE, Essex — GUEST ACCOMMODATION

★★★★
GUEST ACCOMMODATION

Bufo Villae Guest House 31 Beatrice Road, Walton-on-the-Naze CO14 8HJ
t (01255) 672644
e bufo@ukgateway.net   w bufovillae.co.uk

WANGFORD, Suffolk — GUEST ACCOMMODATION

★★★★
GUEST ACCOMMODATION

The Plough Inn London Road, Wangford, Southwold, Beccles NR34 8AZ
t (01502) 578239
e enquiries@the-plough.biz   w wangfordplough.co.uk

WATTISFIELD, Suffolk — SELF CATERING

★★★
SELF CATERING

Jayes Holiday Cottages contact Mrs Denise Williams, Walsham Road, Wattisfield IP22 1NZ   t (01359) 251255
e booking@jayesholidaycottages.co.uk   w jayesholidaycottages.co.uk

At-a-glance symbols are explained on the flap inside the back cover.

WEST RUDHAM, Norfolk — GUEST ACCOMMODATION

★★★★
BED & BREAKFAST
SILVER AWARD

Oyster House King's Lynn PE31 8RW
t (01485) 528327
e oyster-house@tiscali.co.uk **w** oysterhouse.co.uk

WHITBOURNE, Herefordshire — SELF CATERING

★★★
SELF CATERING

Crumplebury Farmhouse contact Mrs Anne Evans, Dial House,
Whitbourne Hall Park, Whitbourne, Worcester WR6 5SG
t (01886) 821534
e a.evans@candaevans.fsnet.co.uk **w** whitbourne-estate.co.uk/crumplebury

WHITCHURCH, Herefordshire — SELF CATERING

★★★
SELF CATERING

Tump Farm contact Mrs Williams, Tump Farm, Ross-on-Wye HR9 6DQ
t (01600) 891029
e clinwilcharmaine@hotmail.com

WICKHAM SKEITH, Suffolk — SELF CATERING

★★★
SELF CATERING

Netus Barn contact Mrs Joy Homan, Street Farm, Eye IP23 8LP
t (01449) 766275
e joygeoff@homansf.freeserve.co.uk

WIGSTHORPE, Northamptonshire Map ref 3A2 — SELF CATERING

★★★★★
SELF CATERING

Units	**3**
Sleeps	**2–4**

Low season per wk
£250.00–£350.00
High season per wk
£350.00–£600.00

Nene Valley Cottages, Wigsthorpe

contact Heather Ball, The Cottage, Glapthorn PE8 5BQ
t (01832) 273601
e stay@nenevalleycottages.co.uk **w** nenevalleycottages.co.uk

General 🐎 **P** ⚡ ⓢ

Unit 🛁🍳▦🍴🖥️🔲📻📶🔌🍳
🍽️🎛️❄️

Payment Cash/cheques

*The single bedroom cottage is a
luxury M3I property that has
been created with all the needs of
the less mobile in mind.*

Idyllic rural setting with
commanding views over the
Nene Valley. All home comforts
and more in two units, each with
two twin bedrooms and one with
a single twin bedroom that
interconnects with a larger unit.
This smaller cottage is adapted
for those with impaired mobility
and has a sofa bed for a carer.

open All year
nearest shop 4 miles
nearest pub 2 miles

WIRKSWORTH, Derbyshire — GUEST ACCOMMODATION

★★★★★
GUEST ACCOMMODATION GOLD AWARD

The Old Lock-Up North End, Wirksworth DE4 4FG
t (01629) 826272
e wheeler@theoldlockup.co.uk
w theoldlockup.co.uk

WISBECH, Cambridgeshire — SELF CATERING

★★★★
SELF CATERING

Common Right Barns contact Mrs Teresa Fowler, Common Right Barns,
Wisbech St Mary PE13 4SP t (01945) 410424 f (01945) 410424
e teresa@commonrightbarns.co.uk w commonrightbarns.co.uk

WISSETT, Suffolk — SELF CATERING

★★★★
SELF CATERING

Wissett Lodge contact Mrs Claire Kiddy, Lodge Lane, Wissett,
Halesworth IP19 0JQ t (01986) 873173
e geoffrey.kiddy@farmersweekly.net

WOODHALL SPA, Lincolnshire Map ref 4D2 — HOTEL

★★★
HOTEL

B&B per room per night
s £95.00
d £140.00
HB per person per night
£90.00–£134.00

Petwood Hotel

Stixwould Road, Woodhall Spa LN10 6QG t (01526) 352411 f (01526) 353473
e reception@petwood.co.uk w petwood.co.uk

Originally built in the early 1900s,
the Petwood Hotel stands in a 30-
acre estate and is famous for its
magnificent gardens. Individually
designed bedrooms. Short holidays
available.
open All year
bedrooms 21 double, 13 twin,
6 single, 8 family, 5 suites
bathrooms All en suite

Access	
General	
Rooms	
Payment	Credit/debit cards, cash/cheques, euros

WOODHALL SPA, Lincolnshire — SELF CATERING

★★
SELF CATERING

Mill Lane Cottage contact Mr & Mrs Ian & Jane Williamson, 72 Mill Lane,
Woodhall Spa LN10 6QZ t (01526) 353101
e will@williamsoni.freeserve.co.uk w skegness.net/woodhallspa.htm

Key to symbols

Symbols at the end of each entry help you pick out the services and facilities which are most important for your stay. A key to the symbols can be found inside the back-cover flap. Keep this open for easy reference.

At-a-glance symbols are explained on the flap inside the back cover.

WORKSOP, Nottinghamshire Map ref 4C2 | **CAMPING & CARAVANNING**

★★★★
TOURING PARK

Clumber Park Caravan Club Site

🚐(183)
£14.30–£27.70
🚐(183)
£14.30–£27.70
183 touring pitches

Limetree Avenue, Clumber Park, Worksop S80 3AE **t** (01909) 484758
w caravanclub.co.uk

General 🖼 P 🖼 🖰 🎒 🗑 ⟨🖼⟩ 🙂 🗄
🖾 ☼

Leisure ⟨△⟩

Payment Credit/debit cards,
cash/cheques

Midweek discount; pitch fees
reduced by 50% for stays on Tue,
Wed or Thu night outside peak
season.

THE
CARAVAN
CLUB

There's a great feeling of
spaciousness here, the site is on
20 acres within 4,000 acres of
parkland where you can walk,
cycle or ride. Children will enjoy
Clumber Park as it is part of what
was once Sherwood Forest, and
there are plenty of reminders of
the Forest's most famous
resident, Robin Hood.

open All year

*From the junction of the A1 and
A57, take the A614 signposted to
Nottingham for 0.5 miles. Turn
right into Clumber Park site. The
club is signposted thereafter.*

Bank holiday
dates for your diary

holiday	2008	2009
New Year's Day (England & Wales)	1 January	1 January
New Year's Day (Scotland)	1 January	1 January
January Bank Holiday (Scotland)	2 January	2 January
Good Friday	21 March	10 April
Easter Monday (England & Wales)	24 March	13 April
Early May Bank Holiday	5 May	4 May
Spring Bank Holiday	26 May	25 May
Summer Bank Holiday (Scotland)	4 August	3 August
Summer Bank Holiday (England & Wales)	25 August	31 August
Christmas Day	25 December	25 December
Boxing Day Holiday	26 December	28 December

CLACTON-ON-SEA, Essex Map ref 3B3 — SELF CATERING

Groomhill, Clacton-on-Sea

Units **1**
Sleeps **1–7**

Low season per wk
Min £215.00
High season per wk
Max £435.00

Awaiting NAS rating

contact Gail Lewis, PO Box 36, Cowbridge CF71 7GB t 08456 584478
f (01446) 775060 e selfcatering@johngrooms.org.uk w groomsholidays.org.uk

Holiday bungalow specially adapted for disabled people, near town centre and seafront. Three twin bedrooms and sofa bed. Roll-in shower, hoist and shower-chair available.
open All year
nearest shop 2 miles
nearest pub 2 miles

Access abc
General
Unit
Payment Credit/debit cards, cash/cheques, euros

HOVETON, Norfolk Map ref 3C1 — SELF CATERING

Broomhill, Hoveton

Units **2**
Sleeps **2–7**

Low season per wk
Min £225.00
High season per wk
Max £435.00

Awaiting NAS rating

contact Gail Lewis, PO Box 36, Cowbridge CF71 7GB t 08456 584478
f (01446) 775060 e selfcatering@johngrooms.org.uk w groomsholidays.org.uk

Two self-contained flats by Wroxham Broad, owned by Grooms Holidays, Designed for wheelchair users. One on ground floor, other has lift access to first floor. Each has double twin and bunk bedrooms, sofa bed, roll-in shower, shower-chair and hoist available. Can be booked separately.
open All year
nearest shop 1 mile
nearest pub 1 mile

Access abc
General
Unit
Payment Credit/debit cards, cash/cheques, euros

To your credit

If you book by phone you may be asked for your credit card number. If so, it is advisable to check the proprietor's policy in case you have to cancel your reservation at a later date.

At-a-glance symbols are explained on the flap inside the back cover.

STAFFORD, Staffordshire Map ref 4B3 HOTEL

Swan Hotel

B&B per room per night
s £80.00
d £95.00–£130.00

46 Greengate Street, Stafford ST16 2JA **t** (01785) 258142
f (01785) 223372
e info@theswanstafford.co.uk **w** theswanstafford.co.uk

Access

General

Rooms

Payment Credit/debit cards, cash/cheques

The Swan Hotel has been part of Stafford's history for over 250 years. A former coaching inn, it has welcomed visitors since the 18th century. Now sympathetically restored and boasting 31 luxurious bedrooms, an award-winning brasserie restaurant, two popular bar areas and relaxing coffee shop.

open All year
bedrooms 18 double, 2 twin, 6 single, 2 family, 3 suites
bathrooms All en suite

M6 jct 13 A449, M6 jct 14 A5013. A518 town centre. Turn into Tenterbanks, left into Water Street, into Mill Street, car park on left.

Welcome to the Heart of England!

Welcome to the Heart of England – a region of contrasts.

From the rolling beauty of the Malvern Hills to the magic of Shakespeare's Stratford, from the world-class shopping of Birmingham to the iconic Ironbridge Gorge World Heritage site.

The Heart of England offers a diversity of landscapes, people, food & drink, accommodation and attractions that is hard to match anywhere in the country.

Come and enjoy the Heart of England!

www.advantagewm.co.uk

For further information log on to:

Shakespeare Country
www.shakespeare-country.co.uk

Birmingham
www.visitbirmingham.com

Black Country
www.blackcountrytourism.co.uk

Staffordshire
www.enjoystaffordshire.com

Shropshire
www.shropshiretourism.org

Herefordshire
www.visitherefordshire.co.uk

Worcestershire
www.visitworcestershire.org

Coventry & Warwickshire
www.visitcoventryandwarwickshire.co.uk

Fun for all at Cadbury World

For a day packed full of interactive fun, come to Cadbury World. Visit Purple Planet for hands-on fun with virtual chocolate rain. Then discover the secret of Cadbury Dairy Milk in Essence.

We offer discounts for groups of 15+ and a free preview visit for the group organiser. We also boast excellent disabled access and facilities so everyone can fully enjoy their day out.

For more information or to book tickets call **0845 450 3599** or visit **www.cadburyworld.co.uk**

Cadbury WORLD

The National Forest: open to all!

THE NATIONAL FOREST

The National Forest prides itself on being open to all. Many woodlands and attractions within its 200 square miles offer facilities for disabled visitors, with accessible areas for wheelchairs and pushchairs.

Rosliston Timber Lodges nestle within 154 acres of this forest in the making, with loads of activities on site. Each of the four lodges accommodates up to ten people and is purpose-built to welcome visitors of all abilities.

To find out more about the wealth of things to do and see, including our 'Access for All' walks pack, contact us:

www.nationalforest.org
enquiries@nationalforest.org
01283 551211

Back to Life

Discover the beautifully restored 160 acre Italian Gardens, originally designed by Capability Brown for the second Duke of Sutherland.

Now they have been brought back to life with a vast contemporary planting scheme by Tom Stuart Smith and Piet Oudolf's new Prairie Garden.

You may also wish to discover the Shopping Village, Monkey Forest, 750 acre Woodland Estate and Lake, and a multitude of coffee shops, bars and restaurants.

It's a breath of fresh air. Access information available on request.

The Trentham Estate

The Trentham Estate, Trentham, Stoke-on-Trent, Staffs ST4 8AX
Tel: (01782) 646 646 www.trentham.co.uk 5 minutes from J15, M6

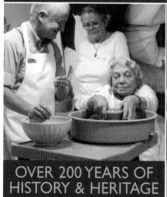

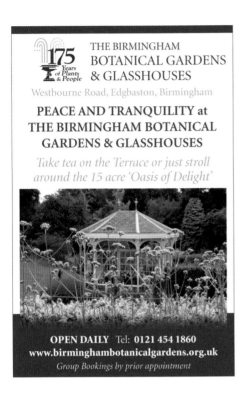

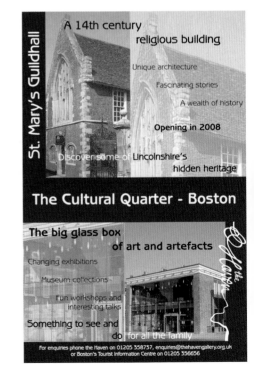

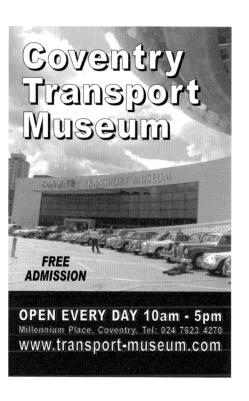

Grosvenor Centre Northampton
Where the shops are

all under one roof

GROSVENOR CENTRE

Tel: 01604 637268
www.grosvenorshoppingcentre.co.uk

Discover the
WORLD'S FIRST GARDEN CITY

- **Speciality Shopping**
- **Art Deco Cinema**
- **Award Winning Tourist Information Centre**
- **Shopmobility**

Letchworth Garden City Tourist Information Centre, 33-35 Station Road, SG6 3BB   Tel: 01462 487868   www.letchworthgc.com

Letchworth Garden City Heritage Foundation is an Industrial and Provident Society with charitable status, Registered No. 28211R

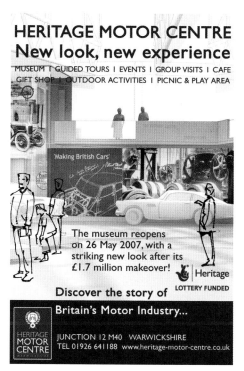

HERITAGE MOTOR CENTRE
New look, new experience
MUSEUM I GUIDED TOURS I EVENTS I GROUP VISITS I CAFE
GIFT SHOP I OUTDOOR ACTIVITIES I PICNIC & PLAY AREA

'Making British Cars'

The museum reopens on 26 May 2007, with a striking new look after its £1.7 million makeover!

Heritage LOTTERY FUNDED

Discover the story of
Britain's Motor Industry...

HERITAGE MOTOR CENTRE   JUNCTION 12 M40   WARWICKSHIRE
TEL 01926 641188 www.heritage-motor-centre.co.uk

Always something new to see and do

- Free admission
- Open Tues to Sat: 10am - 5pm
  Sun: 12pm - 5pm
  and Bank Holiday Mondays
- Fully accessible with lifts to all floors

The New Art Gallery
Walsall

The New Art Gallery
Gallery Square
Walsall
WS2 8LG
Tel: 01922 654400
www.artatwalsall.org.uk

Walsall Council

ARTS COUNCIL ENGLAND

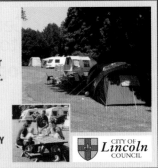

Bank holiday
dates for your diary

holiday	2008	2009
New Year's Day (England & Wales)	1 January	1 January
New Year's Day (Scotland)	1 January	1 January
January Bank Holiday (Scotland)	2 January	2 January
Good Friday	21 March	10 April
Easter Monday (England & Wales)	24 March	13 April
Early May Bank Holiday	5 May	4 May
Spring Bank Holiday	26 May	25 May
Summer Bank Holiday (Scotland)	4 August	3 August
Summer Bank Holiday (England & Wales)	25 August	31 August
Christmas Day	25 December	25 December
Boxing Day Holiday	26 December	28 December

Newcastle under Lyme

is an easily accessible and attractive town centre with excellent shopping facilities and a wide variety of restaurants, cafes, pubs and bars. With the New Vic Theatre, Dorothy Clive Garden and Museum and Art Gallery all situated within the Borough - there's something for everyone in Newcastle.

www.newcastle-staffs.gov.uk

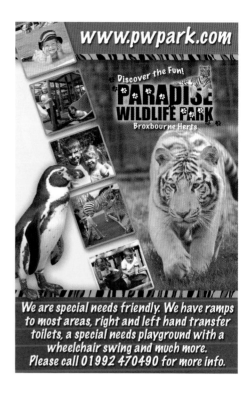

www.pwpark.com

Discover the Fun!

PARADISE WILDLIFE PARK
Broxbourne Herts

We are special needs friendly. We have ramps to most areas, right and left hand transfer toilets, a special needs playground with a wheelchair swing and much more.
Please call 01992 470490 for more info.

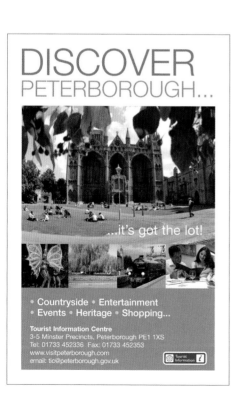

DISCOVER
PETERBOROUGH...

...it's got the lot!

• Countryside • Entertainment
• Events • Heritage • Shopping...

Tourist Information Centre
3-5 Minster Precincts, Peterborough PE1 1XS
Tel: 01733 452336 Fax: 01733 452353
www.visitpeterborough.com
email: tic@peterborough.gov.uk

Redwings
Horse Sanctuary

Home to rescued horses, ponies and donkeys!

FREE ADMISSION

Meet rescued horses, ponies and donkeys at one of our visitor centres in Norfolk, Suffolk, Essex and Warwickshire.

All centres open 10am to 5pm seven days a week April to October.

For all enquiries including accessibility and winter opening times, call

REDWINGS
HORSE SANCTUARY
Registered Charity
No.1068911
Incorporating Ada Cole
Memorial Stables

0870 040 0033
Please visit www.redwings.co.uk

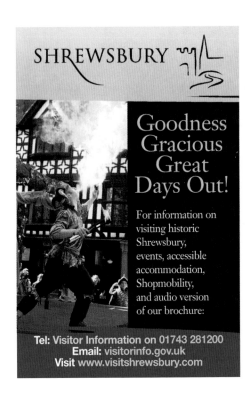

www.shropshirehillsdiscoverycentre.co.uk

discover
secrets in the landscape

what to **do**, what to **see**, where to **stay**

Visitor Information at the
Shropshire Hills
Discovery Centre
01588 676000

*Just off the A49 at
Craven Arms, seven
miles north of Ludlow.*

Shropshire Hills
Discovery Centre

Coors
Visitor Centre
& The Museum of Brewing

EXPERIENCE THE LIVING HISTORY
at the
**Coors Visitor Centre
& the Museum of Brewing**
Horninglow Street
Burton upon Trent

www.coorsvisitorcentre.com
Tel **0845 600 0598**

▪ Vintage Vehicles
▪ Shire Horse Stables
▪ Bar and Restaurant
▪ Café Coors
▪ Beer Gift Shop

Bedfordshire
county council

For information on local bus services in
Bedfordshire contact **The Bedfordshire
County Council Bus Information Line**
on **01234 228333.**

Alternatively please contact:

 traveline
public transport info
0871 200 22 33
www.traveline.info

**SEVERN VALLEY
RAILWAY**
the line for all seasons

T he best way to see the beauty of the River
Severn is from a steam-hauled train on the
Severn Valley Railway.

Kidderminster – Bewdley – Bridgnorth
Specially adapted carriges in certain trains.
Access to toilets and buffet at each terminus.

THE RAILWAY STATION, BEWDLEY, WORCESTERSHIRE, DY12 1BG

TEL: 01299 403816 www.svr.co.uk

Enjoy **Braintree** *district*

Braintree, Coggeshall, Halstead and Witham
Historic market towns set in the most beautiful rolling
countryside of North Essex with:
*designer shopping, street markets, historical sites,
country pursuits, picturesque villages & wedding venues*

Braintree District Museum
Discover a vibrant heritage at this award winning museum

Warners textile Archive
A visual record of 200 years of textile design

Tourist Information: 01376 550066
www.enjoybraintreedistrict.co.uk

TYSELEY LOCO WORKS
VISITOR CENTRE
BIRMINGHAM
RAILWAY MUSEUM
670 WARWICK RD,
TYSELEY, B'HAM B11 2HL
TEL:0121 708 4962
Home of the "Shakespeare Express"
OPEN SAT/SUN 10.00 - 16.00
www.vintagetrains.co.uk

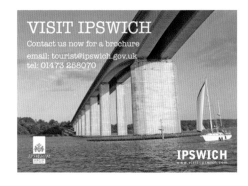

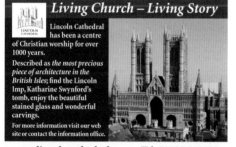

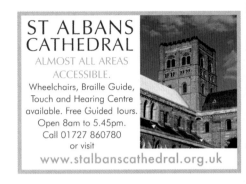

Calling Britain from overseas

Telephone numbers in this guide can be used if you are dialling from within Britain. If you are an overseas visitor and wish to call Britain from another country, start with the international dialling code 00. Next, dial the country code for the UK, which is **44**. Finally, dial the UK number, **without the first 0**.

Finding accommodation

VisitBritain's official guides to quality accommodation make it quick and easy to find a place to stay. There are several ways to use this guide.

1 PROPERTY INDEX
If you know the name of the establishment you wish to book, turn to the property index at the back where the relevant page number is shown.

2 PLACE INDEX
The place index at the back lists all locations with accommodation featured in the regional sections. A page number is shown where you can find full accommodation and contact details.

3 QUICK REFERENCE INDEXES
The quick reference indexes list accommodation with particular accessible facilities. There are indexes for accommodation with level entry showers, hoists, induction loop systems at reception, typetalk, adapted kitchens and facilities for service dogs.

4 COLOUR MAPS
All the place names in black on the colour maps at the front have an entry in the regional sections. Refer to the place index for the page number where you will find one or more establishments offering accommodation in your chosen town or village.

South West England

Stonehenge, Wiltshire

Bristol, Cornwall, Devon, Dorset, Gloucestershire, Isles of Scilly, Somerset, Wiltshire

St Michael's Mount,
Marazion, Cornwall

Wonders of the **west**

Indulge your love of cream teas and clotted cream fudge. Explore the South West Coast Path, Exmoor, Dartmoor and honey-coloured Cotswold villages. Wonder at the mysteries of Avebury and Stonehenge and stunning gardens across the region. **There's so much to experience in South West England.**

Secret gardens

The South West boasts three of the most extraordinary gardens in Britain. Its balmy, subtropical climate is perfect for more exotic flora. Start with the remarkable Eden Project, near St Austell, home to thousands of plants. Wander around the enormous glass biomes, where nature and technology meet, or set the children off on one of the fun, interactive trails. Delight in the Lost Gardens of Heligan at Pentewan – an 80-acre garden neglected for more than 70 years until 1991 – or take a helicopter ride to Tresco, one of the Scilly Isles, to see more unexpected exotic plants at the Abbey Garden. For more inspiration, follow The Forest of Dean Sculpture Trail where you can discover thought-provoking works of art nestling between the trees. Or stroll around Westonbirt: The National Arboretum in Gloucestershire and allow the colours to mesmerise you whatever the season.

Feeling free

Find your bearings along sections of the South West Coast Path which stretches for 630 miles from Minehead to Poole, with dramatic views of the coastline along the way. A selection of short walks are suitable for people with limited mobility, wheelchairs or motor scooters (southwestcoastpath.com). Catch a glimpse of wild red deer or grazing ponies in the stunning Exmoor National Park and gaze at reflections in beautiful lake-like reservoirs on heather-clad Dartmoor.

After all that fresh air, indulge in the South West's delicious specialities. A Cornish pasty tastes especially good washed down with a pint of sweet cider. Or take afternoon tea with mouthwatering scones straight from the oven, topped with indulgent clotted cream!

Down by the sea

How's this for the perfect antidote to modern life? The South West has more Blue Flag beaches than anywhere else in England. The region's sandy bays and sheltered coves are perfect for building sandcastles and enjoying secluded picnics. If you are seeking adventure, the hip centres of Newquay, Bude, Croyde and Woolacombe are great places for watersports. Discover Devon's English Riviera – the bustling seaside towns of Torquay, Paignton and Brixham – and get acquainted with coastal creatures from penguins to puffins at Living Coasts in Torquay. Away from the beach, charming fishing villages, such as Clovelly, Port Isaac and Beer, are the perfect setting for a relaxing lunch.

Looking for something different? Take a fossil hammer for an ammonite hunt on the Jurassic Coast, a World Heritage Site, where you can see 185 million years of earth history along 95 miles of spectacular coastline.

Bibury, Gloucestershire

Fascinating history at
SS Great Britain, Bristol

Inset pictures
Biomes at The Eden
Project, near St Austell;
Forest of Dean Sculpture
Trail, Gloucestershire;
Tate St Ives, Cornwall;
Oceanarium,
Bournemouth, Dorset

Great days out

If you're looking for a great day out, try these for starters! Uncover the history of the railway at Swindon's interactive attraction Steam – Museum of the Great Western Railway, and find out about the abolition of slavery at the Breaking Chains exhibition at Bristol's British Empire & Commonwealth Museum.

The Roman Baths, Bath

See how many animals the kids can spot at Longleat's famous Safari Park and enjoy a close encounter with friendly mute swans and their fluffy cygnets at Abbotsbury Swannery. Relive the seafaring history of the South West at the National Maritime Museum Cornwall in Falmouth, or catch a performance at the stunning cliffside setting of The Minack Theatre at Porthcurno.
Ponder the mysteries of the ancient stone circles of Stonehenge and Avebury or try to spot Gwyn ap Nudd, King of the Fairies, at Glastonbury Tor. Take a tour around the honey-coloured limestone villages of the Cotswolds, exploring the beautiful towns of Cheltenham and Cirencester, and the lovely villages of Bourton-on-the-Water and Castle Combe on the way. Saddle up on Exmoor, Dartmoor or Bodmin (disabled riding is available), or soar skywards in a hot-air balloon.

City splendours

The buzzing cities of Bristol and Bath are filled with attractions. Revel in the Georgian beauty of Bath; tour round the best-preserved Roman religious spa from the ancient world, lying under the watchful gaze of Bath Abbey; or sink into the natural thermal waters of the newly opened Thermae Bath Spa.

> Spectacular coastlines, perfect beaches, enchanting gardens and tasty treats – indulge your every whim in the South West

Sample Bristol's infectious vitality and head for the rejuvenated harbour front to discover vibrant bars and restaurants. Take an interactive adventure of a lifetime at magical At-Bristol – a unique destination bringing science, nature and art to life. Check out the feat of engineering that is the Clifton Suspension Bridge, the brainchild of Isambard Kingdom Brunel, and then continue your journey with a trip to some of the West's other great cathedral cities. Discover Exeter, Wells and Gloucester and marvel at Salisbury Cathedral with the tallest spire in Britain.

Useful regional contacts

For information before you travel, check out the useful regional contacts below. Local Tourist Information Centres will also be able to give you information on accessible attractions and accommodation.

South West Tourism
t 0870 442 0880
w visitsouthwest.co.uk

Publications

Access Salisbury
Available free from Salisbury Tourist Information Centre.
Call (01722) 334956.

Easy Going Dartmoor and Access Guide to Dartmoor
Available from the Dartmoor National Park Authority. Call (01822) 890414 or visit dartmoor-npa.gov.uk.

Handbook For Disabled Visitors
Available from Isle of Wight Tourism. Call (023) 9081 3818 or visit islandbreaks.co.uk.

South Somerset: a Guide for People with Disabilities
Available from South Somerset District Council. Call (01935) 462462 or visit tourism@southsomerset.gov.uk.

The English Riviera: Access for All
An information leaflet on Torbay, Paignton and Brixham. Available from Tourist Information Centres and the English Riviera Tourist Board on (01803) 296296.

West Dorset for Visitors with Disabilities
Available from West Dorset District Council Tourist Information Centres. Email tourism@westdorset-dc.gov.uk.

Resources

Accessible South West
w accessiblesouthwest.co.uk
A directory designed to assist visitors with disabilities travelling to the South West of England find suitable places to stay and visit.

Forest of Dean Council Tourism and Marketing
w visitforestofdean.co.uk
Has information for visitors with disabilities.

South West Coastal Path
w southwestcoastpath.com
A national trail website with details of walks for everyone. Includes pictures so that you can assess whether a walk is right for you.

Visit Kennet
w visitkennet.co.uk
Includes a guide to assist and enable disabled visitors to enjoy Kennet and its attractions.

Visit Somerset
w visitsomerset.net
Contains information for disabled people, including where to find accessible toilets and accommodation.

Tourist Information Centres

When you arrive at your destination, visit a Tourist Information Centre for help with accommodation and information about local attractions and events, or email your request before you go.

Bristol & Bath

Bath	Abbey Church Yard	0906 711 2000**	tourism@bathnes.gov.uk
Bristol	Harbourside	0906 711 2191**	ticharbourside@destinationbristol.co.uk

Cornwall & the Isles of Scilly

Bodmin	Mount Folly Square	(01208) 76616	bodmintic@visit.org.uk
Bude	The Crescent	(01288) 354240	budetic@visitbude.info
Camelford*	The Clease	(01840) 212954	manager@camelfordtic.eclipse.co.uk
Falmouth	11 Market Strand	(01326) 312300	info@falmouthtic.co.uk
Fowey	5 South Street	(01726) 833616	info@fowey.co.uk
Isles of Scilly	Hugh Street, Hugh Town	(01720) 422536	tic@scilly.gov.uk
Launceston	Market Street	(01566) 772321	launcestontica@btconnect.com
Looe*	Fore Street	(01503) 262072	looetic@btconnect.com
Newquay	Marcus Hill	(01637) 854020	info@newquay.co.uk
Padstow	North Quay	(01841) 533449	padstowtic@btconnect.com
Penzance	Station Road	(01736) 362207	pztic@penwith.gov.uk
St Austell	Southbourne Road	0845 094 0428	tic@cornish-riviera.co.uk
St Ives	Street-an-Pol	(01736) 796297	ivtic@penwith.gov.uk
Truro	Boscawen Street	(01872) 274555	tic@truro.gov.uk
Wadebridge	Eddystone Road	0870 122 3337	wadebridgetic@btconnect.com

Devon

Axminster*	Church Street	(01297) 34386	axminstertic@btopenworld.com
Barnstaple	The Square	(01271) 375000	info@staynorthdevon.co.uk
Bideford	Victoria Park	(01237) 477676	bidefordtic@torridge.gov.uk
Braunton	Caen Street	(01271) 816400	info@brauntontic.co.uk
Brixham	The Quay	0870 707 0010	brixham.tic@torbay.gov.uk
Budleigh Salterton	Fore Street	(01395) 445275	budleigh.tic@btconnect.com
Combe Martin*	Cross Street	(01271) 883319	mail@visitcombemartin.co.uk
Crediton	High Street	(01363) 772006	info@devonshireheartland.co.uk
Dartmouth	Mayor's Avenue	(01803) 834224	holidays@discoverdartmouth.com
Dawlish	The Lawn	(01626) 215665	dawtic@Teignbridge.gov.uk
Exeter	Dix's Field	(01392) 265700	tic@exeter.gov.uk
Exmouth	Alexandra Terrace	(01395) 222299	info@exmouthtourism.co.uk
Honiton	Lace Walk Car Park	(01404) 43716	honitontic@btconnect.com
Ilfracombe	The Seafront	(01271) 863001	info@ilfracombe-tourism.co.uk
Ivybridge	19 Fore Street	(01752) 897035	bookends.ivybridge@virgin.net
Kingsbridge	The Quay	(01548) 853195	advice@kingsbridgeinfo.co.uk

Lynton and Lynmouth	Lee Road	0845 660 3232	info@lyntourism.co.uk
Modbury*	5 Modbury Court	(01548) 830159	modburytic@lineone.net
Newton Abbot	6 Bridge House	(01626) 215667	natic@Teignbridge.gov.uk
Okehampton	3 West Street	(01837) 53020	okehamptontic@westdevon.gov.uk
Ottery St Mary	10a Broad Street	(01404) 813964	info@otterytourism.org.uk
Paignton	The Esplanade	0870 707 0010	paignton.tic@torbay.gov.uk
Plymouth (Plymouth Mayflower)	3-5 The Barbican	(01752) 306330	barbicantic@plymouth.gov.uk
Salcombe	Market Street	(01548) 843927	info@salcombeinformation.co.uk
Seaton	The Underfleet	(01297) 21660	info@seatontic.freeserve.co.uk
Sidmouth	Ham Lane	(01395) 516441	sidmouthtic@eclipse.co.uk
South Molton	1 East Street	(01769) 574122	visitsouthmolton@btconnect.com
Tavistock	Bedford Square	(01822) 612938	tavistocktic@westdevon.gov.uk
Teignmouth	The Den	(01626) 215666	teigntic@teignbridge.gov.uk
Tiverton	Phoenix Lane	(01884) 255827	tivertontic@btconnect.com
Torquay	Vaughan Parade	0870 707 0010	torquay.tic@torbay.gov.uk
Torrington	Castle Hill	(01805) 626140	info@great-torrington.com
Totnes	Coronation Road	(01803) 863168	enquire@totnesinformation.co.uk
Woolacombe	The Esplanade	(01271) 870553	info@woolacombetourism.co.uk

Dorset

Blandford Forum	1 Greyhound Yard	(01258) 454770	blandfordtic@north-dorset.gov.uk
Bournemouth	Westover Road	(01202) 451700	info@bournemouth.gov.uk
Bridport	47 South Street	(01308) 424901	bridport.tic@westdorset-dc.gov.uk
Christchurch	49 High Street	(01202) 471780	enquiries@christchurch.gov.uk
Dorchester	11 Antelope Walk	(01305) 267992	dorchester.tic@westdorset-dc.gov.uk
Lyme Regis	Church Street	(01297) 442138	lymeregis.tic@westdorset-dc.gov.uk
Poole	Poole Quay	(01202) 253253	info@poole.gov.uk
Shaftesbury	8 Bell Street	(01747) 853514	shaftesburytic@north-dorset.gov.uk
Sherborne	3 Tilton Court	(01935) 815341	sherborne.tic@westdorset-dc.gov.uk
Swanage	Shore Road	(01929) 422885	mail@swanage.gov.uk
Wareham	South Street	(01929) 552740	tic@purbeck-dc.gov.uk
Weymouth	The Esplanade	(01305) 785747	tic@weymouth.gov.uk
Wimborne Minster	29 High Street	(01202) 886116	wimbornetic@eastdorset.gov.uk

Gloucestershire & the Cotswolds

Bourton-on-the-Water	Victoria Street	(01451) 820211	bourtonvic@btconnect.com
Cheltenham	77 Promenade	(01242) 522878	tic@cheltenham.gov.uk
Cirencester	Market Place	(01285) 654180	cirencestervic@cotswold.gov.uk
Coleford	High Street	(01594) 812388	tourism@fdean.gov.uk
Gloucester	28 Southgate Street	(01452) 396572	tourism@gloucester.gov.uk
Newent	7 Church Street	(01531) 822468	newent@fdean.gov.uk
Stow-on-the-Wold	The Square	(01451) 831082	stowvic@cotswold.gov.uk
Stroud	George Street	(01453) 760960	tic@stroud.gov.uk
Tetbury	33 Church Street	(01666) 503552	tourism@tetbury.org

| Tewkesbury | 64 Barton Street | (01684) 295027 | tewkesburytic@tewkesburybc.gov.uk |
| Winchcombe* | High Street | (01242) 602925 | winchcombetic@tewkesbury.gov.uk |

Somerset

Bridgwater	King Square	(01278) 436438	bridgwater.tic@sedgemoor.gov.uk
Burnham-on-Sea	South Esplanade	(01278) 787852	burnham.tic@sedgemoor.gov.uk
Cartgate	A303/A3088 Cartgate Picnic Site	(01935) 829333	cartgate.tic@southsomerset.gov.uk
Chard	Fore Street	(01460) 65710	chardtic@chard.gov.uk
Cheddar*	The Gorge	(01934) 744071	cheddar.tic@sedgemoor.gov.uk
Frome	Justice Lane	(01373) 467271	frome.tic@ukonline.co.uk
Glastonbury	9 High Street	(01458) 832954	glastonbury.tic@ukonline.co.uk
Minehead	17 Friday Street	(01643) 702624	info@mineheadtic.co.uk
Sedgemoor Services	M5 Southbound	(01934) 750833	somersetvisitorcentre@somerset.gov.uk
Shepton Mallet	48 High Street	(01749) 345258	sheptonmallet.tic@ukonline.co.uk
Street	Farm Road	(01458) 447384	street.tic@ukonline.co.uk
Taunton	Paul Street	(01823) 336344	tauntontic@tauntondeane.gov.uk
Wellington	30 Fore Street	(01823) 663379	wellingtontic@tauntondeane.gov.uk
Wells	Market Place	(01749) 672552	touristinfo@wells.gov.uk
Weston-super-Mare	Beach Lawns	(01934) 888800	westontouristinfo@n-somerset.gov.uk
Yeovil Heritage & Visitor Information Centre	Hendford	(01935) 845946	yeoviltic@southsomerset.gov.uk

Wiltshire – Salisbury & Stonehenge

Amesbury	Smithfield Street	(01980) 622833	amesburytic@salisbury.gov.uk
Avebury	Green Street	(01672) 539425	all.atic@kennet.gov.uk
Bradford-on-Avon	50 St Margaret's Street	(01225) 865797	tic@bradfordonavon.co.uk
Chippenham	Market Place	(01249) 665970	tourism@chippenham.gov.uk
Corsham	31 High Street	(01249) 714660	enquiries@corshamheritage.org.uk
Devizes	Market Place	(01380) 729408	all.dtic@kennet.gov.uk
Malmesbury	Market Lane	(01666) 823748	malmesburyip@northwilts.gov.uk
Marlborough	High Street	(01672) 513989	all.tic's@kennet.gov.uk
Melksham	Church Street	(01225) 707424	info@visit-melksham.com
Mere	Barton Lane	(01747) 861211	MereTIC@Salisbury.gov.uk
Salisbury	Fish Row	(01722) 334956	visitorinfo@salisbury.gov.uk
Swindon	37 Regent Street	(01793) 530328	infocentre@swindon.gov.uk
Trowbridge	St Stephen's Place	(01225) 710535	tic@trowbridge.gov.uk
Warminster	off Station Rd	(01985) 218548	visitwarminster@westwiltshire.gov.uk

* seasonal opening   ** calls to this number are charged at premium rate

ABBOTSBURY, Dorset Map ref 2A3 | SELF CATERING

★★★★
SELF CATERING

Units **7**
Sleeps **2–9**

Low season per wk
£200.00–£500.00
High season per wk
£370.00–£950.00

Character Farm Cottages, Weymouth

contact Mrs AE Mayo, Higher Farm, Rodden, Weymouth DT3 4JE
t (01305) 871187 **e** jane@mayo.fsbusiness.co.uk
w characterfarmcottages.co.uk

Nestling on the World Heritage Jurassic coast between picturesque Abbotsbury and Weymouth, our personally-run quality character cottages are suitable for the less mobile. 'Chestnuts' is suitable for wheelchair access and three cottages have ground-floor bedrooms, showers/bathrooms.
open All year
nearest shop 2 miles
nearest pub 2 miles

Access	
General	
Leisure	
Unit	
Payment	Cash/cheques

ABBOTSBURY, Dorset | SELF CATERING

★★★★
SELF CATERING

Gorwell Farm Cottages contact Mrs Mary Pengelly, M J Pengelly Ltd, Gorwell, Abbotsbury, Weymouth DT3 4JX **t** (01305) 871401
e mary@gorwellfarm.co.uk **w** gorwellfarm.co.uk

ALBASTON, Cornwall | SELF CATERING

★★★★
SELF CATERING

Todsworthy Farm Holidays contact Mr Pellow, Todsworthy Farm Holidays, Albaston, Gunnislake PL18 9AW **t** (01822) 834744
w todsworthyfarmholidays.co.uk

ALTON PANCRAS, Dorset | SELF CATERING

★★★★–★★★★★★★
SELF CATERING

Bookham Court contact Mr & Mrs Andrew Foot, Whiteways, Bookham, Alton Pancras, Dorchester DT2 7RP **t** (01300) 345511 **f** (01300) 345511
e andy.foot1@btinternet.com **w** bookhamcourt.co.uk

ASHBURTON, Devon | SELF CATERING

★★★–★★★★★
SELF CATERING

Wooder Manor Holiday Homes contact Mrs Angela Bell, Wooder Manor Holiday Homes, Widecombe-in-the-Moor, Newton Abbot TQ13 7TR
t (01364) 621391 **f** (01364) 621391
e angela@woodermanor.com **w** woodermanor.com

ASHBURTON, Devon Map ref 1C2 — SELF CATERING

Wren & Robin Cottages, Ashburton

★★★★
SELF CATERING

Units **2**
Sleeps **2–6**

Low season per wk
Min £245.00
High season per wk
Max £450.00

contact Mrs Margaret Phipps, Wren & Robin Cottages, New Cott Farm, Newton Abbot TQ13 7PD **t** (01364) 631421 **f** (01364) 631421
e enquiries@newcott-farm.co.uk **w** newcott-farm.co.uk

Within Dartmoor National Park Robin and Wren cottages sit in a peaceful location with uninterrupted views over farmland and woodland. Beautifully furnished, well equipped, own garden and veranda. Safe parking. Christmas and New Year breaks. Prices all inclusive.
open All year
nearest shop 4 miles
nearest pub 1 mile

General ☳3 P ⚡ Ⓢ

Unit ⬚ ⬚, ⬚ ⬚ ⬚ ⬚ ⬚ ⬚ ⬚
⬚ ✳

Payment Credit/debit cards, cash/cheques

ASHWATER, Devon Map ref 1C2 — SELF CATERING

Blagdon Farm Country Holidays, Beaworthy

★★★★–★★★★★★
SELF CATERING

Units **8**
Sleeps **2–6**

Low season per wk
£240.00–£740.00
High season per wk
£460.00–£938.00

contact Mr & Mrs M Clark & Mr & Mrs H O'Brien, Blagdon Farm Country Holidays, Nr Ashwater, Beaworthy EX21 5DF
t (01409) 211509
e info@blagdon-farm.co.uk **w** blagdon-farm.co.uk

Access abc ⚠

General ☳ ⬚ ♿ P ⚡ Ⓢ

Leisure ⬚

Unit ⬚ ⬚ ⬚, ⬚ ⬚ ⬚ ⬚ ⬚ ⬚
⬚ ⬚ ⬚ ⬚ ⬚ ✳

Payment Cash/cheques

The swimming pool has a ceiling hoist. Mobility equipment is available for hire. Level parking directly outside the cottages.

Fully accessible (M3A) luxury cottages set in 12 acres of Devon countryside, yet only 20 minutes from the coast. South facing, each cottage enjoys stunning views towards its own 2.5-acre coarse-fishing lake, forest and fields beyond. Facilities include a heated indoor hydrotherapy swimming pool, licensed bar and bistro, games room and woodland walks.
open All year
nearest shop 1.5 miles
nearest pub 1.5 miles

From the A30 at Launceston, take the A388 Holsworthy Road. After 9 miles, take the 2nd Ashwater turning, following the brown tourist signs for Blagdon Farm.

BARNSTAPLE, Devon | **SELF CATERING**

★★★★
SELF CATERING

Country Ways contact Mrs Kate Price, Country Ways, Little Knowle Farm, High Bickington, Umberleigh EX37 9BJ **t** (01769) 560503 **f** (01769) 560819
e kate@country-ways.net **w** country-ways.net

BATH, Somerset Map ref 2B2 | **GUEST ACCOMMODATION**

★★★★★
GUEST ACCOMMODATION
B&B per room per night
s £71.00–£81.00
d £99.00–£150.00
Evening meal per person
£8.50–£16.50

The Carfax

13-15 Great Pulteney Street, Bath BA2 4BS **t** (01225) 462089
f (01225) 443257
e reservations@carfaxhotel.co.uk **w** carfaxhotel.co.uk

A trio of Georgian townhouses in the centre of Bath. Lifts to all floors, private car park and garages, wheelchair access to public rooms and affordable prices.
open All year
bedrooms 13 double, 7 twin, 6 single, 4 family, 1 suite
bathrooms All en suite

From M4 jct 18, A4 to London Road. At city traffic lights over Cleveland Bridge, sharp right at Holburne Museum.

Access   abc ☑

General ☎ P♿ ✂ ✗ 🍽 ⬇

Rooms ♨ 📺 🛁 🧴 ♨ 🖂

Payment Credit/debit cards, cash/cheques

Check our website for seasonal offers and special discounts.

BATH, Somerset | **SELF CATERING**

★★★★
SELF CATERING

Church Farm Country Cottages contact Mrs Trish Bowles, Church Farm, Winsley, Bradford-on-Avon BA15 2JH **t** (01225) 722246 **f** (01225) 722246
e stay@churchfarmcottages.com **w** churchfarmcottages.com

BATH, Somerset | **SELF CATERING**

★★★★ – ★★★★★★
SELF CATERING

Greyfield Farm Cottages contact Mrs June Merry, Greyfield Farm Cottages, Greyfield Road, High Littleton, Bristol BS39 6YQ **t** (01761) 471132 **f** (01761) 471132
e june@greyfieldfarm.com **w** greyfieldfarm.com

BEAMINSTER, Dorset | **SELF CATERING**

★★★★
SELF CATERING

Lewesdon Farm Holidays contact Mr & Mrs Michael & Linda Smith, Lewesdon Farm Holidays, Lewesdon Farm, Stoke Abbott, Beaminster DT8 3JZ
t (01308) 868270
e lewesdonfarmholiday@tinyonline.co.uk **w** lewesdonfarmholidays.co.uk

BEAMINSTER, Dorset | **SELF CATERING**

★★★★
SELF CATERING

Stable Cottage contact Mrs Diana Clarke, Stable Cottage, Meerhay Manor, Beaminster DT8 3SB **t** (01308) 862305 **f** (01308) 863972
e meerhay@aol.com **w** meerhay.co.uk

At-a-glance symbols are explained on the flap inside the back cover.

BEESON, Devon | SELF CATERING

★★★★
SELF CATERING

Beeson Farm Holiday Cottages contact Mr & Mrs Robin & Veronica Cross, Beeson Farm Holidays, Beeson Farm, Beeson, Kingsbridge TQ7 2HW
t (01548) 581270 **f** (01548) 581270
e info@beesonhols.co.uk **w** beesonhols.co.uk

BEETHAM, Somerset | CAMPING & CARAVANNING

★★★★
TOURING PARK

Five Acres Caravan Club Site Beetham, Chard TA20 3QA
t (01460) 234519
w caravanclub.co.uk

BERWICK ST JOHN, Wiltshire | SELF CATERING

★★★★
SELF CATERING

Priory Cottage, Awre
t (01747) 828170
e enq@hideaways.co.uk **w** hideaways.co.uk

BETTISCOMBE, Dorset | SELF CATERING

★★★
SELF CATERING

Conway Bungalow contact Mrs Margaret Smith, Conway Bungalow, Bettiscombe, Bridport DT6 5NT **t** (01308) 868313 **f** (01308) 868313
e info@conway-bungalow.co.uk **w** conway-bungalow.co.uk

BLANDFORD FORUM, Dorset Map ref 2B3 | SELF CATERING

★★★★★
SELF CATERING

Units **1**
Sleeps **10**

Low season per wk
£1,650.00–£1,850.00
High season per wk
£1,995.00–£2,495.00

Houghton Lodge, Blandford Forum

contact Lucy Fiander, Houghton Lodge, Winterborne Houghton, Blandford Forum DT11 0PE **t** (01258) 882170
e enquiries@houghtonlodge.com **w** houghtonlodge.com

Access 🅰

General 🐾 ▥ 🚹 P ✂ 🔘 Ⓢ

Leisure 🏊

Unit 🛏 🚿 🪜 🍽 🛢 🖥 📺 🧺

Payment Cash/cheques

Use of heated indoor pool with Wispa hoist. Infra-red sauna. Hydrotherapy hot tub. Accessible gardens and patios.

Set in the beautiful Dorset Downs yet just a short drive from the Jurassic Coast and seaside towns of Poole, Bournemouth and Weymouth (host to the 2012 Paralympic sailing events). Accessible accommodation with a touch of luxury for the whole family. Large wheel-in wet room. Indoor pool with hoist.

open All year
nearest shop 1 mile
nearest pub 1 mile

From Blandford Forum take A354 to Winterborne Whitechurch and turn right. Follow signs to Winterborne Clenston/Stickland. At Stickland follow sign to Winterborne Houghton opposite pub, house approx 1 mile on right.

BODMIN, Cornwall — HOTEL

★★★
HOTEL

Lanhydrock Hotel & Golf Course Lostwithiel Road, Bodmin PL30 5AQ
t (01208) 262570 f (01208) 262579
e info@lanhydrockhotel.com w lanhydrockhotel.com

BOSCASTLE, Cornwall — GUEST ACCOMMODATION

Rating Applied For
GUEST ACCOMMODATION

Old Coach House Tintagel Road, Boscastle PL35 0AS
t (01840) 250398 f (01840) 250346
e jackiefarm@btinternet.com w old-coach.co.uk

BOURNEMOUTH, Dorset — GUEST ACCOMMODATION

★★★★
GUEST HOUSE

Wood Lodge Hotel 10 Manor Road, Bournemouth BH1 3EY
t (01202) 290891 f (01202) 290892
e enquiries@woodlodgehotel.co.uk w woodlodgehotel.co.uk

BRATTON, Somerset Map ref 1D1 — SELF CATERING

★★★★
SELF CATERING

Units **8**
Sleeps **2–11**

Low season per wk
Min £170.00
High season per wk
Max £1,250.00

Woodcombe Lodges, Minehead

contact Mrs Nicola Hanson, Woodcombe Lodges, Bratton Lane,
Minehead TA24 8SQ t (01643) 702789 & 07860 667325 f (01643) 702789
e nicola@woodcombelodge.co.uk w woodcombelodge.co.uk

Cherry Lodge and Holly Lodge are both wheelchair-accessible with Holly Lodge having the additional benefit of a wheel-in shower with seat. Both lodges are very comfortable with wonderful views.
open All year
nearest shop 1 mile
nearest pub 1 mile

General
Unit
Payment Credit/debit cards, cash/cheques

BRATTON FLEMING, Devon — GUEST ACCOMMODATION

★★★★★
GUEST ACCOMMODATION

Bracken House Country Hotel Bratton Fleming, Barnstaple EX31 4TG
t (01598) 710320
e steve@brackenhousehotel.co.uk w brackenhousehotel.co.uk

BRIDGWATER, Somerset — SELF CATERING

★★★★
SELF CATERING

Ash-Wembdon Farm Cottages contact Mr Clarence Rowe, Ash-Wembdon Farm Cottages, Ash-Wembdon Farm, Hollow Lane, Bridgwater TA5 2BD
t (01278) 453097 f (01278) 445856
e c.a.rowe@btinternet.com w ukcottageholiday.com

BRISTOL, City of Bristol — CAMPING & CARAVANNING

★★★★
TOURING PARK

Baltic Wharf Caravan Club Site Cumberland Road, Bristol BS1 6XG
t (0117) 926 8030 f (0117) 926 8030
w caravanclub.co.uk

At-a-glance symbols are explained on the flap inside the back cover.

BRIXHAM, Devon Map ref 1D2 — CAMPING & CARAVANNING

★★★★★
TOURING & CAMPING PARK

(239)
£14.30–£32.00
(239)
£14.30–£32.00
239 touring pitches

THE
CARAVAN CLUB

Hillhead Holiday Park Caravan Club Site

Hillhead, Brixham TQ5 0HH **t** (01803) 853204
w caravanclub.co.uk

Set in 22 acres of Devon countryside this site offers some of the finest facilities on the network. In a great location with many pitches affording stunning views of the sea. There's plenty of entertainment, including an outdoor heated swimming pool, games room, play area, bar and restaurant. Open March to January.

General P 🚗 🏧 🍴 WP 🔫 ☺ 📞🗄 🛒 ✗ ☼

Leisure ⚓ 📺 🍴 ♪ ⚲ ⁄⁀

Payment Credit/debit cards, cash/cheques

Right off A380 (Newton Abbot). Three miles onto ring road (Brixham). Seven miles turn right, A3022. In 0.75 miles, right onto A379. Two miles keep left onto B3025. Site entrance on left.

BROADCLYST, Devon Map ref 1D2 — SELF CATERING

★★★★
SELF CATERING

Units **1**
Sleeps **4**

Low season per wk
£230.00–£495.00
High season per wk
£580.00–£735.00

Hue's Piece, Exeter

contact Mrs Anna Hamlyn, Hue's Piece, Paynes Farm, Broadclyst, Exeter EX5 3BJ **t** (01392) 466720 **e** annahamlyn@paynes-farm.co.uk **w** paynes-farm.co.uk

Characterful wheelchair-accessible cottage on friendly National Trust farm. Peaceful open views across fields, level parking and private garden. One double and two single bedrooms, wet room-style shower room.
open All year
nearest shop 1 mile
nearest pub 1 mile

General 🐚 🏛 🛢 P ✂ Ⓢ

Unit ♨ 🏢 🍳 📺 🍴 🗄 🚿 🔥 🍳 🗄 ❀

Payment Cash/cheques

BROMHAM, Wiltshire — SELF CATERING

★★★
SELF CATERING & SERVICED APARTMENTS

Park Farm Cottages contact Mrs Valerie Bourne, Westbrook, Bromham, Chippenham SN15 2EE
t (01380) 850966
e valandtom2003@aol.com

BUCKLAND IN THE MOOR, Devon — SELF CATERING

★★★
SELF CATERING

Pine Lodge contact Ian Butterworth, Holiday Homes & Cottages South West, 365a Torquay Road, Paignton TQ3 2BT **t** (01803) 663650 **f** (01803) 664037
e holcotts@aol.com **w** swcottages.co.uk

BUDE, Cornwall — SELF CATERING

★★★★ – ★★★★★
SELF CATERING
&

Forda Lodges and Cottages contact Mr & Mrs Chibbett, Forda Lodges and Cottages, Kilkhampton, Bude EX23 9RZ
t (01288) 321413 **f** (01288) 321413
e forda.lodges@virgin.net **w** forda.co.uk

CANNINGTON, Somerset — GUEST ACCOMMODATION

★★★
FARMHOUSE
&

Blackmore Farm Blackmore Lane, Cannington, Bridgwater TA5 2NE
t (01278) 653442 **f** (01278) 653427
e dyerfarm@aol.com **w** dyerfarm.co.uk

CASTLE CARY, Somerset — SELF CATERING

★★★★
SELF CATERING
&

Clanville Manor Tallet and Lone Oak Cottage contact Mrs Snook, Clanville Manor Tallet and Lone Oak Cottage, Clanville Manor, Clanville, Castle Cary BA7 7PJ **t** (01963) 350124 **f** (01963) 350719
e info@clanvillemanor.co.uk **w** clanvillemanor.co.uk

CHARMOUTH, Dorset — SELF CATERING

★★★
SELF CATERING
&

The Poplars contact Mrs Jane Bremner, Wood Farm Caravan Park, Axminster Road, Bridport DT6 6BT **t** (01297) 560697 **f** (01297) 561243
e holiday@woodfarm.co.uk **w** woodfarm.co.uk

CHEDZOY, Somerset — GUEST ACCOMMODATION

★★★★
FARMHOUSE
SILVER AWARD
&

Apple View Chedzoy Lane, Bridgwater TA7 8QR
t (01278) 423201 **f** (01278) 423201
e temple_farm@hotmail.com **w** apple-view.co.uk

CHELTENHAM, Gloucestershire — HOTEL

★★★
HOTEL
&

The Prestbury House Hotel The Burgage, Prestbury, Cheltenham GL52 3DN
t (01242) 529533 **f** (01242) 227076
e enquiries@prestburyhouse.co.uk **w** prestburyhouse.co.uk

COLEFORD, Gloucestershire — HOTEL

★★★
HOTEL
&

Best Western Speech House Hotel Forest of Dean, Coleford GL16 7EL
t (01594) 822607 **f** (01594) 823658
e relax@thespeechhouse.co.uk **w** thespeechhouse.co.uk

COLYFORD, Devon — SELF CATERING

★★★★★
SELF CATERING
&

Whitwell Farm Cottages contact Mr Mike Williams, Whitwell Farm Cottages, Whitwell Lane, Colyford, Colyton EX24 6HS **t** 0800 092 0419 **f** (01297) 552911
e 100755.66@compuserve.com **w** a5star.co.uk

COLYTON, Devon — GUEST ACCOMMODATION

★★★★
GUEST ACCOMMODATION
SILVER AWARD
&

Smallicombe Farm Northleigh, Colyton EX24 6BU
t (01404) 831310 **f** (01404) 831431
e maggie_todd@yahoo.com **w** smallicombe.com

At-a-glance symbols are explained on the flap inside the back cover.

COLYTON, Devon Map ref 1D2 — SELF CATERING

★★★★
SELF CATERING

Units **4**
Sleeps **2–6**

Low season per wk
Min £175.00
High season per wk
Max £695.00

Smallicombe Farm, Colyton

contact Mrs Todd, Smallicombe Farm, Northleigh, Colyton EX24 6BU
t (01404) 831310 **f** (01404) 831431
e maggie_todd@yahoo.com **w** smallicombe.com

General 🐾 🛏 🏠 P 🖵 S

Unit 🧎 🛁 🎞 S 🖾 📺 ⊡ 🚲 🔌 🗐 🐾

Payment Credit/debit cards,
cash/cheques

Short breaks from £125 a couple.

Relax in award-winning converted barns in an Area of Outstanding Natural Beauty. Superb rural views yet close to the World Heritage Coastline between Lyme Regis and Sidmouth. The accommodation is designed to suit the needs of wheelchair users and their carers. It is entirely ground floor and has wheel-in shower rooms.

open All year
nearest shop < 0.5 miles
nearest pub 2 miles

From Honiton High Street take New Street past station, up hill, left at mini-roundabout, then 1st right to top of hill. Left after 2 miles signed 'Slade'.

CORFE CASTLE, Dorset — HOTEL

★★★
HOTEL
GOLD AWARD

Mortons House Hotel East Street, Corfe Castle, Wareham BH20 5EE
t (01929) 480988 **f** (01929) 480820
e stay@mortonshouse.co.uk **w** mortonshouse.co.uk

CREDITON, Devon — SELF CATERING

★★★★
SELF CATERING

Creedy Manor contact Mrs Sandra Turner, Creedy Manor, Long Barn Farm,
Crediton EX17 4AB **t** (01363) 772684
e sandra@creedymanor.com **w** creedymanor.com

CREDITON, Devon — SELF CATERING

★★★★
SELF CATERING

White Witches and Stable Lodge contact Mrs Gillian Gillbard, Hele Barton,
Black Dog, Crediton EX17 4QJ **t** (01884) 860278 **f** (01884) 860278
e gillbard@eclipse.co.uk **w** eclipse.co.uk/helebarton

DEERHURST, Gloucestershire — SELF CATERING

★★★★
SELF CATERING

Deerhurst Cottages contact Mrs Nicole Samuel, Abbots Court Farm, Deerhurst,
Gloucester GL19 4BX **t** (01684) 275845 **f** (01684) 275845
e enquiries@deerhurstcottages.co.uk **w** deerhurstcottages.co.uk

---

DEVIZES, Wiltshire — GUEST ACCOMMODATION

★★★
BED & BREAKFAST

Longwater Lower Road, Erlestoke, Devizes SN10 5UE
t (01380) 830095 **f** (01380) 830095
e pam.hampton@talk21.com

DULVERTON, Somerset — CAMPING & CARAVANNING

★★★★
TOURING PARK

Exmoor House Caravan Club Site Dulverton TA22 9HL
t (01398) 323268
w caravanclub.co.uk

EXETER, Devon — SELF CATERING

★★★★★
SELF CATERING

Coach House Farm contact Mr & Miss John & Polly Bale, Coach House Farm,
Exeter EX5 3JH **t** (01392) 461254 **f** (01392) 460931
e selfcatering@mpprops.co.uk

EXFORD, Somerset — SELF CATERING

★★★–★★★★★
SELF CATERING

Westermill Farm contact Mr & Mrs Oliver & Jill Edwards, Westermill Farm, Exford,
Minehead TA24 7NJ **t** (01643) 831238 **f** (01643) 831216
e swt@westermill.com **w** westermill.com

FIFEHEAD MAGDALEN, Dorset Map ref 2B3 — SELF CATERING

★★★
SELF CATERING

Units **1**
Sleeps **1–5**

Low season per wk
Min £280.00
High season per wk
Max £500.00

Top Stall, Fifehead Magdalen, Gillingham
contact Mrs Kathleen Jeanes, Top Stall, Factory Farm, Fifehead Magdalen,
Gillingham SP8 5RS **t** (01258) 820022 **f** (01258) 820022
e kathy@topstallcottage.co.uk **w** topstallcottage.co.uk

A spacious, comfortable, well-equipped, converted cowstall on a dairy farm, with ramp entry, wet room, three ground-floor bedrooms. Ample parking in a level garden, with views of the Blackmore Vale. Enjoy the peaceful surroundings.
open All year
nearest shop 1 mile
nearest pub 1 mile

General
Unit
Payment Cash/cheques

GODNEY, Somerset — GUEST ACCOMMODATION

★★★★
FARMHOUSE
GOLD AWARD

Double-Gate Farm Godney, Wells BA5 1RX
t (01458) 832217 **f** (01458) 835612
e doublegatefarm@aol.com **w** doublegatefarm.com

GODNEY, Somerset — SELF CATERING

★★★★
SELF CATERING

Swallow Barn contact Mrs Hilary Millard, Double-Gate Farm Holidays,
Double Gate Farm, Godney, Wells BA5 1RX **t** (01458) 832217 **f** (01458) 835612
e doublegatefarm@aol.com **w** doublegatefarm.com

GOLANT, Cornwall — SELF CATERING

★★★★–★★★★★★
SELF CATERING

Penquite Farm Holidays contact Mr & Mrs Varco, Penquite Farm Holidays,
Penquite Farm, Golant PL23 1LB **t** (01726) 833319 **f** (04017) 2683 3319
e varco@farmersweekly.net **w** penquitefarm.co.uk

HAMWORTHY, Dorset

See entry on p203

At-a-glance symbols are explained on the flap inside the back cover.

HELSTON, Cornwall Map ref 1B3 · **SELF CATERING**

★★★★
SELF CATERING

Units **1**
Sleeps **3–9**

Low season per wk
Min £470.00
High season per wk
Max £1,707.00

Tregoose Farmhouse, Helston

contact Mrs Hazel Bergin, Southern Cross, Boundervean Lane, Penponds, Camborne TR14 7QP **t** (01209) 714314 & 07977 269936
e hazel.bergin@dsl.pipex.com **w** tregooselet.co.uk

General 🐎 🏛 🏕 P ✂

Leisure 🎣

Unit ♿ 🛏 🖥 ▣ 📺 ☕ 🗄 ⚏

Payment Cash/cheques

Ground floor offered at separate tariff off-peak and late availability. Mobility and rehabilitation products available for hire through local supplier.

A spacious and luxuriously renovated farmhouse in a peaceful rural setting. Indoor swimming pool. Games room. Sleeps three (plus one cot) or nine (plus two cots). Two ground-floor bedrooms and wet-room. Far-reaching views. Conveniently positioned for exploring south and west Cornwall's coastline, gardens and attractions. Three doubles, one twin and two singles.

open All year
nearest shop 1 mile
nearest pub 2 miles

From A394 (Helston to Penzance), turn right onto B3302. Take 2nd right signposted Gwavas/Lowertown. Left at crossroad. 30yds turn right. Top of hill on left.

LONG BREDY, Dorset · **SELF CATERING**

★★★★
SELF CATERING

Whatcombe Stables contact Ms Margarette Stuart-Brown, Long Bredy, Dorchester DT2 9HN
t (01305) 789000 **f** (01305) 761346
e admin@dream-cottages.co.uk

LOOE, Cornwall · **SELF CATERING**

★★★★
SELF CATERING

Bocaddon Holiday Cottages contact Mrs Alison Maiklem, Bocaddon Holiday Cottages, Bocaddon Farm, Lanreath PL13 2PG
t (01503) 220192
e holidays@bocaddon.com **w** bocaddon.com

LOOE, Cornwall · **SELF CATERING**

★★★★–★★★★★★
SELF CATERING

Bucklawren Farm contact Mrs Henly, Bucklawren Farm, St Martins, Looe PL13 1NZ
t (01503) 240738 **f** (01503) 240481
e bucklawren@btopenworld.com **w** bucklawren.com

LOOE, Cornwall Map ref 1C2   SELF CATERING

★★★★
SELF CATERING

Units   **6**
Sleeps   **2–6**

Low season per wk
Min £225.00
High season per wk
Max £755.00

Tudor Holiday Lodges, Looe

contact Mr & Mrs Mike & Molly Tudor, Tudor Holiday Lodges, Morval, Looe, Pl13 1pr PL14 6QN **t** (01579) 320344
e mollytudor@aol.com **w** tudorlodges.co.uk

Six new (2007) individual country holiday lodges. Three double/twin bedrooms. Sleep two to six. Discounts for two and four persons. Large, fitted kitchen, open-plan lounge with vaulted ceilings and balconies. Tarmac driveway to adjacent country restaurant and bar. Ideal touring base for Eden Project, National Trust and Cornish gardens.
open All year
nearest shop 2 miles
nearest pub < 0.5 miles

Access

General

Unit

Payment Cash/cheques

Weekend and midweek short breaks. Two bedrooms have balconies. Tarmac parking outside lodges. Level entry throughout. Pocket doors. Hoist available.

A38 from Plymouth to Liskeard 2 miles. Before Liskeard turn left onto B3252. After 3 miles turn right A387 to Morval. We are on right entering Morval.

LOSTWITHIEL, Cornwall Map ref 1B2 — SELF CATERING

★ ★ ★ ★ ★
SELF CATERING

Units	**1**
Sleeps	**8**

Low season per wk
Min £1,195.00
High season per wk
Max £1,995.00

Brean Park, Lostwithiel

contact Mrs Janet Hoskins, Brean Park Farm, Lostwithiel PL22 0LP
t (01208) 872184 **f** (01208) 872184
e breanpark@btconnect.com **w** breanpark.co.uk

General 🛏 🖥 👤 **P** ✂

Unit 🍳 🎚 💻 📺 🔌 📻 ♨ 🍽 ⬆
🔲 🧺 ✳

Payment Cash/cheques

Single-storey property, two en suite wetrooms.

The perfect choice for those seeking quality and luxury in a rural idyll. Our luxurious mobility-assisted property is situated in a picturesque valley with breathtaking views of the Lanhydrock estate and parkland within easy reach of Eden. Spaciously accommodates eight plus cot. Four en suite bedrooms.
open All year
nearest shop 4 miles
nearest pub 4 miles

From A30 Bodmin exit, 3rd left, T-junction turn left, roundabout 1st exit, next roundabout 3rd exit towards Lostwithiel, 1st left towards Respryn. After bridge 0.75 miles on left.

LOSTWITHIEL, Cornwall — SELF CATERING

★ ★ ★ ★
SELF CATERING

Chark Country Holidays contact Mrs Littleton, Chark Country Holidays, Redmoor, Bodmin PL30 5AR **t** (01208) 871118
e charkholidays@tiscali.co.uk **w** charkcountryholidays.co.uk

Gold and Silver Awards

VisitBritain's unique Gold and Silver Awards recognise exceptional quality in serviced accommodation.

Enjoy England assessors make recommendations for Gold and Silver Awards during assessments in recognition of levels of quality over and above that expected of a particular rating.

Look for the Gold and Silver Awards in the regional sections.

LOSTWITHIEL, Cornwall Map ref 1B2 **SELF CATERING**

★★★–★★★★★
SELF CATERING

Units **2**
Sleeps **1–6**
Low season per wk
£300.00 £450.00
High season per wk
£500.00–£680.00

Hartswheal Barn, Lostwithiel

contact Mrs Wendy Jordan, Saint Winnow, Downend, Lostwithiel PL22 0RB **t** (01208) 873419 **f** (01208) 873419
e hartswheal@connexions.co.uk
w connexions.co.uk/hartswheal/index.htm

Access abc

General 6 P

Unit

Payment Cash/cheques

3-day breaks available in Mar and Apr. Lowered kitchen units in 'Stables'.

The Barn and Stables are part of an old converted granary, within a working farm, with breathtaking views just five miles from the Eden Project. The Stables has a double bedroom, with en suite shower, twin with electric bed, and ceiling hoist tracking to en suite bathroom/wc. The Barn has a double, twin and bunks.

open All year
nearest shop 1 mile
nearest pub 1 mile

Take A38 to Plymouth and Cornwall. Just past Liskeard at Dobwalls, left onto A390 for St Austell. Entrance is off A390, one mile before Lostwithiel.

MALMESBURY, Wiltshire **SELF CATERING**

★★★★
SELF CATERING

The Cottage contact Mrs Ross Eavis, Manor Farm, Corston, Malmesbury SN16 0HF
t (01666) 822148 **f** (01666) 826565
e ross@johneavis.wanadoo.co.uk **w** manorfarmbandb.co.uk

Awaiting a rating

If you are considering accommodation that is awaiting a National Accessible Scheme rating, please confirm with the proprietor what facilities you can expect before booking.

 At-a-glance symbols are explained on the flap inside the back cover.

MINEHEAD, Somerset Map ref 1D1 — GUEST ACCOMMODATION

★★★
GUEST ACCOMMODATION

HB per person per night
£36.61–£56.43

Awaiting NAS rating

The Promenade

The Esplanade, Minehead TA24 5QS **t** (01643) 702572
f (01643) 702572
e promenadehotel@johngrooms.org.uk **w** groomsholidays.org.uk

Access ☺ abc ⚠

General 🛏 P♿ ♿✂ ♉ ✗ 📺▣ ✳

Rooms 🛏 🍴 ♨ 📺

Payment Credit/debit cards, cash/cheques, euros

Turkey and Tinsel breaks (Nov).
Spring Harvest breaks (Feb, Mar).

Property owned by Grooms Holidays specially adapted for disabled guests. Eleven bedrooms with eight fully accessible. Some equipment available, including fixed and manual hoists. Guests needing personal help should be accompanied or make arrangements through local agency. Tail-lift bus for outings.
open All year
bedrooms 9 twin, 1 single, 1 family
bathrooms All en suite

A358 from Taunton. Collections from Taunton railway station can be arranged.

MODBURY, Devon Map ref 1C3 **CAMPING & CARAVANNING**

★★★★
TOURING PARK

🚐(112)
£12.10–£24.90
🚚(112)
£12.10–£24.90
112 touring pitches

THE
CARAVAN
CLUB

Broad Park Caravan Club Site

Higher East Leigh, Modbury, Ivybridge PL21 0SH **t** (01548) 830714
w caravanclub.co.uk

Situated between moor and sea, not far from the ancient village of Modbury – a splendid base from which to explore South Devon. Make for Dartmoor and the silence and solitude, the tumbling streams and the long views, or go south and seek out the small villages of the South Hams. Open March to November.

From B3207, site on left.

General P 🚐 🄰 🆆🄿 🄵 📱📷

Payment Credit/debit cards, cash/cheques

Midweek discount; pitch fees reduced by 50% for stays on Tue, Wed or Thu night outside peak season.

MORETON-IN-MARSH, Gloucestershire Map ref 2B1 **CAMPING & CARAVANNING**

★★★★★
TOURING &
CAMPING PARK

🚐(182)
£14.30–£27.70
🚚(182)
f14.30–£27.70
182 touring pitches

THE
CARAVAN
CLUB

Moreton-in-Marsh Caravan Club Site

Bourton Road, Moreton-in-Marsh GL56 0BT **t** (01608) 650519
w caravanclub.co.uk

A well-wooded site with a pleasant openness nonetheless, and within easy walking distance of an interesting, lively market town. Moreton-in-Marsh nestles in the heart of beautiful Cotswold countryside. This attractive town with many interesting shops, is perhaps today most famous for the Tuesday street market.

open All year

From Moreton-in-Marsh on A44 the site entrance is on the right 250yds past the end of the speed limit sign.

General 🔌 P 🚐 🄰 🍴 🆆🄿 🄵 ☺ 📱
📷 ☼

Leisure ⚠

Payment Credit/debit cards, cash/cheques

At-a-glance symbols are explained on the flap inside the back cover.

MORETONHAMPSTEAD, Devon — SELF CATERING

★★–★★★
SELF CATERING

Budleigh Farm contact Mrs Judith Harvey, Budleigh Farm,
Moretonhampstead TQ13 8SB **t** (01647) 440835 **f** (01647) 440436
e harvey@budleighfarm.co.uk **w** budleighfarm.co.uk

MOUNT HAWKE, Cornwall — SELF CATERING

★★★★
SELF CATERING

Ropers Walk Barns contact Mr & Mrs Pollard, Ropers Walk Barns,
Rope Walk Farm, Mount Hawke, Truro TR4 8DW **t** (01209) 891632
e peterandliz@roperswalkbarns.co.uk **w** roperswalkbarns.co.uk

NEWQUAY, Cornwall

See entry on p203

NORTH PETHERWIN, Cornwall — SELF CATERING

★★★★
SELF CATERING

Waterloo Farm contact Lucy Ellison, Farm & Cottage Holidays, Victoria House,
12 Fore Street, Bideford EX39 1AW **t** (01237) 479146 **f** (01237) 421512
e enquiries@farmcott.co.uk **w** farmcott.co.uk

OGWELL, Devon — SELF CATERING

★★★★
SELF CATERING

Rydon Ball contact Mr Ian Butterworth, Holiday Homes & Cottages South West,
365a Torquay Road, Paignton TQ3 2BT **t** (01803) 663650 **f** (01803) 664037
e holcotts@aol.com **w** swcottages.co.uk

OKEHAMPTON, Devon — SELF CATERING

★★★★
SELF CATERING

Beer Farm contact Bob & Sue Annear, Beer Farm, Okehampton EX20 1SG
t (01837) 840265 **f** (01837) 840245
e info@beerfarm.co.uk **w** beerfarm.co.uk

PADSTOW, Cornwall — GUEST ACCOMMODATION

★★★★★
GUEST ACCOMMODATION
SILVER AWARD

Woodlands Country House Treator, Padstow PL28 8RU
t (01841) 532426 **f** (01841) 533353
e info@woodlands-padstow.co.uk **w** woodlands-padstow.co.uk

PADSTOW, Cornwall — SELF CATERING

★★★–★★★★★
SELF CATERING

Yellow Sands Cottages contact Mrs Sharon Keast, Yellow Sands Cottages,
Harlyn Bay, Padstow PL28 8SE **t** (01637) 881548
e yellowsands@btinternet.com **w** yellowsands.co.uk

PENZANCE, Cornwall — HOTEL

★★★
HOTEL
SILVER AWARD

Hotel Penzance Britons Hill, Penzance TR18 3AE
t (01736) 363117 **f** (01736) 350970
e enquiries@hotelpenzance.com **w** hotelpenzance.com

PLYMOUTH, Devon — HOTEL

★★★
HOTEL

Kitley House Hotel and Restaurant Kitley Estate, Yealmpton, Plymouth PL8 2NW
t (01752) 881555 **f** (01752) 881667
e sales@kitleyhousehotel.com **w** kitleyhousehotel.com

PLYMOUTH, Devon — SELF CATERING

★★★★
SELF CATERING

Haddington House Apartments contact Mr Fairfax Luxmoore,
42 Haddington Road, Plymouth PL2 1RR **t** (01752) 500383
w abudd.co.uk

PLYMOUTH, Devon — SELF CATERING

★★★–★★★★★
SELF CATERING

Traine Farm contact Mrs Sheila Rowland, Traine Farm, Train Road, Wembury,
Plymouth PL9 0EW **t** (01752) 862264 **f** (01752) 862264
e traine.cottages@btopenworld.com **w** traine-holiday-cottages.co.uk

PLYMOUTH, Devon — CAMPING & CARAVANNING

★★★★
TOURING PARK

Plymouth Sound Bovisand Lane, Down Thomas, Plymouth PL9 0AE
t (01752) 862325
w caravanclub.co.uk

POLZEATH, Cornwall — SELF CATERING

★★★★
SELF CATERING

Manna Place contact Mrs Ann Jones, Manna Place, 14 Trenant Close,
Wadebridge PL27 6SW **t** (01208) 863258
e anniepolzeath@hotmail.com **w** mannaplace.co.uk

POOLE, Somerset — CAMPING & CARAVANNING

★★★★
TOURING PARK

Cadeside Caravan Club Site Nynehead Road, Wellington TA21 9HN
t (01823) 663103
e enquiries@caravanclub.co.uk **w** caravanclub.co.uk

PORTREATH, Cornwall Map ref 1B3 — SELF CATERING

★★★★★
SELF CATERING

Units **3**
Sleeps **1–5**

Low season per wk
£220.00–£300.00
High season per wk
£300.00–£750.00

Higher Laity Farm, Redruth

contact Mrs Lynne Drew, Higher Laity Farm, Portreath Road,
Redruth TR16 4HY **t** (01209) 842317 **f** (01209) 842317
e info@higherlaityfarm.co.uk **w** higherlaityfarm.co.uk

General 🛏 🏛 🕭 P ✂ Ⓢ

Unit 🔌 🎚 📺 📱 🍳 📻 ♨ 🗄 🖨
🍽 📶 ❀

Payment Credit/debit cards,
cash/cheques

*Special weekend and mid-week
breaks available.*

Tastefully converted luxury barns
set amidst the Cornish
countryside. One cottage,
offering master bedroom with en
suite and second twin-bedded
room, has a fully adapted
accessible bathroom with level-
access shower. The exceptional
accommodation and its proximity
to the A30 makes this an ideal
base from which to explore.
Service dogs welcome.

open All year
nearest shop 1 mile
nearest pub 0.5 miles

*From M5 take A30 to Redruth/
Porthtowan slip road towards
Redruth. For full travel directions
please contact us directly.*

PORTREATH, Cornwall — SELF CATERING

★★★–★★★★★
SELF CATERING

Trengove Farm Cottages contact Mrs Richards, Trengove Farm Cottages,
Trengove Farm, Cot Road, Illogan, Redruth TR16 4PU
t (01209) 843008 **f** (01209) 843682
e richards@farming.co.uk

At-a-glance symbols are explained on the flap inside the back cover.

PORTSCATHO, Cornwall — SELF CATERING

★★★★–★★★★★★ **SELF CATERING**

Pollaughan Farm contact Mrs Valerie Penny, Pollaughan Farm, Portscatho, Truro TR2 5EH **t** (01872) 580150 **f** (01872) 580150 **e** pollaughan@yahoo.co.uk **w** pollaughan.co.uk

RUAN HIGH LANES, Cornwall — GUEST ACCOMMODATION

★★★ **FARMHOUSE**

Trenona Farm Holidays Ruan High Lanes, Truro TR2 5JS **t** (01872) 501339 **f** (01872) 501253 **e** info@trenonafarmholidays.co.uk **w** trenonafarmholidays.co.uk

ST AUSTELL, Cornwall Map ref 1B3 — SELF CATERING

★★★★ **SELF CATERING**

Units **1**
Sleeps **2–5**
Low season per wk
£300.00–£450.00
High season per wk
£650.00–£800.00

Owls Reach, Roche, St Austell

contact Diana Pride, Owls Reach, Colbiggan Farm, Roche PL26 8LJ
t (01208) 831597 **e** info@owlsreach.co.uk **w** owlsreach.co.uk

Spacious detached luxury cottage, designed for accessibility needs on single level. Three bedrooms, wheel-in shower room and second bathroom. Parking very close to doors. Peaceful country location.
open All year
nearest shop 2 miles
nearest pub 2 miles

General 🐶 🎬 🛏 P ✄
Leisure 🎣 ✎
Unit 🛁 🍳 ⬛ 💻 📺 🎧 📻 🧹 🧺 📠 📱 📷 ❄

Payment Cash/cheques, euros

ST ENDELLION, Cornwall — SELF CATERING

★★★★ **SELF CATERING**

Tolraggott Farm Cottages contact Mrs Harris, Barton Cottage, Tolraggott Farm, St Endellion, Port Isaac PL29 3TP **t** (01208) 880927 **f** (01208) 880927

Bank holiday
dates for your diary

holiday	2008	2009
New Year's Day (England & Wales)	1 January	1 January
New Year's Day (Scotland)	1 January	1 January
January Bank Holiday (Scotland)	2 January	2 January
Good Friday	21 March	10 April
Easter Monday (England & Wales)	24 March	13 April
Early May Bank Holiday	5 May	4 May
Spring Bank Holiday	26 May	25 May
Summer Bank Holiday (Scotland)	4 August	3 August
Summer Bank Holiday (England & Wales)	25 August	31 August
Christmas Day	25 December	25 December
Boxing Day Holiday	26 December	28 December

ST JUST-IN-PENWITH, Cornwall Map ref 1A3 — SELF CATERING

★ ★ ★ ★
SELF CATERING

Units **1**
Sleeps **2–4**

Low season per wk
£200.00–£350.00
High season per wk
£450.00–£595.00

Swallow's End, Nr St Just-in-Penwith

contact Mr & Mrs Beer, Swallow's End, Kelynack Moor Farmhouse,
Bosworlas, St Just TR19 7RQ t (01736) 787011 f (01736) 787011
e db.properties@virgin.net w westcornwalllets.co.uk

Modern annexe to traditional farmhouse in peaceful valley with lovely countryside views. Close to Sennen and Land's End. Lovely garden with private patio and barbecue. One double room and one twin room. All one level. Specialist equipment available. Low-level kitchen.

open All year
nearest shop 1 mile
nearest pub 1 mile

Turn off the A30 Land's End road onto the A3071 towards St Just, then B3306 towards Sennen. Turn left before Kelynach village. Third house on the right.

Access abc 🅰

General 🛏 📷 ♿ P ✂ ▣

Unit ♿ 🛋 🖿 🔲 📺 📀 📻 📻

Payment Credit/debit cards,
cash/cheques

Special reductions for short breaks for two people out of season. Special Christmas break offers.

SALISBURY, Wiltshire — SELF CATERING

★ ★ ★ ★
SELF CATERING

The Old Stables contact Mr Giles Gould, The Old Stables, Bridge Farm,
Lower Road, Salisbury SP5 4DY t (01722) 349002 f (01722) 349003
e mail@old-stables.co.uk w old-stables.co.uk

SANDFORD, Devon — GUEST ACCOMMODATION

★ ★ ★ ★
BED & BREAKFAST

Ashridge Ashridge Farm, Crediton EX17 4EN
t (01363) 774292
e info@ashdridgefarm.co.uk w ashdridgefarm.co.uk

Awaiting a rating

If you are considering accommodation that is awaiting a National Accessible Scheme rating, please confirm with the proprietor what facilities you can expect before booking.

SHAFTESBURY, Dorset Map ref 2B3

★★–★★★★★
SELF CATERING

Units **4**
Sleeps **4–5**

Low season per wk
£380.00–£405.00
High season per wk
£740.00–£795.00

Hartgrove Farm, Shaftesbury

contact Mrs Susan Smart, Hartgrove Farm, Hartgrove,
Shaftesbury SP7 0JY **t** (01747) 811830 **f** (01747) 811066
e cottages@hartgrovefarm.co.uk **w** hartgrovefarm.co.uk

Access

General

Leisure

Unit

Payment Credit/debit cards,
cash/cheques

A working organic farm in glorious countryside. Our disabled guests have returned year after year. A special place and a holiday that works. 'Holiday Care' Award. Cottages have log fires, full central heating, wheel-in shower, mobile hoist and various aids. Tennis court. Accessible swimming. Lots of good local pubs.

open All year
nearest shop 1.5 miles
nearest pub 1.5 miles

Take A350 south from Shaftesbury to Fontmell Magna, 4 miles, turn right at pub. Farm is 1.75 miles on left, immediately past Hartgrove village sign.

Country ways

The Countryside Rights of Way Act gives people new rights to walk on areas of open countryside and registered common land.

To find out where you can go and what you can do, as well as information about taking your dog to the countryside, go online at countrysideaccess.gov.uk.

And when you're out and about...

Always follow the Country Code

● Be safe – plan ahead and follow any signs
● Leave gates and property as you find them
● Protect plants and animals, and take your litter home
● Keep dogs under close control
● Consider other people

SIDBURY, Devon Map ref 1D2 —

★★★★★
TOURING PARK

(113)
£12.10–£24.90
(113)
£12.10–£24.90
113 touring pitches

Putts Corner Caravan Club Site

Sidbury, Sidmouth EX10 0QQ **t** (01404) 42875
w caravanclub.co.uk

A quiet site in pretty surroundings high up but sheltered from the wind. Spring brings a fantastic display of bluebells followed by foxgloves, and you'll see a wide variety of birds and even the occasional deer. There is a choice of walks from the site and Sidmouth is a restful resort with a long pebble beach. Open March to November.

From M5 jct 25, A375 signposted Sidmouth. Turn right at Hare and Hounds onto B3174. In about 0.25 miles turn right into site entrance.

General

Leisure

Payment Credit/debit cards, cash/cheques

THE
CARAVAN
CLUB

SOUTH MOLTON, Devon —

★★★★★
SELF CATERING

Stable Cottage contact Mrs Victoria Huxtable, Stable Cottage, Stable Cottages, Stitchpool Farm, South Molton EX36 3EL **t** (01598) 740130

STATHE, Somerset —

★★★★
SELF CATERING

Walkers Farm Cottages contact Mrs Dianne Tilley, Walkers Farm Cottages, Walkers Farm, Stathe, Bridgwater TA7 0JL **t** (01823) 698229
e info@walkersfarmcottages.co.uk **w** walkersfarmcottages.co.uk

---

STOKE ST GREGORY, Somerset —

★★★★
SELF CATERING

Holly Farm contact Mr & Mrs Robert & Liz Hembrow, Meare Green, Stoke St Gregory, Taunton TA3 6HS **t** (01823) 490828
e robhembrow@btinternet.com **w** holly-farm.com

SWANAGE, Dorset —

★★★
SELF CATERING

9 Quayside Court contact Ms Anne Bennett, 14 Lilliput Avenue, Chipping Sodbury BS37 6HX **t** (01454) 311178
e info@bythequayholidays.co.uk **w** bythequayholidays.co.uk

SWANAGE, Dorset —

★★★★★
TOURING PARK

Haycraft Caravan Club Site Haycrafts Lane, Swanage BH19 3EB
t (01929) 480572
w caravanclub.co.uk

TAUNTON, Somerset —

★★★★
SELF CATERING

Linnets contact Mrs Patricia Grabham, Linnets, Taunton TA4 3JX
t (01823) 400658 **f** (01823) 400658
e patricia.grabham@onetel.net

At-a-glance symbols are explained on the flap inside the back cover.

TEWKESBURY, Gloucestershire — CAMPING & CARAVANNING

★★★★
**TOURING &
CAMPING PARK**

Tewkesbury Abbey Caravan Club Site Gander Lane, Tewkesbury GL20 5PG
t (01684) 294035
e natalie.tiller@caravanclub.co.uk **w** caravanclub.co.uk

TINCLETON, Dorset — SELF CATERING

★★★★★
SELF CATERING

Tincleton Lodge and Clyffe Dairy Cottage contact Mrs Jane Coleman,
The Old Dairy Cottage and Clyffe Dairy Cottage, Eweleaze Farm, Tincleton,
Dorchester DT2 8QR **t** (01305) 848391 **f** (01305) 848702
e enquiries@dorsetholidaycottages.net **w** dorsetholidaycottages.net

TINTAGEL, Cornwall — CAMPING & CARAVANNING

★★★★★
**TOURING &
CAMPING PARK**

Trewethett Farm Caravan Club Site Trethevy, Tintagel PL34 0BQ
t (01840) 770222 **f** (01840) 779066
e uksitesbookingservice@caravanclub.co.uk **w** caravanclub.co.uk

TORQUAY, Devon — HOTEL

★★
HOTEL

Frognel Hall Hotel Higher Woodfield Road, Torquay TQ1 2LD
t (01803) 298339 **f** (01803) 215115
e mail@frognel.co.uk **w** frognel.co.uk

TORQUAY, Devon Map ref 1D2 — SELF CATERING

★★★
SELF CATERING

Units   **3**
Sleeps   **2–4**

Low season per wk
£200.00–£420.00
High season per wk
£370.00–£620.00

Atlantis Holiday Apartments, Torquay

contact Mrs Pauline Roberts, Atlantis Holiday Apartments, Solsbro Road,
Chelston, Torquay TQ2 6PF **t** (01803) 607929
e enquiry@atlantistorquay.co.uk **w** atlantistorquay.co.uk

Near seafront. Non smoking. Car park. Wheelchair access. Wetfloor shower room. Heated outdoor pool. Central heating. Dishwasher and washer/dryer in apartments. Tranquillity holistic therapies for massage and reflexology. Green Tourism Business Scheme Silver Award. BSL used.
open All year
nearest shop < 0.5 miles
nearest pub < 0.5 miles

Access	abc
General	🛖 ⊞ ⚲ P ✄ Ⓢ
Leisure	⇗
Unit	icons
Payment	Credit/debit cards, cash/cheques

TORQUAY, Devon — SELF CATERING

★★★
SELF CATERING

South Sands Apartments contact Mr & Mrs Paul & Deborah Moorhouse,
South Sands Apartments, Torbay Road, Livermead, Torquay TQ2 6RG
t (01803) 293521 **f** (01803) 293502
e info@southsands.co.uk **w** southsands.co.uk

TORQUAY, Devon

See also entry on p203

TRURO, Cornwall — GUEST ACCOMMODATION

★★★★
GUEST ACCOMMODATION

Tregoninny Farm Tresillian, Truro TR2 4AR **t** (01872) 520145
w tregoninny.com

UGBOROUGH, Devon — SELF CATERING

★★★★
SELF CATERING

Venn Farm contact Mrs Stephens, Venn Farm, Ugborough, Ivybridge PL21 0PE
t (01364) 73240 **f** (01364) 73240

VERYAN, Cornwall Map ref 1B3 — SELF CATERING

★★★★
SELF CATERING

Units	**1**
Sleeps	**6**

Low season per wk
£240.00–£350.00
High season per wk
£350.00–£760.00

Trenona Farm Holidays, Veryan, Truro

contact Mrs Pamela Carbis, Trenona Farm, Ruan High Lanes,
Truro TR2 5JS **t** (01872) 501339 **f** (01872) 501253
e pam@trenonafarmholidays.co.uk **w** trenonafarmholidays.co.uk

Chy Whel is a single-storey cottage with three en suite bedrooms (a double and two twin-bedded rooms). The open-plan lounge/kitchen/diner has all modern comforts and conveniences. The property also has a private garden with patio and lawn area.

open All year
nearest shop 1 mile
nearest pub 2 miles

A30 past Bodmin, A391 to St Austell, A390 towards Truro. Just beyond Probus take A3078 to St Mawes. After 8 miles pass Esso garage, Trenona Farm 2nd on left.

Access ⚑

General ⌂ ▥ ♿ P ✂

Unit ⛄ 🔥 ▥ ▢ ▣ ▣ ⚲ ▢ ⚒ ▨ ▣ ▢ ▢ ❄

Payment Credit/debit cards, cash/cheques

*Short breaks Oct-Mar.
2 bedrooms accessible for wheelchair users.*

Country ways

The Countryside Rights of Way Act gives people new rights to walk on areas of open countryside and registered common land.

To find out where you can go and what you can do, as well as information about taking your dog to the countryside, go online at countrysideaccess.gov.uk.

Always follow the Country Code
- Be safe – plan ahead and follow any signs
- Leave gates and property as you find them
- Protect plants and animals, and take your litter home
- Keep dogs under close control
- Consider other people

At-a-glance symbols are explained on the flap inside the back cover.

WARMINSTER, Wiltshire Map ref 2B2   **CAMPING & CARAVANNING**

★★★★★
TOURING PARK

Longleat Caravan Club Site

Longleat, Warminster BA12 7NL **t** (01985) 844663

(165)
£14.30–£27.70

(165)
£14.30–£27.70

165 touring pitches

The only Club site where you can hear lions roar at night. Longleat is one of the Club's most beautiful parkland sites, in the middle of the lovely Longleat estate, with miles of paths to walk amid the pleasures of woodland, bluebell, azalea and rhododendron. Open March to November.

General   ⚑ P 🅿 🚰 🛖 WP 🐾 ☺ 🏪   📷 ☼

Leisure   /⚠\

Payment   Credit/debit cards, cash/cheques

Take A362, signed Frome, 0.5 miles at roundabout turn left (2nd exit) onto Longleat estate. Through toll booths, follow caravan and camping pennant signs for 1 mile.

THE
CARAVAN
CLUB

WELLINGTON, Somerset   **SELF CATERING**

★★★★
SELF CATERING

Lime Kiln Cottages contact Mrs Sue Gallagher, Hopper Cottage c/o Whipcott Heights, Holcombe Rogus, Wellington TA21 0NA **t** (01823) 672339 **f** (01823) 672339 **e** bookings@oldlimekiln.freeserve.co.uk

---

WELLS, Somerset   **SELF CATERING**

★★★★
SELF CATERING

St Marys Lodge contact Mrs Jane Hughes, St Mary Mead, Long Street, Croscombe, Wells BA5 3QL **t** (01749) 342157 **e** janehughes@trtopbox.net **w** st-marys-lodge.co.uk

---

WEST BEXINGTON, Dorset Map ref 2A3   **SELF CATERING**

★★★★
SELF CATERING

Tamarisk Farm Cottages, West Bexington

contact Mrs Josephine Pearse, Tamarisk Farm Cottages, Beach Road, West Bexington, Dorchester DT2 9DF **t** (01308) 897784 **e** holidays@tamariskfarm.com **w** tamariskfarm.com/holidays

Units   **2**
Sleeps   **4–7**

Low season per wk
Min £365.00
High season per wk
Max £960.00

Beautiful views of Lyme Bay – Portland to Start Point, Devon. Quiet, extensive patios. Roll-in showers, low-level stove and sink. Extra aids available.
open All year
nearest shop 3 miles
nearest pub < 0.5 miles

Access   🐾

General   📺 🛏 ♿ P Ⓢ

Leisure   🎣

Unit   🛁 📶 🖥 🖵 📺 📞 ⛰ 🛋 🍴 🍳 🍲 ✿

Payment   Credit/debit cards, cash/cheques

WEST DOWN, Devon — CAMPING & CARAVANNING

★★★★
TOURING PARK

Brook Lea Caravan Club Site, Ilfracombe EX34 8NE
t (01271) 862848
e debby.towers@caravanclub.co.uk
w caravanclub.co.uk

WEST QUANTOXHEAD, Somerset — GUEST ACCOMMODATION

★★★★★
GUEST ACCOMMODATION

Stilegate Bed and Breakfast West Quantoxhead, Taunton TA4 4DN
t (01984) 639119 f (01984) 639119
e stilegate@aol.com w stilegate.co.uk

WESTON-SUPER-MARE, Somerset Map ref 1D1 — HOTEL

★★★
HOTEL

B&B per room per night
s £62.00–£66.00
d £83.00–£99.00

Royal Hotel

South Parade, Weston-super-Mare BS23 1JP t (01934) 423100
f (01934) 415135 e reservations@royalhotelweston.com
w royalhotelweston.com

Situated in the heart of Weston, the Royal Hotel is set in its own extensive lawns which extend to the promenade, offering views across the bay.
open All year
bedrooms 20 double, 3 twin, 6 single, 5 family, 3 suites
bathrooms All en suite

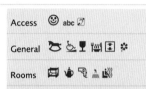

WESTON-SUPER-MARE, Somerset — GUEST ACCOMMODATION

★★★
GUEST HOUSE

Milton Lodge Hotel 15 Milton Road, Weston-super-Mare BS23 2SH
t (01934) 623161 f (01934) 623210
e miltonlodgehotel@btconnect.com

WESTON-SUPER-MARE, Somerset — GUEST ACCOMMODATION

★★★
GUEST HOUSE

Saxonia Guest House 95 Locking Road, Weston-super-Mare BS23 3EW
t (01934) 424850 f (01934) 623141
e saxoniahotel@btinternet.com w saxoniaguesthouse.co.uk

WESTON-SUPER-MARE, Somerset — GUEST ACCOMMODATION

★★★
GUEST HOUSE

Spreyton Guest House 72 Locking Road, Weston-super-Mare BS23 3EN
t (01934) 416887 f (01934) 416887
e Info@spreytonguesthouse.fsnet.co.uk w spreytonguesthouse.com

WESTON-SUPER-MARE, Somerset

See also entry on p204

Check it out

Information on accommodation listed in this guide has been supplied by proprietors. As changes may occur you should remember to check all relevant details at the time of booking.

At-a-glance symbols are explained on the flap inside the back cover.

WEYMOUTH, Dorset Map ref 2B3  **CAMPING & CARAVANNING**

★★★★
TOURING PARK

🚐 (120)
£11.20–£22.40
🚍 (120)
£11.20–£22.40
120 touring pitches

Crossways Caravan Club Site

Dorchester DT2 8BE **t** (01305) 852032
w caravanclub.co.uk

General 🔌 P 🍴 🚿 🚽 WP 🐾 ☺ 🎒
🔘 ☀

Leisure ⚠

Payment Credit/debit cards,
cash/cheques

*Midweek discount; pitch fees
reduced by 50% for stays on Tue,
Wed or Thu night outside peak
season.*

A most imaginatively landscaped
site in 35 acres of woodland, with
pitching in open groves linked by
a snaking road which leads you
round the site from Iron Horse
Meadows to Poacher's Paradise.
If you want to leave the car
behind for the day, the railway
station is just 5 minutes' walk
from the site. Open March to
October.

*North from A35 or south from
A352, join B3390. Site on right
within 1 mile. Entrance to site by
forecourt of filling station. For
details on other routes visit
caravanclub.co.uk.*

THE
**CARAVAN
CLUB**

WEYMOUTH, Dorset

See also entry on p204

Discover Britain's heritage

Our travel map and guide is perfectly tailored
to your needs. Discover the history and
beauty of over 250 of Britain's best-known
historic houses, castles, gardens and smaller
manor houses. You can purchase Britain's
Historic Houses and Gardens – Guide and
Map from good bookshops and online at
visitbritaindirect.com

★★★★
GUEST ACCOMMODATION

B&B per room per night
s £37.50–£42.50
d £60.00–£70.00

Overcombe House

Old Station Road, Yelverton PL20 7RA   **t** (01822) 853501
f (01822) 853602
e enquiries@overcombehotel.co.uk   **w** overcombehotel.co.uk

Access   🖐 abc

General   🐾5 ✂ 🍷 ❀

Rooms   🖉 📺 🍵 🛋 💷

Payment Credit/debit cards,
cash/cheques

Offering a warm, friendly welcome in relaxed comfortable surroundings with a substantial breakfast using local and home-made produce. Situated between Tavistock and Plymouth with beautiful views over the village and Dartmoor. Conveniently located for exploring both Devon and Cornwall, in particular Dartmoor National Park and the adjacent Tamar Valley.

open All year
bedrooms 3 double, 2 twin, 1 single, 2 family
bathrooms All en suite

Situated between Plymouth and Tavistock. Located on the edge of the village of Horrabridge and just over a mile north-west of Yelverton heading towards Tavistock.

Gold and Silver Awards

VisitBritain's unique Gold and Silver Awards recognise exceptional quality in serviced accommodation.

Enjoy England assessors make recommendations for Gold and Silver Awards during assessments in recognition of levels of quality over and above that expected of a particular rating.

Look for the Gold and Silver Awards in the regional sections.

NATIONAL ACCESSIBLE SCHEME RATINGS ONLY

The following establishments hold a National Accessible Scheme rating as shown in their entry, but do not participate in VisitBritain's Enjoy England quality assessment scheme. However, to participate in the National Accessible Scheme accommodation must meet a minimum level of quality. In addition to being assessed under the National Accessible Scheme the entries listed below may hold a quality rating from another organisation.

HAMWORTHY, Dorset Map ref 2B3 — SELF CATERING

Grooms Chalet, Hamworthy

contact Gail Lewis, PO Box 36, Cowbridge CF71 7GB **t** 08456 584478
f (01446) 775060 **e** selfcatering@johngrooms.org.uk **w** groomsholidays.org.uk

Units	**1**
Sleeps	**2–6**

Low season per wk
Min £340.00
High season per wk
Max £430.00

Awaiting
NAS rating

Chalet adapted for disabled holidaymakers. Sleeps up to six in two bedrooms, plus sofa bed in lounge. Roll-in shower and shower-chair, and mobile hoist. Open April to October.

nearest shop 1 mile
nearest pub 1 mile

Access	abc ⚡ ♿
General	🐎 P ⚡ Ⓢ
Leisure	⚡
Unit	♿ 🛏 ▣ 🔥 🕯 ✉ 📶
Payment	Credit/debit cards, cash/cheques, euros

NEWQUAY, Cornwall — GUEST ACCOMMODATION

Dewolf Guest House 100 Henver Road, Newquay TR7 3BL
t (01637) 874746
e holidays@dewolfguesthouse.co.uk **w** dewolfguesthouse.co.uk

---

TORQUAY, Devon Map ref 1D2 — SELF CATERING

Park House, St Mary Church, Babbacombe

contact Gail Lewis, PO Box 36, Cowbridge CF71 7GB **t** 08456 584478
f (01446) 775060 **e** selfcatering@johngrooms.org.uk **w** groomsholidays.org.uk

Units	**1**
Sleeps	**2–4**

Low season per wk
Min £145.00
High season per wk
Max £375.00

Awaiting
NAS rating

Ground-floor flat. Double bedroom and two sofa beds in lounge. Fully adapted for wheelchair users. Roll-in shower. Electric hoist and shower-chair available.

open All year
nearest shop 1 mile
nearest pub 1 mile

Access	abc ♿
General	🐎 ⚡
Unit	♿ 🛏 🖼 ▣ 🔲 🔥 🕯 ✉
Payment	Credit/debit cards, cash/cheques, euros

To your credit

If you book by phone you may be asked for your credit card number. If so, it is advisable to check the proprietor's policy in case you have to cancel your reservation at a later date.

Official tourist board guide **Easy Access Britain**

WESTON-SUPER-MARE, Somerset Map ref 1D1 — SELF CATERING

Casa Ryall, Worle

contact Gail Lewis, PO Box 36, Cowbridge CF71 7GB **t** 08456 584478
f (01446) 775060 **e** selfcatering@johngrooms.org.uk **w** groomsholidays.org.uk

Units **1**
Sleeps **1–8**

Low season per wk
Min £235.00
High season per wk
Max £435.00

Awaiting
NAS rating

Newly-adapted property, with four bedrooms, large lounge, dining area and decked area. Fully fitted kitchen. Three miles from Weston-super-Mare seafront.
open All year
nearest shop 1 mile
nearest pub 1 mile

Access abc 🦮 ♿

General 🛏 P ✂ Ⓢ

Unit ♿ 🛁 📖 🖥 🖵 📱 📠 🔥 🛏 🍴 📋 ✿

Payment Credit/debit cards, cash/cheques, euros

WEYMOUTH, Dorset Map ref 2B3 — SELF CATERING

Anchor House, Weymouth

contact Gail Lewis, PO Box 36, Cowbridge CF71 7GB **t** 08456 584478
f (01446) 775060 **e** selfcatering@johngrooms.org.uk **w** groomsholidays.org.uk

Units **1**
Sleeps **2–10**

Low season per wk
Min £330.00
High season per wk
Max £500.00

Awaiting
NAS rating

Victorian house owned by Grooms Holidays, adapted for wheelchair users. Ramp to entrance. Lift to first floor. Accommodation for up to ten people in six bedrooms of which three are accessible. Roll-in shower, shower-chair and hoist available.
open All year
nearest shop 1 mile
nearest pub 1 mile

Access abc 🦮 ♿

General 🛏 P ✂ Ⓢ

Unit ♿ 🛁 📖 🖥 🖵 📱 📠 🔥 🛏 🍴 📋 ✿

Payment Credit/debit cards, cash/cheques, euros

At-a-glance symbols are explained on the flap inside the back cover.

Summer special at the Lauriston Hotel

During July and August, four nights' accommodation, including dinner bed and breakfast, will cost just £150 per person.

The Lauriston Hotel is one of four hotels owned and operated by Action for Blind People. 2007 marks our 150th anniversary and we would like to present this special offer to you in celebration of our birthday.

We hope to see you this summer.

Best wishes,

Greg Ballesty
Hotel Manager

Please note that trips and excursions will incur additional cost. This offer cannot be used in conjunction with any other offer.

To book your break, or for more information, please contact:

The Lauriston Hotel,

6-12 Knightstone Road, Weston-super-Mare, BS23 2AN

Tel: 01934 620758   **Fax:** 01934 621154

Email: lauriston.hotel@actionforblindpeople.org.uk

Website: www.actionforblindpeople.org.uk

0290

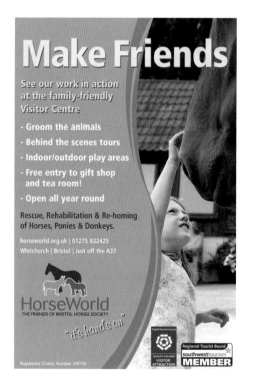

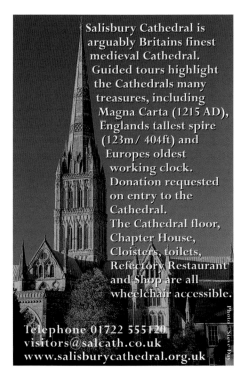

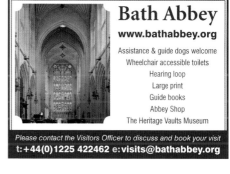

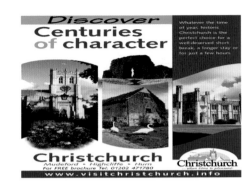

South East England

The Long Walk leading to
Windsor Castle, Berkshire

**Berkshire, Buckinghamshire,
East Sussex, Hampshire,
Isle of Wight, Kent, London,
Oxfordshire, Surrey, West Sussex**

Royal Pavilion, Brighton, East Sussex

Southern **delight**

The South East is your quintessential slice of England. Stroll around an English country garden, explore outstanding castles, experience colourful festivals and savour English wine. From 400 miles of glorious coastline to the dizzy heights of the London Eye, your feet won't touch the ground!

Making history

Explore a region that has witnessed some of the most momentous events of British history, from the Battle of Hastings in 1066 to the air raids of the Second World War. At Battle Abbey, stand on the exact spot where tradition says King Harold fell and take the interactive audio tour of the battlefield. Discover the world-famous HMS Victory at Portsmouth Historic Dockyard, where you can also go into battle with the Royal Marines at Action Stations, an interactive showcase of the modern navy.

Discover a life of privilege when you explore the South East's many awe-inspiring castles. Windsor, Hever, Bodiam, Scotney and Arundel, to name but five. Dreamy Leeds Castle in Kent, 'the loveliest castle in the world', was restored by Henry VIII for his first queen, Catherine of Aragon. Visit too the historic cities of Oxford, Canterbury and Chichester to discover elegant cathedrals and listen to the gentle sound of evensong. If you're looking for 'the finest view in England', according to Winston Churchill's mother, take a trip to stunning Blenheim Palace in Oxfordshire.

RHS Garden Wisley, Surrey

Full-on fun

For non-stop entertainment set your course for London where you can swashbuckle with Captain Jack Sparrow and croon with Robbie Williams at the world-famous Madam Tussauds. Submerge yourself in one of Europe's largest displays of aquatic life at the London Aquarium, then come up for air on the British Airways London Eye for a bird's-eye view of this buzzing city. Surreal! Check out surreal for real at the Dali Universe on the South Bank, where mind-boggling furniture and original sculptures will puzzle and amuse. On rainy days, cower at the dinosaurs at the Natural History Museum – admission is free.

Is the Queen at home? Peer into Buckingham Palace's windows at Legoland, Windsor, or prepare for a wet and wild voyage on the Vikings' River Splash ride! Get nose to nose with a multitude of furry and feathered friends at Drusillas Park, Alfriston, where children can learn as they have fun with hands-on activities.

A shore thing

Leave the hurly-burly behind and head to the beaches of the south coast. Eastbourne, Bournemouth, Brighton and Margate were all popular playgrounds for the Victorians – Queen Victoria would frequently stay at her Isle of Wight home, Osborne House. Save your small change for the slot machines on the pier where it's hot doughnuts or fish and chips all round. If you're looking for something a bit more peaceful, there are still many gems on this stretch of coastline. Run in and out of the sand dunes at West Wittering, just down the Sussex coast from Bognor Regis and watch the zigzagging

The splendid HMS Victory at Portsmouth, Hampshire

Inset pictures
Oxford spires, Oxfordshire; relaxing at the Royal Regatta, Henley; Osbourne House, Isle of Wight; Arundel Castle, West Sussex

kite-surfers at Pevensey Bay. Try your hand at an unrivalled number of watersports, including sailing on the Solent at the Calshot Activities Centre.

Kings and queens, castles and palaces, museums and zoos; the South East has them all

At one with nature

It's not for nothing that Kent is called the Garden of England. Sample the beauty of country gardens such as Sissinghurst Castle Garden near Cranbrook, the loving creation of Vita Sackville-West. Play hide and seek in and out of the paths and bridleways of the New Forest, now a National Park, and watch out for wild ponies as they gently graze. Follow the ancient tracks of the South Downs Way or the Ridgeway that eventually meets the Thames Path. Spend hours in the Royal Botanic Gardens at Kew, the jewel in the crown of English gardens: explore the 300 incredible acres or wonder at the exotic plants in the world-famous Palm House. Sister garden to Kew, Wakehurst Place in West Sussex, displays plants from across the world and aims to house seeds from 10% of the world's flora by 2009 to save species from extinction in the wild.

Never a dull moment

Catch the buzz of a festival or event, whatever the time of year. From rock 'n' pop to hops, from rowing to sailing, from Dickens to dancing round a maypole – the rich tapestry of life. In London, there's the Notting Hill Carnival or The Lord Mayor's Show. The Brighton Festival comes to the hip

Bodiam Castle, Kent

seaside town every May – a true celebration of the arts. If you're looking for the epitome of elegance, dress up for Glyndebourne's season of opera, or see the streets of Broadstairs thronged with Victorian costumes during the Dickens Festival. There's rock, pop and hip hop mixed with a liberal dose of mud at August's Reading Festival. Don't forget the Henley Royal Regatta or Cowes Week – two internationally famous spectacles. Cheer on your heroes at the London Marathon, Lord's cricket ground and Wimbledon.

Tate Modern, London

South East England
The warmest of welcomes

Visitors to South East England are benefiting from the tourism sector's continued commitment to making it an even more accessible region.

From B&Bs and hotels to historic properties, gardens, new family attractions and entire towns and cities, there are many great places to visit that have gone the extra mile to make tourists more welcome. Investment in special facilities, adaptations and new internal and external building work are all improving accessibility.

Just a few are featured below. More details on accommodation and great destinations and attractions can be found at **visitsoutheastengland.com.**

Dickens World, at Chatham Maritime, Kent is a stunning new £62 million indoor visitor complex, themed around the life, books and times of Charles Dickens, and developed with accessibility very much in mind. Marwell Zoological Park in Hampshire offers added benefits like Shopmobility scooters for hire, manual wheelchairs, easy wheelchair accessibility across the site and free road trains including a special carriage accessible to wheelchairs.

Many historic properties and sites across the region have been modernised to offer excellent accessibility for all visitors including Waddesdon Manor in

Main: Brighton's Palace Pier, East Sussex
Above: Blenheim Palace, Oxfordshire

Buckinghamshire, Oxfordshire's Blenheim Palace, and the abbey and battlefield at Hastings, Sussex.

For something completely different, Farming World in Kent, Denbies Wine Estate in Surrey, and the historic Eton College in Berkshire all offer a special experience. The South East is famed for its beautiful accessible gardens, such as Paradise Park in East Sussex and Emmetts Gardens in Kent.

Brighton recently became one of the first cities in the UK to undergo a full city centre 'Destination Disability Audit' and a similar investment is planned for Windsor.

As the 2012 Paralympics approaches, the South East is keen to maintain its reputation for offering the warmest of welcomes to all visitors. The very first Paralympics were hosted here, in Stoke Mandeville in 1948, and we have retained the very highest commitment to accessibility for all visitors.

South East | ENGLAND

www.visitsoutheastengland.com

Find out more:
visitsoutheastengland.com
dickensworld.co.uk
marwell.org.uk
blenheimpalace.com
waddesdon.org.uk
discoverhastings.co.uk
farming-world.com
denbiesvineyard.co.uk
etoncollege.com
paradisepark.co.uk
nationaltrust.org.uk
visitbrighton.com

Below: Waddesdon Manor, Buckinghamshire

Useful regional contacts

For information before you travel, check out the useful regional contacts below. Local Tourist Information Centres will also be able to give you information on accessible attractions and accommodation.

Tourism South East
t (023) 8062 5505
w visitsoutheastengland.com

Visit London
t 0870 156 6366
w visitlondon.com

Publications

A Town Centre Shopping Guide For People With Disabilities
A Maidstone Borough Council publication available to download from digitalmaidstone.co.uk.

Access Guide
A guide to Tunbridge Wells for people with disabilities. Available to download from tunbridgewells.gov.uk or call (01892) 526121 for alternative formats.

Accessible Portsmouth – A Guide For Visitors With Disabilities
Available to download from visitportsmouth.co.uk. For alternative formats, call (023) 9283 4109 or email lorraine.hawthorne@portsmouthcc.gov.uk.

Accessible Worthing
Information on accessibility in Worthing is available Tourist Information Centre. Call (01903) 239999 or visit visitworthing.co.uk.

Places In And Around Eastbourne
Available from Eastbourne Tourist Information Centre. Call 0906 711 2212 or for textphone users (01323) 415111.

Walks For All In Kent And Medway
A Kent County Council series of leaflets available to download from kent.gov.uk/explorekent.

Resources

Access to London
w bloomsbury.com
A detailed guide on getting around and using the facilities in London.

Artsline
t (020) 7388 2227
w artsline.org.uk
A resource for finding accessible attractions in London.

City of London
Access Office, City of London, PO Box 270, Guildhall, London EC2P 2EJ
t (020) 7332 1995
t (020) 7332 3929 (textphone)
e access@cityoflondon.gov.uk
w cityoflondon.gov.uk
Provides online information on accessible parking bays and toilets, and access to places of interest. A number of leaflets may be downloaded from the website.

Congestion charge

t 0845 900 1234
t (020) 7649 9123 (textphone)
w cclondon.com
Blue badge holders are entitled to 100% discount for an initial registration of £10 – worthwhile if you pay more than 2 weekday visits to London in a year. Call for a registration pack.

Disabledgo

w disabledgo.info
An online service with detailed information on access to premises and attractions in London, including Croydon, Lewisham, Richmond, Tower Hamlets and Wandsworth.

London Eye

t 0870 500 0600
w ba-londoneye.com
Operates a fast track policy for visitors with disabilities and can take up to eight wheelchairs per revolution, with a maximum of two in a capsule.

Society of London Theatres

t (020) 7557 6751
e access@solttma.co.uk
w officiallondontheatre.co.uk/access
Runs Access London Theatre, a three-year project aiming to increase audiences with sensory impairments, as well as families and 16-25 year olds. There is a free brochure of audio-described, captioned and sign language performances.

Taxis

All London Black Cabs have space for a passenger in a manual wheelchair, and carry a ramp.

Transport for London

t (020) 7222 1234
t (020) 7918 3015 (textphone)
w tfl.gov.uk
Responsible for London's public transport. Search for accessible routes on tfl.gov.uk/journeyplanner. See also their shared information on directenquiries.com.

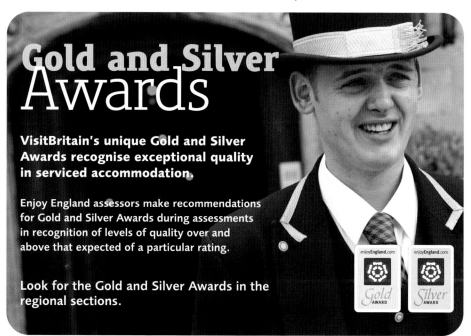

Gold and Silver Awards

VisitBritain's unique Gold and Silver Awards recognise exceptional quality in serviced accommodation.

Enjoy England assessors make recommendations for Gold and Silver Awards during assessments in recognition of levels of quality over and above that expected of a particular rating.

Look for the Gold and Silver Awards in the regional sections.

Tourist Information Centres

When you arrive at your destination, visit a Tourist Information Centre for help with accommodation and information about local attractions and events, or email your request before you go.

Berkshire

Bracknell	Nine Mile Ride	(01344) 354409	TheLookOut@bracknell-forest.gov.uk
Maidenhead	St Ives Road	(01628) 796502	maidenhead.tic@rbwm.gov.uk
Newbury	The Wharf	(01635) 30267	tourism@westberks.gov.uk
Reading	Chain Street	(0118) 956 6226	touristinfo@reading.gov.uk
Windsor	24 High Street	(01753) 743900	windsor.tic@rbwm.gov.uk

Buckinghamshire

Aylesbury	Kings Head Passage	(01296) 330559	tic@aylesburyvaledc.gov.uk
Buckingham	Market Hill	(01280) 823020	buckingham.t.i.c@btconnect.com
High Wycombe	Paul's Row	(01494) 421892	tourism_enquiries@wycombe.gov.uk
Marlow	31 High Street	(01628) 483597	tourism_enquiries@wycombe.gov.uk
Wendover	High Street	(01296) 696759	tourism@wendover-pc.gov.uk

East Sussex

Battle	High Street	(01424) 773721	battletic@rother.gov.uk
Brighton	10 Bartholomew Square	0906 711 2255**	brighton-tourism@brighton-hove.gov.uk
Eastbourne	Cornfield Road	0906 711 2212**	tic@eastbourne.gov.uk
Hastings (Old Town)*	The Stade	(01424) 781111	hic@hastings.gov.uk
Hastings	Queens Square	(01424) 781111	hic@hastings.gov.uk
Lewes	187 High Street	(01273) 483448	lewes.tic@lewes.gov.uk
Rye	Strand Quay	(01797) 226696	ryetic@rother.gov.uk
Seaford	25 Clinton Place	(01323) 897426	seaford.tic@lewes.gov.uk

Hampshire

Aldershot	39 High Street	(01252) 320968	mail@rushmoorvic.com
Alton	7 Cross and Pillory Lane	(01420) 88448	altoninfo@btconnect.com
Andover	6 Church Close	(01264) 324320	andovertic@testvalley.gov.uk
Fareham	West Street	(01329) 221342	touristinfo@fareham.gov.uk
Fordingbridge*	Salisbury Street	(01425) 654560	fordingbridgetic@tourismse.com
Gosport	South Street	(023) 9252 2944	tourism@gosport.gov.uk
Hayling Island*	Seafront	(023) 9246 7111	tourism@havant.gov.uk
Lymington	New Street	(01590) 689000	information@nfdc.gov.uk
Lyndhurst & New Forest	Main Car Park	(023) 8028 2269	information@nfdc.gov.uk
Petersfield	27 The Square	(01730) 268829	petersfieldinfo@btconnect.com
Portsmouth	Clarence Esplanade	(023) 9282 6722	vis@portsmouthcc.gov.uk
Portsmouth	The Hard	(023) 9282 6722	vis@portsmouthcc.gov.uk
Ringwood	The Furlong	(01425) 470896	information@nfdc.gov.uk
Romsey	13 Church Street	(01794) 512987	romseytic@testvalley.gov.uk

Southampton	9 Civic Centre Road	(023) 8083 3333	tourist.information@southampton.gov.uk
Winchester	High Street	(01962) 840500	tourism@winchester.gov.uk

Isle of Wight

Cowes	9 The Arcade	(01983) 813818	info@islandbreaks.co.uk
Newport	High Street	(01983) 813818	info@islandbreaks.co.uk
Ryde	81-83 Union Street	(01983) 813818	info@islandbreaks.co.uk
Sandown	8 High Street	(01983) 813818	info@islandbreaks.co.uk
Shanklin	67 High Street	(01983) 813818	info@islandbreaks.co.uk
Yarmouth	The Quay	(01983) 813818	info@islandbreaks.co.uk

Kent

Ashford	18 The Churchyard	(01233) 629165	tourism@ashford.gov.uk
Broadstairs	2 Victoria Parade	0870 264 6111	
Canterbury	12/13 Sun Street	(01227) 378100	canterburyinformation@canterbury.gov.uk
Deal	129 High Street	(01304) 369576	tic@doveruk.com
Dover	Biggin Street	(01304) 205108	tic@doveruk.com
Faversham	13 Preston Street	(01795) 534542	fata@visitfaversham.com
Folkestone	Harbour Street	(01303) 258594	
Gravesend	18a St George's Square	(01474) 337600	info@towncentric.co.uk
Herne Bay	Central Parade	(01227) 361911	hernebayinformation@canterbury.gov.uk
Hythe	Scanlons Bridge Road	(01303) 266421	
Maidstone	High Street	(01622) 602169	tourism@maidstone.gov.uk
Margate	12-13 The Parade	0870 264 6111	margate.tic@visitor-centre.net
New Romney	New Romney Station	(01797) 362353	
Ramsgate	17 Albert Court	0870 264 6111	ramsgate.tic@visitor-centre.net
Rochester	95 High Street	(01634) 843666	visitor.centre@medway.gov.uk
Royal Tunbridge Wells	The Pantiles	(01892) 515675	touristinformationcentre@tunbridgewells.gov.uk
Sandwich*	Cattle Market	(01304) 613565	info@ticsandwich.wanadoo.co.uk
Sevenoaks	Buckhurst Lane	(01732) 450305	tic@sevenoakstown.gov.uk
Tenterden*	High Street	(01580) 763572	tentic@ashford.gov.uk
Tonbridge	Castle Street	(01732) 770929	tonbridge.castle@tmbc.gov.uk
Whitstable	7 Oxford Street	(01227) 275482	whitstableinformation@canterbury.gov.uk

London

Bexley (Hall Place)	Bourne Road	(01322) 558676	hallplaceshoptic@tiscali.co.uk
Britain & London Visitor Centre	1 Regent Street	08701 566 366	blvcenquiry@visitlondon.com
Croydon	Katharine Street	(020) 8253 1009	tic@croydon.gov.uk
Greenwich	2 Cutty Sark Gardens	0870 608 2000	tic@greenwich.gov.uk
Harrow	Station Road	(020) 8424 1102	info@harrow.gov.uk
Hillingdon	14-15 High Street	(01895) 250706	libraryinfoteam@hillingdongrid.org
Hounslow	High Street	0845 456 2929	tic@cip.org.uk
Kingston	Market Place	(020) 8547 5592	tourist.information@rbk.kingston.gov.uk
Lewisham	199-201 Lewisham High Street	(020) 8297 8317	tic@lewisham.gov.uk
Richmond	Whittaker Avenue	(020) 8940 9125	info@visitrichmond.co.uk
Southwark	Level 2, Tate Modern	(020) 7401 5266	tourisminfo@southwark.gov.uk

Swanley	London Road	(01322) 614660	touristinfo@swanley.org.uk
Twickenham	44 York Street	(020) 8891 7272	info@visitrichmond.co.uk
Waterloo International	Arrivals Hall	(020) 7620 1550	london.visitorcentre@iceplc.com

Oxfordshire

Banbury	Spiceball Park Road	(01295) 259855	banbury.tic@cherwell-dc.gov.uk
Bicester	Bicester Village	(01869) 369055	bicester.vc@cherwell-dc.gov.uk
Burford	Sheep Street	(01993) 823558	burford.vic@westoxon.gov.uk
Faringdon	5 Market Place	(01367) 242191	tourism@faringdontowncouncil.org.uk
Henley-on-Thames	Kings Road	(01491) 578034	henleytic@hotmail.com
Oxford	15/16 Broad Street	(01865) 726871	tic@oxford.gov.uk
Witney	26a Market Square	(01993) 775802	witney.vic@westoxon.gov.uk
Woodstock	Park Street	(01993) 813276	woodstock.vic@westoxon.gov.uk

Surrey

Guildford	14 Tunsgate	(01483) 444333	tic@guildford.gov.uk

West Sussex

Arundel	61 High Street	(01903) 882268	arundel.vic@arun.gov.uk
Bognor Regis	Belmont Street	(01243) 823140	bognorregis.vic@arun.gov.uk
Burgess Hill	96 Church Walk	(01444) 238202	touristinformation@burgesshill.gov.uk
Chichester	29a South Street	(01243) 775888	chitic@chichester.gov.uk
Horsham	9 The Causeway	(01403) 211661	tourist.information@horsham.gov.uk
Littlehampton	63-65 Surrey Street	(01903) 721866	littlehampton.vic@arun.gov.uk
Midhurst	North Street	(01730) 817322	midtic@chichester.gov.uk
Petworth*	The Old Bakery	(01798) 343523	
Worthing	Chapel Road	(01903) 221307	tic@worthing.gov.uk
Worthing*	Marine Parade	(01903) 221307	tic@worthing.gov.uk

seasonal opening ** calls to this number are charged at a premium rate*

Bank holiday
dates for your diary

holiday	2008	2009
New Year's Day	1 January	1 January
January Bank Holiday (Scotland)	2 January	2 January
Good Friday	21 March	10 April
Easter Monday (England & Wales)	24 March	13 April
Early May Bank Holiday	5 May	4 May
Spring Bank Holiday	26 May	25 May
Summer Bank Holiday (Scotland)	4 August	3 August
Summer Bank Holiday (England & Wales)	25 August	31 August
Christmas Day	25 December	25 December
Boxing Day Holiday	26 December	28 December

BATTLE, East Sussex Map ref 3B4 | **CAMPING & CARAVANNING**

★★★★★
TOURING PARK

(150)
£12.10–£24.90
(150)
£12.10–£24.90
150 touring pitches

THE
CARAVAN
CLUB

Normanhurst Court Caravan Club Site

Stevens Crouch, Battle TN33 9LR **t** (01424) 773808
w caravanclub.co.uk

A gracious site in a former garden with magnificent specimen trees. There is a choice between pitches in open areas or in small groups surrounded with shrubs – the rhododendrons are a riot of colour in the spring. The site is located close to the 1066 Trail which will appeal to walkers, nature lovers and families. Open March to November.

From Battle, turn left onto A271. Site is 3 miles on left.

General   🚋 **P** 🅿 🛗 🚻 🆆🅿 📶 ☉ 🛈
       🖻 ☼

Leisure   ⛰

Payment   Credit/debit cards, cash/cheques

BEMBRIDGE, Isle of Wight | **HOTEL**

★★★
HOTEL

Bembridge Coast Hotel Fishermans Walk, Bembridge PO35 5TH
t (01983) 873931 **f** (01983) 874693
e reception.bembridge@bourne-leisure.co.uk
w warnerholidays.co.uk

BICESTER, Oxfordshire | **SELF CATERING**

★★★★
SELF CATERING

Pimlico Farm Country Cottages contact Mr & Mrs John & Monica Harper,
Pimlico Farm Country Cottages, Pimlico Farm, Tusmore, Bicester OX27 7SL
t (01869) 810306 **f** (01869) 810309
e enquiries@pimlicofarm.co.uk

Quality assessment

Our commitment to quality involves wide-ranging accommodation assessment. Ratings and awards were correct at the time of going to press but may change following a new assessment. Please check at the time of booking.

BOGNOR REGIS, West Sussex Map ref 2C3 — CAMPING & CARAVANNING

★★★★★
TOURING & CAMPING PARK

(94) £12.10–£24.90
(94) £12.10–£24.90
94 touring pitches

CARAVAN CLUB

Rowan Park Caravan Club Site

Rowan Way, Bognor Regis PO22 9RP **t** (01243) 828515
f (01243) 869189

This site is conveniently situated alongside the A29 and about two miles from the beach and is most attractive with its screen of trees in a park-like setting. The town of Bognor Regis is a traditional seaside resort with a shingle and sand beach and entertainments. Open March to November.

From roundabout on A29, 1 mile north of Bognor, turn left into Rowan Way, site 100yds on right, opposite Halfords superstore.

General

Leisure   🏛

Payment   Credit/debit cards, cash/cheques

BOGNOR REGIS, West Sussex

See also entry on p237

BORTHWOOD, Isle of Wight — SELF CATERING

★★★
SELF CATERING

Borthwood Cottages   **t** (01983) 403967
e mail@netguides.co.uk **w** netguides.co.uk

BRACKLESHAM BAY, West Sussex

See entry on p237

BRACKNELL, Berkshire — HOTEL

★★★★
HOTEL SILVER AWARD

Coppid Beech Hotel John Nike Way, Bracknell RG12 8TF
t (01344) 303333 **f** (01344) 301200
e reservations@coppid-beech-hotel.co.uk **w** coppidbeech.com

BRIGHTON & HOVE, East Sussex — CAMPING & CARAVANNING

★★★★★
TOURING & CAMPING PARK

Sheepcote Valley Caravan Club Site East Brighton Park, Brighton BN2 5TS
t (01273) 626546
w caravanclub.co.uk

Accessible index

If you have specific accessible requirements, the Accessible index at the back of the guide lists accommodation under different categories for mobility, hearing and visual impairment.

   At-a-glance symbols are explained on the flap inside the back cover.

BURFORD, Oxfordshire Map ref 2B1 — CAMPING & CARAVANNING

★★★★★
TOURING PARK

(120)
£12.10–£24.90
🚐(120)
£12.10–£24.90
120 touring pitches

THE
CARAVAN CLUB

Burford Caravan Club Site

Bradwell Grove, Burford OX18 4JJ **t** (01993) 823080
w caravanclub.co.uk

An attractive and spacious site – you can't miss it as it is located opposite the Cotswold Wildlife Park, a popular family attraction in the area. With rhinos, zebras and leopards, children love it and the brass rubbing centre, beautiful gardens and narrow gauge railway make this a good value and special day out. Open March to November.

From roundabout at A40/A361 junction in Burford, take A361 signposted Lechlade. Site on right after 2.5 miles. Site signposted from roundabout.

General 📺 P 🔌 🕐 🕯 📶 🎣 ☉ 🚰
📷 ☼

Leisure /🎿\

Payment Credit/debit cards, cash/cheques

CHALE, Isle of Wight Map ref 2C3 — SELF CATERING

★★★★
SELF CATERING

Units **4**
Sleeps **2–10**

Low season per wk
£150.00–£733.00
High season per wk
£395.00–£990.00

Atherfield Green Farm Holiday Cottages, Ventnor

contact A Jupe, Atherfield Green Farm Holiday Cottages, The Laurels, High Street, Newchurch PO36 0NJ **t** (01983) 867613 & 07974 946738
e agfh@btinternet.com **w** btinternet.com/~Alistair.Jupe

Converted farm buildings near to the south western coast of the island near to the fossil beaches. Ideal for walking in relaxing countryside. Specifically designed for the disabled with level access and wheelchair-accessible wetrooms in each unit.
open All year
nearest shop 2 miles
nearest pub 2 miles

General 🛏 🏠 ♿ P

Unit ♿ 🏠 📺 📷 🔥 🛢 🍳 📠 🧺 ❄

Payment Cash/cheques

CHICHESTER, West Sussex — SELF CATERING

★★★★
SELF CATERING

Cornerstones contact Mrs Higgins, Greenacre, Goodwood Gardens, Chichester PO20 1SP **t** (01243) 839096
e v.r.higgins@dsl.pipex.com **w** cornercottages.com

COLDWALTHAM, West Sussex — GUEST ACCOMMODATION

★★★★
INN

The Labouring Man Old London Road, Pulborough RH20 1LF **t** (01798) 872215
e philip.beckett@btconnect.com **w** thelabouringman.co.uk

DORKING, Surrey — SELF CATERING

★★★
SELF CATERING

Bulmer Farm contact Mrs Gill Hill, Bulmer Farm, Holmbury St Mary, Dorking RH5 6LG **t** (01306) 730210

DUCKLINGTON, Oxfordshire — GUEST ACCOMMODATION

★★★
FARMHOUSE

Ducklington Farm Course Hill Lane, Ducklington, Witney OX29 7YL
t (01993) 772175
w countryaccom.co.uk

EASTBOURNE, East Sussex — HOTEL

★★★
HOTEL
SILVER AWARD

Hydro Hotel Mount Road, Eastbourne BN20 7HZ
t (01323) 720643 **f** (01323) 641167
e sales@hydrohotel.com **w** hydrohotel.com

FARNHAM, Surrey — SELF CATERING

★★★
SELF CATERING

High Wray contact Mrs Alexine G N Crawford, High Wray, 73 Lodge Hill Road, Farnham GU10 3RB **t** (01252) 715589
e crawford@highwray73.co.uk **w** highwray73.co.uk

FELPHAM, West Sussex

See entry on p238

FOLKESTONE, Kent — GUEST ACCOMMODATION

★★★★
GUEST ACCOMMODATION

Garden Lodge 324 Canterbury Road, Densole, Folkestone CT18 7BB
t (01303) 893147 **f** (01303) 894581
e stay@garden-lodge.com **w** garden-lodge.com

FOLKESTONE, Kent Map ref 3B4 — CAMPING & CARAVANNING

★★★★★
TOURING &
CAMPING PARK

🚐 (140)
£12.10–£24.90
🚏 (140)
£12.10–£24.90
140 touring pitches

Black Horse Farm Caravan Club Site

385 Canterbury Road, Densole, Folkestone CT18 7BG
t (01303) 892665
w caravanclub.co.uk

Set in the heart of farming country in the Kentish village of Densole, on the Downs. This is a quiet and relaxed country site, ideally suited for families wishing to visit the many interesting local attractions including the historic city of Canterbury. For nature lovers there are many walks.
open All year

From M20 jct 13 on A260 to Canterbury, 2 miles from junction with A20, site on left 200yds past Black Horse inn.

General 🔲 **P** 🔌 🕒 🛋 📶 🐾 ☺ 📠
🔲 ☼

Leisure 🅰

Payment Credit/debit cards, cash/cheques

THE
CARAVAN
CLUB

At-a-glance symbols are explained on the flap inside the back cover.

HEATHFIELD, East Sussex Map ref 3B4   GUEST ACCOMMODATION

★★★★
BED & BREAKFAST

Spicers

Spicers Cottages, 21 Cade Street, Heathfield TN21 9BS   t (01435) 866363
f (01435) 866363   e spicersbb@btinternet.com   w spicersbb.co.uk

B&B per room per night
s £28.00–£35.00
d £48.00–£60.00
Evening meal per person
£12.00–£15.00

Beamed cottage on the High Weald
of East Sussex. Convenient for many
places of interest. Level entrance.
Spacious wheel-in shower. A warm
welcome awaits you.
open All year
bedrooms 1 double, 1 twin,
1 single
bathrooms 2 en suite, 1 private

Access 🦮

General ♨ ✗ 🍴 🖼 ❀

Rooms 🛏 📺 🛁 🎣 ⬛ 🛎 🗄

Payment Credit/debit cards

HEATHROW AIRPORT, Outer London

See entry on p238

HIGH HALDEN, Kent   SELF CATERING

★★★★–★★★★★★
SELF CATERING

The Granary and The Stables contact Mrs Serena Maundrell,
Vintage Years Company Ltd, Hales Place, High Halden, Ashford TN26 3JQ
t (01233) 850871 & 07715 488804   f (01233) 850717
e serena@vintage-years.co.uk   w vintage-years.co.uk

LECKHAMPSTEAD, Buckinghamshire   GUEST ACCOMMODATION

★★★★
FARMHOUSE

Weatherhead Farm Leckhampstead, Buckingham MK18 5NP
t (01280) 860502   f (01280) 860535
e weatherheadfarm@aol.com

LEEDS, Kent   SELF CATERING

★★★
SELF CATERING

1 & 2 Orchard View contact Mr Stuart Winter, Garden of England Cottages,
The Mews Office, 189a High Street, Tonbridge TN9 1BX
t (01732) 369168   f (01732) 358817
e holidays@gardenofenglandcottages.co.uk   w gardenofenglandcottages.co.uk

LENHAM, Kent   SELF CATERING

★★★★
SELF CATERING

Apple Pye Cottage   t (01622) 858878
e diane@bramleyknowlefarm.co.uk   w bramleyknowlefarm.co.uk

Don't forget www.

Web addresses throughout this guide are
shown without the prefix www. Please
include www. in the address line of your
browser. If a web address does not follow
this style it is shown in full.

LEWES, East Sussex Map ref 2D3   SELF CATERING

★★★★
SELF CATERING

Units **2**
Sleeps **1–10**

Low season per wk
£385.00–£465.00
High season per wk
£460.00–£625.00

Heath Farm, Plumpton Green, Lewes

contact Mrs Marilyn Hanbury, Heath Farm, South Road, Plumpton Green, Lewes BN8 4EA   **t** (01273) 890712   **f** (01273) 890712
e hanbury@heath-farm.com   **w** heath-farm.com

General 🐎 🏛 ♣ P ✂ ▣ S

Unit ♿ ♨ 🏠 ▣ ▣ 🍳 ▣ ♨ 📻
📻 🍽 🛁 ❄

Payment Cash/cheques

Former milking parlour and stables converted into luxury cottages on working family farm. Beautifully and comfortably furnished to highest standard. Level-entry showers. Wonderful countryside, easy access to Brighton, Gatwick, London, National Trust gardens and historic towns and villages. An ideal holiday base.
open All year
nearest shop 1 mile
nearest pub < 0.5 miles

Directions given at time of booking.

Bank holiday
dates for your diary

holiday	2008	2009
New Year's Day (England & Wales)	1 January	1 January
New Year's Day (Scotland)	1 January	1 January
January Bank Holiday (Scotland)	2 January	2 January
Good Friday	21 March	10 April
Easter Monday (England & Wales)	24 March	13 April
Early May Bank Holiday	5 May	4 May
Spring Bank Holiday	26 May	25 May
Summer Bank Holiday (Scotland)	4 August	3 August
Summer Bank Holiday (England & Wales)	25 August	31 August
Christmas Day	25 December	25 December
Boxing Day Holiday	26 December	28 December

CAMPING & CARAVANNING

★★★★★
TOURING &
CAMPING PARK

 (220)
£14.30–£27.70
(220)
£14.30–£27.70
220 touring pitches

Abbey Wood Caravan Club Site

Federation Road, Abbey Wood, London SE2 0LS t (020) 8311 7708
w caravanclub.co.uk

General

Leisure

Payment Credit/debit cards,
cash/cheques

*Midweek discount; pitch fees
reduced by 50% for stays on Tue,
Wed or Thu night outside peak
season.*

It feels positively rural when you
reach this verdant, gently
sloping, secure site with its
mature-tree screening and
spacious grounds. Good railway
connections (35 mins) into
central London's attractions are
within walking distance of the
site. As an alternative to the busy
city centre, nearby Greenwich
offers its own blend of fascinating
attractions.

open All year

*On M2 turn off at A221. Then
turn right into McLeod Road,
right into Knee Hill and the site is
the 2nd turning on the right.*

THE
CARAVAN
CLUB

CAMPING & CARAVANNING

★★★★★
TOURING &
CAMPING PARK

 (126)
£14.30–£27.70
(126)
£14.30–£27.70
126 touring pitches

Crystal Palace Caravan Club Site

Crystal Palace Parade, London SE19 1UF t (020) 8778 7155
w caravanclub.co.uk

General

Payment Credit/debit cards,
cash/cheques

London is the lure here. The
number 3 bus takes you directly
to Piccadilly and Travelcards can
be bought on-site. Popular with
families from Europe during the
summer months, this is a busy,
but friendly site on the edge of a
pleasant park with many
attractions for children.

open All year

*Turn off the A205 South Circular
Road at West Dulwich into
Croxted Road. The site is adjacent
to the BBC television mast.*

THE
CARAVAN
CLUB

See also entries on p239 and p240

MARLOW, Buckinghamshire — GUEST ACCOMMODATION

★★★
BED & BREAKFAST

Granny Anne's Marlow SL7 3EP
t (01628) 473086
e enquiries@grannyannes.com
w marlowbedbreakfast.co.uk

NEWCHURCH, Isle of Wight — CAMPING & CARAVANNING

★★★★★
**TOURING &
CAMPING PARK**

Southland Camping Park Winford Road, Sandown PO36 0LZ
t (01983) 865385   f (01983) 86/663
e info@southland.co.uk   w southland.co.uk

REDHILL, Surrey Map ref 2D2 — CAMPING & CARAVANNING

★★★★
TOURING PARK

🚐 (79) £12.10–£24.90
🚛 (79) £12.10–£24.90
79 touring pitches

THE
**CARAVAN
CLUB**

Alderstead Heath Caravan Club Site
Dean Lane, Redhill RH1 3AH   t (01737) 644629
w caravanclub.co.uk

General

Payment Credit/debit cards, cash/cheques

A quiet, level site, though the site drops away into rolling wooded countryside. Alderstead Heath is an ideal holiday in a picturesque setting. The Pilgrim's Way provides varied walking options. Its proximity to London makes this an obvious and delightful base to explore the capital (35 mins from Redhill).

open All year

M25 jct 8, A217 towards Reigate, fork left after 300yds towards Merstham. 2.5 miles, left at T-junction onto A23. 0.5 miles turn right into Shepherds Hill (B2031). 1 mile, left into Dean Lane.

RYE, East Sussex — GUEST ACCOMMODATION

★★★★
GUEST ACCOMMODATION

Woodlands Whitebread Lane, Beckley, Rye TN31 6UA
t (01797) 260524
e robson@woodlandsrye.co.uk

Quality assessment

Our commitment to quality involves a wide-ranging assessment. Ratings and awards were correct at the time of going to press but may change following a new assessment. Please check at the time of booking.

SANDWICH, Kent Map ref 3C3 — SELF CATERING

★★★★
SELF CATERING

Units **2**
Sleeps **4–7**

Low season per wk
£300.00–£400.00
High season per wk
£400.00–£695.00

The Old Dairy, Deal

contact Mrs Montgomery, Little Brooksend Farm,
Birchington CT7 0JW **t** (01843) 841656 **f** (01843) 841656
e info@montgomery-cottages.co.uk **w** montgomery-cottages.co.uk

General ☙ ▥ ☗ **P** ⓢ

Unit 🔌 ▥ 📺 🗑 🎛 🍳 📁 ❋

Payment Cash/cheques

Set in 30 acres of Parkland. Two cottages converted from the former dairy. Each having three ground-floor bedrooms, all with own bath/shower rooms, plus twin-bedded room on upper floor. Open-plan living area. Within easy reach of Canterbury, Sandwich, Deal, beaches, Channel ports and Tunnel. Open from March up to and including New Year.

Travel directions given on application.

Each cottage has an en suite double bedroom with wheelchair access. Short weekend/midweek breaks available out of season.

SELSEY, West Sussex

See entry on p240

SHANKLIN, Isle of Wight — SELF CATERING

★★★★
SELF CATERING

Laramie
t (01983) 550510
e sally.ranson@tiscali.co.uk
w laramieholidayhome.co.uk

SWAY, Hampshire — GUEST ACCOMMODATION

★★★★
GUEST ACCOMMODATION

The Nurse's Cottage Station Road, Sway, Lymington SO41 6BA
t (01590) 683402 **f** (01590) 683402
e nurses.cottage@lineone.net

TENTERDEN, Kent — HOTEL

★★★
HOTEL
SILVER AWARD

Little Silver Country Hotel Ashford Road, Tenterden TN30 6SP
t (01233) 850321 **f** (01233) 850647
e enquiries@little-silver.co.uk **w** little-silver.co.uk

TONBRIDGE, Kent — SELF CATERING

★★★★★
SELF CATERING

Goldhill Mill Cottages
t (01732) 851626
e vernon.cole@virgin.net **w** goldhillmillcottages.com

WINCHESTER, Hampshire — CAMPING & CARAVANNING

★★★★
TOURING &
CAMPING PARK

Morn Hill Caravan Club Site Morn Hill, Winchester SO21 2PH
t (01962) 869877
w caravanclub.co.uk

WITNEY, Oxfordshire — GUEST ACCOMMODATION

★★★
GUEST ACCOMMODATION

Springhill Farm Bed & Breakfast Cogges, Witney OX29 6UL
t (01993) 704919
e jan@strainge.fsnet.co.uk

WITNEY, Oxfordshire Map ref 2C1 — SELF CATERING

★★★★
SELF CATERING

Units **1**
Sleeps **4**
Low season per wk
£250.00–£320.00
High season per wk
£420.00–£450.00

Swallows Nest, Witney

contact Mrs Jan Strainge, Springhill Farm Swallows Nest, Cogges, Witney OX29 6UL **t** (01993) 704919 **e** jan@strainge.fsnet.co.uk

Cosy country barn conversion close to Witney, Oxford, Blenheim and nearby Cotswolds. Level access throughout including en suite showers. One zip/link double, one twin (low allergy). Shower chairs etc available.
open All year
nearest shop 1 mile
nearest pub 1 mile

General
Unit
Payment Cash/cheques, euros

WORTHING, West Sussex Map ref 2D3 — CAMPING & CARAVANNING

★★★★
TOURING PARK

(129)
£10.40–£22.40
(129)
£10.40–£22.40
129 touring pitches

THE
CARAVAN
CLUB

Northbrook Farm Caravan Club Site

Titnore Way, Worthing BN13 3RT **t** (01903) 502962
w caravanclub.co.uk

An attractively grassy site with good trees, and only two miles from the coast. If you're a bowler, you'll know about Worthing, for it's where the English Bowls Association has its headquarters. In Worthing itself there's the Lido on the seafront with rides and a restaurant. Open March to November.

From A24 follow signs for Chichester/Littlehampton approx 4 miles on, far side of bridge, signposted Ferring and Goring. After 0.75 miles, left. Caravan site sign Titnore Way is on left.

General
Leisure
Payment Credit/debit cards, cash/cheques

At-a-glance symbols are explained on the flap inside the back cover.

NATIONAL ACCESSIBLE SCHEME RATINGS ONLY

The following establishments hold a National Accessible Scheme rating as shown in their entry, but do not participate in VisitBritain's Enjoy England quality assessment scheme. However, to participate in the National Accessible Scheme accommodation must meet a minimum level of quality. In addition to being assessed under the National Accessible Scheme the entries listed below may hold a quality rating from another organisation.

BOGNOR REGIS, West Sussex Map ref 2C3 — SELF CATERING

Farrell House, Bognor Regis

contact Gail Lewis, PO Box 36, Cowbridge CF71 7GB **t** 08456 584478 **f** (01446) 775060 **e** selfcatering@johngrooms.org.uk **w** groomsholidays.org.uk

Units **1**
Sleeps **2–8**

Low season per wk
Min £235.00
High season per wk
Max £440.00

Awaiting
NAS rating

Chalet bungalow, adapted and equipped for disabled people, sleeping up to eight. Ground-floor lounge, kitchen, bathroom, twin and single bedrooms and bathroom upstairs. Electric hoist and shower-chair. Ramp to garden.
open All year
nearest shop 1 mile
nearest pub 1 mile

Access abc
General
Unit
Payment Credit/debit cards, cash/cheques, euros

BRACKLESHAM BAY, West Sussex Map ref 2C3 — SELF CATERING

Tamarisk, Bracklesham Bay

contact Gail Lewis, PO Box 36, Cowbridge CF71 7GB **t** 08456 584478 **f** (01446) 775060 **e** selfcatering@johngrooms.org.uk **w** groomsholidays.org.uk

Units **1**
Sleeps **2–6**

Low season per wk
Min £235.00
High season per wk
Max £435.00

Awaiting
NAS rating

Bungalow near beach, adapted and equipped for disabled people. Three bedrooms, lounge/dining room, kitchen, roll-in and second shower rooms. Mobile and electric hoists and other equipment available.
open All year
nearest shop 1 mile
nearest pub 1 mile

Access abc
General
Unit
Payment Credit/debit cards, cash/cheques, euros

Place index

If you know where you want to stay, the index at the back of the guide will give you the page number which lists accommodation in your chosen town, city or village. Check out the other useful indexes too.

FELPHAM, West Sussex Map ref 2C3 — SELF CATERING

Beach Lodge, Felpham

Units **1**
Sleeps **2–9**

Low season per wk
Min £300.00
High season per wk
Max £455.00

Awaiting
NAS rating

contact Gail Lewis, PO Box 36, Cowbridge CF71 7GB **t** 08456 584478
f (01446) 775060 **e** selfcatering@johngrooms.org.uk **w** groomsholidays.org.uk

Detached house facing the sea, east of Bognor. Adapted for wheelchair users with a lift and roll-in shower. Sleeps up to nine people. Electric and mobile hoists available.
open All year
nearest shop 1 mile
nearest pub 1 mile

Access	abc 🐾 🏠
General	🛏 P ✂ S
Unit	🔥 🍴 ▦ 🔌 ▭ 📶 📶 🔥

Payment Credit/debit cards, cash/cheques, euros

HEATHROW AIRPORT, Outer London Map ref 2D2 — HOTEL

Crowne Plaza London Heathrow

B&B per room per night
s £93.00–£210.00
d £93.00–£210.00
HB per person per night
£116.00–£234.00

Awaiting
NAS rating

Stockley Road, West Drayton UB7 9NA **t** 0870 400 9140 **f** (01895) 445122
e reservations.cplhr@ihg.com **w** crowneplaza.co.uk

Situated just off M4 junction 4 with easy access to central London, Windsor and Heathrow Airport. Modern refurbished rooms, full leisure facilities, choice of dining options. Facilities available and accessible to all guests equally.
open All year
bedrooms 256 double, 202 twin, 3 suites
bathrooms 461 private

Access	☺ 🛏 abc 📷 🏠
General	🛏 P 🔥 🍴 🎮 ⬆ ✳
Leisure	🏊 🏋 ⛳
Rooms	🛏 S ☕ 🍴 🔥

Payment Credit/debit cards, cash/cheques, euros

Discover Britain's heritage

Our travel map and guide is perfectly tailored to your needs. Discover the history and beauty of over 250 of Britain's best-known historic houses, castles, gardens and smaller manor houses. You can purchase Britain's Historic Houses and Gardens – Guide and Map from good bookshops and online at visitbritaindirect.com

At-a-glance symbols are explained on the flap inside the back cover.

LONDON SW7   HOTEL

Holiday Inn London – Kensington Forum

B&B per room per night
d £99.00–£244.00

97 Cromwell Road, London SW7 4DN   **t** 0870 400 9100
f (020) 7373 1448
e hikensingtonforum@ihg.com   **w** holiday-inn.co.uk

Awaiting
NAS rating

Access ☺ ▥ abc ▨ ⚶ ♿

General ⟆ P♿ ⚒♥ ⛄⊡ ✿

Rooms ▦ ▢ ⑤ ♿ ⛛

Payment Credit/debit cards,
cash/cheques, euros

Large, contemporary hotel in the heart of the Royal Borough of Kensington and Chelsea, providing excellent access to many of London's attractions. Eight newly refurbished bedrooms specially designed for disabled guests, one with a hoist. Easy access to bar, restaurant and conference facilities with accessible washroom. Auxiliary aids on request.

open All year
bedrooms 618 double, 284 twin, 4 suites
bathrooms All en suite

Rail: Victoria (15-minute taxi). Underground: Gloucester Road. Air: within an hour of London's airports. Entrance on Courtfield Gardens.

Bank holiday
dates for your diary

holiday	2008	2009
New Year's Day	1 January	1 January
January Bank Holiday (Scotland)	2 January	2 January
Good Friday	21 March	10 April
Easter Monday (England & Wales)	24 March	13 April
Early May Bank Holiday	5 May	4 May
Spring Bank Holiday	26 May	25 May
Summer Bank Holiday (Scotland)	4 August	3 August
Summer Bank Holiday (England & Wales)	25 August	31 August
Christmas Day	25 December	25 December
Boxing Day Holiday	26 December	28 December

LONDON WC1N | **HOTEL**

Holiday Inn London Bloomsbury

B&B per room per night
d £85.00–£250.00

Coram Street, London WC1N 1HT **t** 0870 400 9222 **f** (020) 7713 5954
e reservations-bloomsbury@ihg.com **w** holiday-inn.com/bloomsbury

Awaiting
NAS rating

Access ☺ 🍴 .: ☒ 🛬 🅰

General 🗝 P♿ ⚬ 🍽 🧺 🔲 ❄

Rooms 📺 Ⓢ 📶 🥂 🎨

Payment Credit/debit cards

Winners of the Best Disabled Facilities award 2007 – Accessibility for All – Meetings and Incentive Travel Awards.

A modern and stylish hotel in London's West End, perfectly located for all of your leisure and business needs. Recently refurbished accessible bedrooms with fully adapted low-level bathrooms. Wide variety of food and drink options – Junction Restaurant, Junction Bar, Callaghan's Irish Pub and 24-hour room service.

open All year
bedrooms 199 double, 84 twin, 26 family, 2 suites
bathrooms All en suite

Nearest tube station Russell Square (Piccadilly Line). 10-minute walk from King's Cross. 18 miles from Heathrow. See website for further directions.

SELSEY, West Sussex Map ref 2C3 | **SELF CATERING**

Seagulls, Selsey

Units **1**
Sleeps **2–6**

Low season per wk
Min £235.00
High season per wk
Max £435.00

Awaiting
NAS rating

contact Gail Lewis, PO Box 36, Cowbridge CF71 7GB **t** 08456 584478
f (01446) 775060 **e** selfcatering@johngrooms.org.uk **w** groomsholidays.org.uk

Bungalow, facing the sea at Selsey Bill, designed and equipped for disabled people. Lounge, kitchen and three bedrooms. Electric hoist, roll-in shower and shower-chair available. Ramp to beach.
open All year
nearest shop 2 miles
nearest pub 2 miles

Access abc 🛬 🅰

General 🗝 P 🍴

Unit ♿ 📺 🍴 🔲 📻 🛁 👕 🎨 🛒 🖼 ❄

Payment Credit/debit cards, cash/cheques, euros

To your credit

If you book by phone you may be asked for your credit card number. If so, it is advisable to check the proprietor's policy in case you have to cancel your reservation at a later date.

At-a-glance symbols are explained on the flap inside the back cover.

Photography: Paul Glendell/English Nature

Immerse yourself in natural beauty in the heart of London

THE ROYAL PARKS

www.royalparks.org.uk

London's Personal Space

DisabledGo guides are available on the website

Bushy Park   The Green Park   Greenwich Park   Hyde Park   Kensington Gardens
The Regent's Park (with Primrose Hill)   Richmond Park   St James's Park

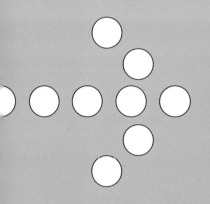

Your journey just got easier

Our new trains now have designated wheelchair spaces, priority seating, tactile surfaces, contrasting colours and on-board announcements.

If your require assistance please pre-book by calling the Assisted Travel freephone number below so that we can be there for you.

While you're there, why not, enquire about rail discounts with the Disabled Person Railcard.

Assisted Travel **0800 783 45 24**
or visit **www.southeasternrailway.co.uk/passengerservices**

southeastern

All day park and ride for £2

Operating hours:

Monday to Saturday from 7am to 7.30pm (from New Dover Road, Sturry Road and Wincheap)

Sunday from 10am to 6pm (from New Dover Road only)

Price is per vehicle and allows the driver and up to six passengers unlimited journeys on all Park and Ride bus services.

Each bus has low floor, easy access suitable for wheelchair users. There are disabled parking spaces, disabled toilets and a waiting room for your comfort at each site and buses run approximately every eight minutes. Each Park and Ride site has staff present during opening hours to help with any questions or problems.

For more information please speak to site staff, call Parking Services on 01227 862 429 or visit www.canterbury.gov.uk/parkandride

Parkand**Ride**
straight into the heart of the city

CANTERBURY
TRAVELWISE.

CANTERBURY
CITY COUNCIL

BRITISH TRANSPORT POLICE

Every day, millions of people travel by train – very few become victims of crime.

Wherever you travel on a mainline train, the London Underground, or Docklands Light Railway, the officers of British Transport Police are there to protect and assist you.

Should you need to contact the police in an emergency, please
- ask any member of the rail staff to contact us;
- call freephone 0800 40 50 40; or
- dial 999

If you would like to know more about British Transport Police, or receive a copy of our *Travel Wise* leaflet, write to:

Media Relations
British Transport Police
25 Camden Road
London
NW1 9LN

Phone: 020 7388 7541

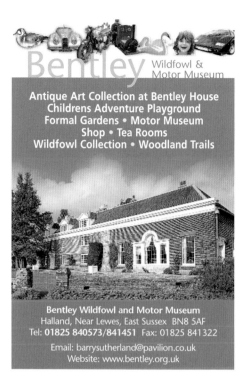
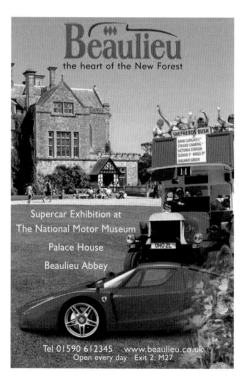

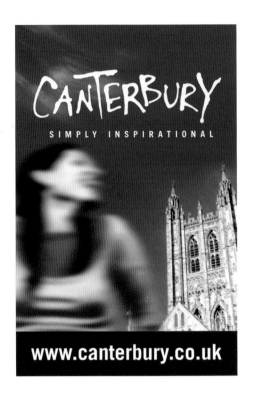

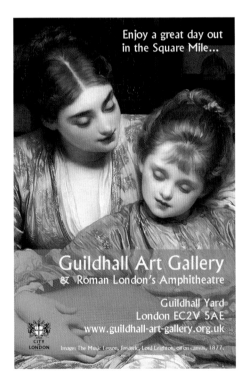

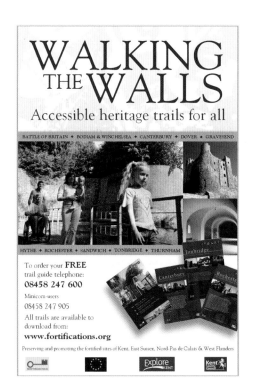

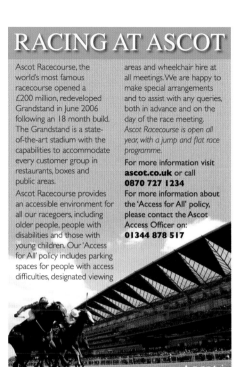

RACING AT ASCOT

Ascot Racecourse, the world's most famous racecourse opened a £200 million, redeveloped Grandstand in June 2006 following an 18 month build. The Grandstand is a state-of-the-art stadium with the capabilities to accommodate every customer group in restaurants, boxes and public areas.

Ascot Racecourse provides an accessible environment for all our racegoers, including older people, people with disabilities and those with young children. Our 'Access for All' policy includes parking spaces for people with access difficulties, designated viewing areas and wheelchair hire at all meetings. We are happy to make special arrangements and to assist with any queries, both in advance and on the day of the race meeting. *Ascot Racecourse is open all year, with a jump and flat race programme.*

For more information visit **ascot.co.uk** or call **0870 727 1234**

For more information about the 'Access for All' policy, please contact the Ascot Access Officer on: **01344 878 517**

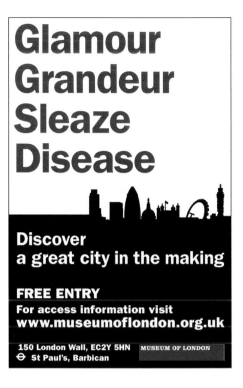

Glamour
Grandeur
Sleaze
Disease

**Discover
a great city in the making**

FREE ENTRY
For access information visit
www.museumoflondon.org.uk

150 London Wall, EC2Y 5HN   MUSEUM OF LONDON
St Paul's, Barbican

BLOOD BLITZ BANANAS

MUSEUM IN DOCKLANDS

How the world came to the East End

**For access information visit
www.museumindocklands.org.uk**

KIDS GO FREE   Canary Wharf   West India Quay
West India Quay, London E14 4AL   Registered charity number: 1060415

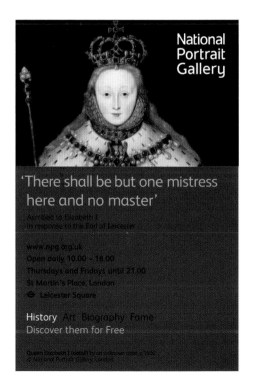

National Portrait Gallery

'There shall be but one mistress here and no master'

Ascribed to Elizabeth I
in response to the Earl of Leicester

www.npg.org.uk
Open daily 10.00 – 18.00
Thursdays and Fridays until 21.00
St Martin's Place, London
Leicester Square

History Art Biography Fame
Discover them for Free

Queen Elizabeth I (detail) by an unknown artist, c.1600
© National Portrait Gallery, London

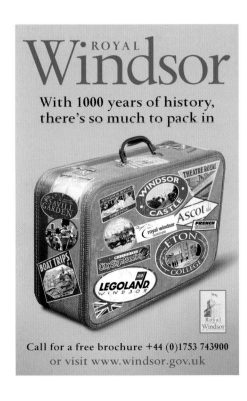

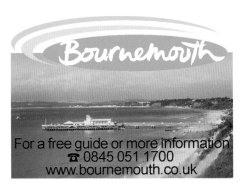

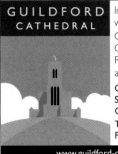
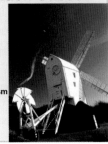

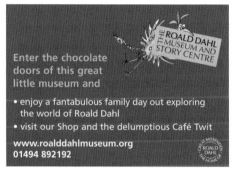

Scotland

Edinburgh from Calton Hill

Kelvingrove Museum, Glasgow

Scotland the **brave**

Dramatic landscapes and mist on the lochs. Or world-class shopping and an unrivalled arts festival. Can you stay the course on the Malt Whisky Trail? **Rediscover yourself in some of Europe's finest landscapes and enjoy a leisurely break or immerse yourself in history and culture.**

Southern delights

Wherever your journey in Scotland takes you, you're in for a treat. For the perfect escape from modern life, start with the magical corner of Dumfries and Galloway. Walk along deserted beaches where Robert Burns journeyed on horseback to catch whisky smugglers or stroll through the rugged grandeur of the Galloway Forest Park, 300 square miles of forest, moorland and lochs. Admire the ancient ruined castles and monuments that set the imagination alight with their whispered hints of what life used to be like. Linger in the Borders to explore the dignified ruins of once-powerful abbeys or follow in the footsteps of Rob Roy and Walter Scott through the Trossachs – heather-clad peaks know as The Highlands in Miniature. Potter around picturesque fishing villages in the Kingdom of Fife or head for Stirling and the battlefield at

> A unique country of soaring peaks, sparkling lochs and fairytale castles

Bannockburn where Robert the Bruce defeated the English. One of Scotland's most sacred sites can be found on the Isle of Iona: take the ferry from Mull and experience first-hand the spiritual atmosphere of Iona Abbey and Monastery.

It's another world

If it's drama you're after, venture north for the Highlands, a vast swathe of untamed wilderness where land and sea collide to create stunning perspectives. Get lucky and you may spot dolphins, whales, eagles, deer, otters and much more besides.

Urquhart Castle overlooking Loch Ness

For stunning views, fascinating history and an opportunity to sight the Loch Ness monster take a trip to Urquhart Castle.

Escape to the islands to truly experience another world. Dreamy beaches are found in the Outer Hebrides and puffins by the million await bird-watchers in Shetland. Folk music draws the finest performers to Orkney. Whilst on the isle take time to visit Skara Brae – the Neolithic ruins dating back more than 4,500 years – and spot auks, kittiwakes and rare birds of prey. Retrace the steps of Sir Walter Scott to the Isle of Skye for more stunning mountain peaks and a visit to Dunvegan Castle.

The Malt Whisky Trail

Piper at Eilean Donan Castle, Highlands

Inset pictures
Fly fishing on the River Tay; Ring of Brodgar, Orkney; Highland cow, Glencoe; Deep Sea World, Fife

City lights

Scotland's great cities beckon. In the capital, Edinburgh, follow the cobbled 'Royal Mile' from the ancient castle, which dominates the skyline, to Holyrood Palace. Visit in August to join in the celebrated arts and fringe festivals and enjoy the pomp and splendour of the Edinburgh Military Tattoo as it lights up the castle esplanade. For a modern day experience explore the extremes of the planet – from the Big Bang, through erupting volcanoes to the chill or polar ice – at Our Dynamic Earth. Beyond the city, explore the beautiful Lothian countryside dotted with historic homes and castles, and discover Rosslyn chapel associated with Dan Brown's best seller, The Da Vinci Code.

Glasgow, Scotland's largest city, has reinvented itself to become one of Europe's great cultural capitals with more than 30 art galleries and museums and an annual programme of performing arts and festivals. Attractions like the Lighthouse, the Burrell Collection, the Gallery of Modern Art and the Kelvingrove Art Gallery and Museum reflect the Glaswegian passion for art. Click your fingers to the music at the International Jazz Festival at the end of June or join in

the celebrations at Celtic Connections – the world's largest winter festival of celtic music and culture in January. Shop 'til you drop with outlets to rival London's best then dine in style – you'll find an abundance of art nouveau brasseries, sophisticated restaurants and cafe bars that will seduce the most adventurous gourmet.

Follow the trail

Aberdeen is Scotland's third largest city, and has one of its most enchanting skylines, while the Old Town has a magical air of time gone by. It's a great place from which to explore the treasures on its doorstep: sample the 'water of life' and visit the eight distilleries on the world's only Malt Whisky Trail, or follow The Castle Trail to visit thirteen gems including the fairy tale magic of Craigievar, the rugged splendour of Kildrummy Castle ruins, and the elegant timelessness of Leith Hall. If you're visiting Orkney, follow the Orkney Craft Trail which includes a range of arts and crafts including contemporary textile and the world-renowned Orcadian jewellery.

Let's celebrate

The Scots are fiercely proud of their heritage which they celebrate in a thousand different ways. Hogmanay, Up-Helly-Aa and Burns Night start the year off with a bang and there's traditional music and celebrations every month of the year! During the summer a visit to a Highland game (which now take place throughout Scotland) is a must. Hammer throwing, tug-o-war and tossing the caber combined with colourful Highland dancers, lively pipers and spectacular scenery – it's an experience you'll never forget.

The Highland Games

Scotland
For the holiday of a lifetime

As a destination for the holiday of a lifetime, Scotland is hard to beat. It has inspiring scenery, fascinating castles, historic houses, beautiful gardens, great places to stay, superb food (and whisky!) – and friendly people.

Wherever you go, there are memories waiting to be captured, whether it be a glimpse of a loch-side castle or a carpet of bluebells in a wood; or exploring Edinburgh's historic Old Town; or the National Trust for Scotland's historic houses; or admiring Scotland's awesome mountains and tumbling rivers. Scotland may be a small country but its landscape includes fertile farmlands, wooded glens, rolling hills, seaside villages and market towns, and a good network of roads makes it easy to get around.

When you plan your holiday, remember that, while Edinburgh and Glasgow have museums, art galleries and entertainment in abundance, lots of towns and villages have fine museums and visitor attractions which highlight the local heritage.

Scotland's a land of festivals of all kinds – as well as the famous Edinburgh International Festival, there are film, folk and rock music, science, walking and story-telling festivals, and, of course, the Highland Games.

As well as reflecting Scotland's traditional fare, restaurants and pubs offer an eclectic choice of international cuisine, often using fresh produce from local farms.

Main: Loch Garry, Highlands
Above: Culzean Castle, Ayrshire

Scotland has a well-deserved reputation for the quality of its food – beef, fish, lamb, fresh produce. Enjoy it on your visit.

Spend a week in Scotland and you'll gather memories for a lifetime!

VisitScotland publishes a guide which lists almost 1,100 places to stay and visit, all of them accessible to people with mobility impairments. For information and a free copy of Accessible Scotland, call VisitScotland.com on 0845 22 55 121 (from within the UK), + 44 1506 832 121 (from outside the UK) or 1800 22 55 121 (from the Republic of Ireland); email info@visitscotland.com or check the website visitscotland.com.

Business Tourism: If you are considering Scotland for a meeting or a conference, our city conference centres are wheelchair accessible, with top-class hotels nearby. Check out conventionscotland.com or email businesstourism@visitscotland.com or call + 44 (0) 131 472 2355.

Live it. Visit Scotland.
visitscotland.com 0845 22 55 121
The No.1 booking and information service for Scotland.

Right: Edinburgh Castle
Above right: Threave Gardens, Dumfries and Galloway

Useful regional contacts

For information before you travel, check out the useful regional contacts below. Local Tourist Information Centres will also be able to give you information on accessible attractions and accommodation.

VisitScotland
t 0845 225 5121
w visitscotland.com

British Airports Authority Scotland

Operates three airports in Scotland:
Aberdeen Airport
t 0870 040 0006
w aberdeenairport.com
Edinburgh Airport
t 0870 040 0007
w edinburghairport.com
Glasgow Airport
t 0870 040 0008
w glasgowairport.com
The textphone for all three airports is (0141) 585 6161.

Historic Scotland

Longmore House, Salisbury Place, Edinburgh EH9 1SH
t (0131) 668 8800
w historic-scotland.gov.uk
Produces a free guide with details of facilities for disabled visitors at 70 historic buildings throughout Scotland.

National Trust for Scotland (NTS)

Wemyss House, 28 Charlotte Square, Edinburgh EH2 4ET
t (01331) 243 9300
e information@nts.org.uk
w nts.org.uk

NTS publishes a booklet giving information about accessibility at sites and buildings throughout Scotland.

Scottish Borders Rangers Service

Scottish Borders Rangers Service, Harestances, Ancrum, Jedburgh TD8 6UQ
t 01835 824000
w scotborders.gov.uk
The Rangers Service produces a free booklet, Countryside visits, on places to visit in the Scottish Borders with access for wheelchair users.

VisitScotland

t 0845 2255121
w visitscotland.com
Produces Accessible Scotland, a guide to accessible accommodation and attractions in Scotland.

Tourist Information Centres

When you arrive at your destination, visit a tourist information centre for help with accommodation and information about local attractions and events. Alternatively call **0845 225 5121** or email info@visitscotland.com to receive information and book accommodation before you depart.

Aberdeen	23 Union Street		Dumfries	64 Whitesands
Aberfeldy	The Square		Dunbar*	141 High Street
Aberfoyle	Trossachs Discovery Centre		Dundee	21 Castle Street
Abington	Junction 13, M74 Services		Dunfermline	1 High Street
			Dunkeld	The Cross
Alford*	Old Station Yard		Dunoon	7 Alexandra Parade
Alva	Mill Trail Visitor Centre		Dunvegan	2 Lochside
Anstruther*	Scottish Fisheries Museum		Durness*	Sangomore
Arbroath	Gravesend		Edinburgh	Princess Mall, 3 Princes Street
Ardgartan*	By Arrochar			
Aviemore	Grampian Road		Edinburgh Airport	Main Concourse
Ayr	22 Sandgate		Elgin	17 High Street
Ballater	Station Square		Eyemouth*	Auld Kirk, Manse Road
Balloch*	The Old Station Building		Falkirk	2-4 Glebe Street
Banchory*	Bridge Street		Forres*	116 High Street
Banff*	Collie Lodge		Fort William	Cameron Square
Biggar*	155 High Street		Fraserburgh*	3 Saltoun Square
Blairgowrie	26 Wellmeadow		Gatehouse of Fleet*	Car Park
Bo'ness*	Union Street		Glasgow	11 George Square
Bowmore	The Square		Glasgow Airport	International Arrivals Hall
Braemar	Mar Road		Grantown on Spey*	54 High Street
Brechin*	Pictavia Centre		Gretna	Gretna Gateway Outlet Village
Brodick	The Pier			
Callander*	Rob Roy Centre		Hawick*	Drumlanrig's Tower
Campbeltown	The Pier		Helensburgh*	The Clock Tower
Castlebay*	Main Street		Huntly*	9a The Square
Castle Douglas*	Market Hill Car Park		Inveraray	Front Street
Craignure	The Pier		Inverness	Castle Wynd
Crail*	Crail Museum, 62 Marketgate		Inverurie*	18 High Street
			Jedburgh	Murrays Green
Crathie*	The Car Park		Kelso	The Square
Crieff	High Street		Killin*	Breadalbane Folklore Centre
Daviot Wood*	Picnic Area, A9			
Drumnadrochit	The Car Park		Kinross*	Junction 6, M90
Dufftown*	The Square		Kirkcaldy	339 High Street
Dumbarton	Milton, A82 Northbound		Kirkcudbright	Harbour Square

Kirkwall	6 Broad Street		Pitlochry	22 Atholl Road
Lanark	Horsemarket, Ladyacre Road		Portree	Bayfield Road
			Rothesay	Winter Gardens
Largs*	Main Street		St Andrews	70 Market Street
Lerwick	The Market Cross		Selkirk*	Halliwells House
Linlithgow*	Burgh Halls, The Cross		Stirling	41 Dumbarton Road
Loch Lomond Gateway Centre	Loch Lomond Shores		Stirling (Pirnhall)	Junction 9, M9 Services
Lochboisdale*	Pier Road		Stonehaven*	66 Allardice Street
Lochgilphead*	Lochnell Street		Stornoway	26 Cromwell Street
Lochinver*	Kirk Lane		Stranraer	Burns House, 28 Harbour Street
Lochmaddy*	Pier Road		Stromness	Ferry Terminal Building
Melrose	Abbey Street		Strontian*	Acharacle
Moffat*	Churchgate		Sumburgh	Sumburgh Airport
Newtongrange*	Scottish Mining Museum		Tarbert (Harris)*	Pier Road
Newton Stewart*	Dashwood Square		Tarbert (Loch Fyne)*	Harbour Street
North Berwick	Quality Street		Tarbet (Loch Lomond)*	Main Street
North Kessock*	Car Park, Picnic Site		Thurso*	Riverside Road
Oban	Argyll Square		Tobermory*	The Pier
Paisley	9A Gilmour Street		Tomintoul*	The Square
Peebles	High Street		Tyndrum	Main Street
Perth	West Mill Street		Ullapool	Argyle Street

seasonal opening

Scottish
accessible scheme

All types of accommodation in Scotland are assessed for wheelchair users and those with limited mobility. Accommodation entries include one of the following three mobility symbols.

Category 1

Accessible to a wheelchair user travelling independently.

Category 2

Accessible to a wheelchair user travelling with assistance.

Category 3

Accessible to a wheelchair user able to walk a few paces and up a maximum of three steps.

ABERDEEN, Aberdeenshire Map ref 7D3 　　　　　　　　　**HOTEL**

★★★★★
HOTEL

B&B per room per night
s £140.00–£295.00
d £150.00–£295.00

Marcliffe Hotel and Spa

North Deeside Road, Pitfodels, Aberdeen AB15 9YA **t** (01224) 861000
f (01224) 868860
e info@marcliffe.com **w** marcliffe.com

Access ☺ ▮ ⚘

General 🛏 P♿ ✂ ♨ ▣ ✿

Leisure ▨ 🏋

Rooms ♿ ▢ 📶 🍵 🛁 ▥

Payment Credit/debit cards, cash/cheques, euros

Many spa/food packages available. Check website and call hotel for details. Available all year, book 4 days in advance.

Situated in 11 acres of wooded grounds on the A93 to Royal Deeside, yet only five minutes from city centre. Restaurant specialises in local and Scottish produce. Ideal location for visiting Aberdeen city and shire, including castles, distilleries and many other attractions. Wonderful health, beauty and hair spa now open.

open All year
bedrooms 30 double, 7 twin, 5 suites
bathrooms All en suite

From Aberdeen ringroad A90, turn west on A93 direction Braemar. Hotel 1 mile on right after turning onto A93.

ANNAN, Dumfries & Galloway Map ref 6C3 　　　　　　　**GUEST ACCOMMODATION**

★★
GUEST HOUSE

Rowanbank Guesthouse 20 St Johns Road, Annan DG12 6AW
t (01461) 204200
e rowanbankguests@btconnect.com **w** rowanbankguesthouse.co.uk

---

BALLATER, Aberdeenshire Map ref 7D3 | SELF CATERING

★★★★
SELF CATERING

Units	**4**
Sleeps	**4–6**

Low season per wk
£289.00–£457.00
High season per wk
£467.00–£572.00

Crathie Opportunity Holidays, Crathie, Royal Deeside

Crathie Opportunity Holidays, The Manse Courtyard, Crathie,
Ballater AB35 5UL **t** (013397) 42100 **f** (013397) 42002
e info@crathieholidays.org.uk **w** crathieholidays.org.uk

Access   abc 🐾 ⚠

General   ♿ 🏠 🚗 P ● S

Unit   🛁 ⚙ 🎞 S 🛏 📺 📞 ♨ 🔔
       🍽 🛋 ❄

Payment Credit/debit cards,
cash/cheques

*Short breaks available from Nov-
Mar from £65 per cottage per
night. (excl Christmas and New
Year).*

Four lovely cottages designed
and equipped to the highest
standard of accessibility. Facilities
include wheel-in-shower, height-
adjustable sink, Clos-o-Mat toilet
and adjustable bed. We also have
a range of other equipment
available. In the heart of the
Cairngorms National Park and
within easy reach of the famous
whisky and castle trails.
open All year
nearest shop 1 mile
nearest pub 4 miles

*Crathie is in the heart of Royal
Deeside situated halfway
between Ballater and Braemar on
the A93, approximately 50 miles
west of Aberdeen.*

Accessible accommodation in Scotland

Establishments in Scotland are awarded one or more
of three mobility categories. If you have visual or
hearing requirements, please contact the
accommodation directly.

At-a-glance symbols are explained on the flap inside the back cover.

DUMFRIES, Dumfries & Galloway Map ref 6C3 — SELF CATERING

SELF CATERING

Units	**1**
Sleeps	**1–4**

Low season per wk
£240.00–£300.00
High season per wk
£300.00–£450.00

Ae Farm Cottages, Dumfries

contact David & Gill Stewart, Ae Farm Cottages, Gubhill Farm, Ae, Dumfries DG1 1RL **t** (01387) 860648
e gill@gubhill.co.uk **w** aefarmcottages.co.uk

General

Unit

Payment Cash/cheques, euros

Ground-floor rooms with adjacent parking and a gentle ramp.

Lovely cosy farm cottage with a country view in the peaceful Southern Uplands of Scotland. It has two bedrooms, sky hook and bars by wc, roll-in shower with fold-down stool, low-level kitchen surface with knee spaces. Children and pets welcome. Farm and wildlife aplenty. Environmentally friendly.

open All year
nearest shop 10 miles
nearest pub 2 miles

From Dumfries, A701 towards Moffat approx 7 miles. Follow Ae village/forest signs on left. Pass village 2 miles. Straight on, river on right. White farm on right 2 miles.

DUMFRIES, Dumfries & Galloway Map ref 6C3 — SELF CATERING

★★★–★★★★★
SELF CATERING

Nunland Country Holidays, Dumfries
t (01387) 730214 **f** (01387) 730364
e mail@nunland.co.uk **w** nunland.co.uk

DUNBAR, East Lothian Map ref 6D2 — CAMPING & CARAVANNING

★★★★
HOLIDAY PARK

Belhaven Bay Caravan Park Belhaven Bay, Dunbar EH42 1TS
t (01368) 865956 **f** (01368) 865022
e belhaven@meadowhead.co.uk **w** meadowhead.co.uk

EDINBURGH, Edinburgh Map ref 6C2 — CAMPING & CARAVANNING

★★★★
HOLIDAY PARK

Mortonhall Caravan Park 38 Mortonhall Gate, Frogston Road East, Edinburgh EH16 6TJ **t** (0131) 664 1533 **f** (0131) 664 5387
e mortonhall@meadowhead.co.uk **w** meadowhead.co.uk

GAIRLOCH, Highland Map ref 7B2 — SELF CATERING

★★★
SELF CATERING

Willow Croft, Gairloch **t** (01445) 712448
e bigsand@waitrose.com **w** sites.ecosse.net/iml

GATEHOUSE OF FLEET, Dumfries & Galloway Map ref 6B3 — SELF CATERING

★★–★★★★★
SELF CATERING

Rusko Holidays, Gatehouse of Fleet

Rusko Holidays, Gatehouse of Fleet, Castle Douglas DG7 2BS
t (01557) 814215 e info@ruskoholidays.co.uk w ruskoholidays.co.uk

Units **2**
Sleeps **1–6**

Low season per wk
£216.00–£763.00
High season per wk
£354.00–£1,278.00

Accessible luxury haven in the hills and charming cottage near historic town and coast. Ideally situated amid magnificent scenery for exploring this beautiful and unspoilt area of Scotland.
open All year
nearest shop 4 miles
nearest pub 4 miles

Access abc 🐾
General 🎠 ▥ 🔥 P Ⓢ
Leisure ✎
Unit ♿ 🛏 Ⓢ 🖥 💻 ◉ ▦ 📻 📺
📼 🏠 ✿

Payment Credit/debit cards, cash/cheques

HOY, Orkney Islands Map ref 7C1 — SELF CATERING

★★★
SELF CATERING

Old Hall Cottage, Hoy

t (01856) 701213 e oldhall@freeuk.com w oldhallcottage.co.uk

Units **1**
Sleeps **1–6**

Low season per wk
£245.00
High season per wk
£315.00

Newly renovated self-catering cottage in extensive gardens. Tranquil location with panoramic views over Scapa Flow and Pentland Firth. One double (full disabled access), one triple. Special interest breaks. Assisted wheelchair access.
open All year
nearest shop 2 miles
nearest pub 1 mile

Access 🐾 🏔
General 🎠 P ✂ ◉ Ⓢ
Unit ♿ 🛏 💻 🍳 ▦ 📻 📺 🏠 ✿

Payment Cash/cheques

ISLE OF SEIL, Argyll and Bute Map ref 6A1 — SELF CATERING

★★★★
SELF CATERING

Oban Seil Croft Cottages, Isle of Seil, Oban t (01852) 300457 f (01852) 300457
e obanseilcroft@btinternet.com w obanseilcroft.co.uk

ISLE OF SKYE

See under Portree, Waternish

KELSO, Scottish Borders Map ref 6D2 — SELF CATERING

★★★–★★★★★
SELF CATERING

Edenmouth Farm Holiday Cottages, Nr Kelso

contact Mr & Mrs O'Driscoll, Edenmouth Holiday Cottages, Edenmouth Farm, Kelso TD5 7QB t (01890) 830391 e edenmouth.odris@virgin.net
w edenmouth.co.uk

Units **3**
Sleeps **1–6**

Low season per wk
£200.00–£400.00
High season per wk
£250.00–£500.00

Quality single-storey cottages set in farmland three miles from Kelso. 300yds from River Tweed. No steps. All bedrooms have en suites.
open All year
nearest shop 3 miles
nearest pub 2 miles

Access 🐾
General 🎠 ▥ 🔥 P ✂ ◉ Ⓢ
Unit ♿ 🛏 ▥ Ⓢ 💻 ◉ ▦ 🏠 🏠
✿

Payment Cash/cheques

At-a-glance symbols are explained on the flap inside the back cover.

NORTH BERWICK, East Lothian Map ref 6D2 — CAMPING & CARAVANNING

★★★★★
HOLIDAY PARK

Tantallon Caravan Park Dunbar Road, North Berwick EH39 5NJ
t (01620) 893348 f (01620) 895623
e tantallon@meadowhead.co.uk w meadowhead.co.uk

ORMSARY, Argyll and Bute Map ref 6A2 — SELF CATERING

★★★
SELF CATERING

Units **1**
Sleeps **11**
Low season per wk
£710.00–£865.00
High season per wk
£1,100.00–£1,350.00

Barnlongart, Lochgilphead
Ormsary Estate Holidays t (01880) 770222 e enquiries@ormsary.co.uk
w ormsary.com

Single-storey, spacious, well-equipped lodge, delightful views, own woodland setting, close to sandy beach. Six bedrooms, six bathrooms (four en suite), full disabled shower room with facilities for wheelchair use.
open All year
nearest shop 12 miles
nearest pub 6 miles

General

Unit

Payment Credit/debit cards, cash/cheques

PEEBLES, Scottish Borders Map ref 6C2 — HOTEL

★★★★
COUNTRY HOUSE HOTEL

B&B per room per night
s £165.00–£325.00
d £220.00–£375.00
HB per person per night
£145.00–£225.00

Cringletie House Hotel
Edinburgh Road, Peebles EH45 8PL t (01721) 725750
f (01721) 725751
e enquiries@cringletie.com w cringletie.com

Access

General

Rooms

Payment Credit/debit cards, cash/cheques

Exceptionally well adapted room for wheelchair users and guests with impaired hearing. Telephone for best available rate and special offers.

A fabulous Scottish baronial castle in stunning surroundings. 28 acres of gardens and woodlands with waterfall and paths throughout. 17thC walled kitchen garden to supply the restaurant kitchen. French dining at its best in the impressive Sutherland dining room with handpainted ceiling.
open All year
bedrooms 7 double, 5 twin, 1 suite
bathrooms All en suite

From Edinburgh City Bypass take A702 (Carlisle); then A703 (Peebles); through Penicuik and Eddleston; 2 miles south of Eddleston on right hand side.

PENCAITLAND, East Lothian Map ref 6C2 — SELF CATERING

★★★★
SELF CATERING

Units **1**
Sleeps **10–12**

Low season per wk
£1,100.00–£1,600.00
High season per wk
£1,500.00–£3,000.00

Winton Cottage, Pencaitland

contact Morag Ramus, Winton House, Pencaitland EH34 5AT
t (01875) 340222
e morag@wintonhouse.co.uk **w** wintonhouse.co.uk

Access 🐾

General 🐕 ▥ ⚱ P ✂ ◉ Ⓢ

Unit 🛁 ▥ Ⓖ ▣ ▱ ☎ 🗑 ❑ ❑ 🔥 ❋

Payment Credit/debit cards,
cash/cheques

*Ground-floor bedroom and
private bathroom with disabled
access. All towels, linen,
bathrobes and slippers included.
Many extras.*

This historic self-catering cottage
has an abundance of character
and is only half an hour's drive
from Edinburgh. Recently
refurbished to a high accessible
standard offering five luxurious
bedrooms and bathrooms, a large
dining room opening to the
secluded south-facing garden,
drawing room with open fire and
games room.

open All year
nearest shop 1 mile
nearest pub 1 mile

*From Edinburgh north follow city
bypass to A1, turn off to Tranent
then follow the B6355 to
Pencaitland.*

PORTREE, Highland Map ref 7B3 — SELF CATERING

★★★
SELF CATERING
♿

No 6 Achachork, Portree, Isle of Skye
t (01478) 613167
e no6chalet@aol.com **w** no6achachork.co.uk

SPEAN BRIDGE, Highland Map ref 6B1 — HOTEL

★★★★
SMALL HOTEL
♿

Old Pines Hotel and Restaurant Gairlochy Road, By Spean Bridge PH34 4EG
t (01397) 712324
e enquiries@oldpines.co.uk **w** oldpines.co.uk

THURSO, Highland Map ref 7C2 — HOTEL

★★★
SMALL HOTEL
♿

Park Hotel Oldfield, Thurso KW14 8RE
t (01847) 893251 **f** (01847) 804044
e easyaccess@parkhotelthurso.co.uk **w** parkhotelthurso.co.uk

At-a-glance symbols are explained on the flap inside the back cover.

★★★★
SELF CATERING

| Units | 1 |
| Sleeps | 2–8 |

Low season per wk
£500.00–£750.00
High season per wk
£750.00–£960.00

La Bergerie, Waternish, Isle of Skye

contact Mrs C Macleod, 33 Lochbay, Waternish, Isle of Skye IV55 8GD
t (01470) 592282   **f** (01470) 592282   **e** enquiries@la-bergerie-skye.co.uk
w la-bergerie-skye.co.uk

Large cottage accommodation built in local stone, sleeping eight people. Fully adapted for four wheelchair-users and their carers. Fabulous sea views, three twin bedrooms, one double, three bathrooms. Open fire.
open All year
nearest shop 6 miles
nearest pub 1 mile

General 🛏 🏠 ♿ P ✗ Ⓢ

Unit ♿ 🏭 📺 📠 💻 🔌 ⭕ 🧹 📶
📺 🔋 ❄

Payment Cash/cheques

Inverclyde is an area of unrivalled beauty, situated along the broad coastal reaches of the River Clyde, with breathtaking views to the Argyll Hills and Scottish Highlands.

Its moorlands, hills and lochs are a haven for the rarest species of Wildlife while its historical attractions celebrate an influential maritime history and industrial past.

A visit to Inverclyde is a visit to remember.

www.inverclyde.gov.uk

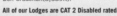

Don't forget www.

Web addresses throughout this guide are shown without the prefix www. Please include www. in the address line of your browser. If a web address does not follow this style it is shown in full.

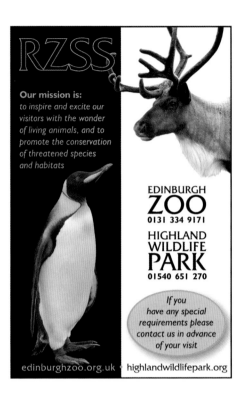

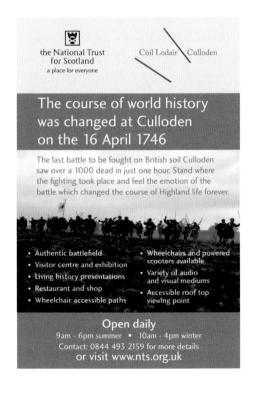

Northern Ireland

Travel a land of legends and folklore and let the ancient tale of Ireland unfold. A tale older than the pyramids of Egypt, full of turmoil and romance, set against a spectacular backdrop of breathtaking scenery.

Discover the natural wonder of the Giant's Causeway in County Antrim, touch the history embedded in the ancient 'Walls of Derry' and visit the magical region of the Kingdoms of Down, famous for the stunning Mountains of Mourne, its dramatic coastline and acres of forest and parks. Experience warm hospitality, delicious traditional dishes and the universal language of music performed anywhere and everywhere!

Above
Carrick a Rede, County Antrim

Wales

Cregennan Lakes and the mountains of Snowdonia beyond

Caernarfon Castle illuminated at dusk

Land of the ancient **Celts**

For a small country Wales is big on things to see and do. To start with it has three National Parks, each one featuring very different landscapes, and a turbulent history which comes alive in its many castles. Search out Wales' fascinating industrial heritage and discover its myths and legends.

Nature at its best

In big, bold Snowdonia National Park ascend to the summit of Mount Snowdon on the little mountain railway for dazzling views across North Wales. In the south, travel in style on a vintage steam locomotive through beautiful Brecon Beacons – you can board the Brecon Mountain Railway near Merthyr Tydfil. Wales has 750 miles of coastline so it's not surprising that it offers a succession of award-winning beaches, bays, headlands and harbours. Let the sea air fill your lungs and the wildlife capture your attention in Pembrokeshire where you'll find Britain's only coastal-based National Park, or discover the hundreds of miles of seashore which have been declared Areas of Outstanding Natural Beauty and Heritage Coast. Take a boat from New Quay or St Davids to spot Bottlenose dolphins along the coast of Cardigan Bay.

Cybermen and science

Europe's youngest capital and home of Dr Who, Cardiff is just a stone's throw from the Beacons' wide open spaces. It's cosmopolitan, lively and busy. Join in the cafe culture and don't miss the stunning new waterfront along Cardiff Bay. Make sure you visit the fabulous city-centre castle then get back to the future, face-to-face with a cyberman and a dalek, at the interactive Dr Who exhibition in the Red Dragon Centre.

Take a trip to Swansea for the largest indoor market in Wales, where you can sample and buy local delicacies such as cockles, laverbread and traditional welshcakes. Then set your course for the Maritime Quarter to visit Wales' newest museum, the National Waterfront Museum. Pushing the boundaries of technology in an interactive interpretation of Wales' industry and innovation, it showcases new technologies in science, manufacturing and medicine.

Great creations

Clough Williams-Ellis aimed to integrate man-made beauty with natural beauty. See the results for yourself at Portmeirion Village and Gardens where a romantic Italian-style village is set in sub-tropical woodlands. Pick up a piece of the attractive Portmeirion Pottery whilst you're there. Make a bee-line for one of the most fascinating gardens in the UK – The National Botanic Garden of Wales in Carmarthenshire where The Great Glasshouse protects and conserves some of the most endangered plants on the planet. Want to entertain the kids? Set them on the Childen's Puzzle Trail at dramatic Lake Vyrnwy, west of Welshpool, where they can seek out beautifully crafted wooden animals hidden in the trees. Surrounded by mountains, its dark waters, forested shores and gothic water tower could be a scene from a Transylvanian fairytale.

Traditional Welsh festivities

Brecon Beacons, Powys

Inset pictures
Hay on Wye, Powys;
boats moored in the
habour at Aberaeron,
Ceredigion; Bodnant
Gardens, Conwy;
Millennium Centre,
Cardiff

Past and future

Wales can stake a strong claim to King Arthur. In the south, Caerleon's magnificent Roman amphitheatre is said to have served as Arthur's Round Table and the castle above Llangollen in the north is the reputed hiding place for the Holy Grail. Discover the legends for yourself. Castles, of course, are what Wales does very well, ranging from Harlech, Beaumaris, Caernarfon and Conwy, part of Edward I's mighty iron ring of castles in the north, to romantic hilltop fortresses such as Carreg Cennen near Llandeilo. If you want to venture inside do check access before you go. Experience the country's fascinating industrial heritage first-hand in places like the Llechwedd Slate Caverns and the Big Pit at Blaenavon where you can go underground and find out exactly what it was like to work there.

> A timeless country of epic mountains and lush green valleys, spectacular coastline and fascinating legends

For all its history, Wales doesn't live in the past. It's an exciting, forward-looking country, full of discovery and adventure. At the Centre for Alternative Technology in mid Wales fill your head with ideas of how to conserve the earth's natural resources: wind, water and solar power, energy conservation, organic growing and more. Or test out the interactive, hands-on exhibits at Techniquest, an amazing science centre, and see stars in the planetarium.

The National Botanic Gardens of Wales, Carmarthenshire

It's all happening

There's plenty going on all over Wales. Begin by checking out sporting fixtures and concerts at Cardiff's Millennium Stadium. Take the tour to imagine being greeted by 72,500 people as you exit the tunnel or see how it feels to sit in the Queen's seat. Give your taste buds a treat in September at the Abergavenny Food Festival or at Caerphilly's Big Cheese extravaganza in July. If words are your inspiration, celebrate great writing in every medium at the world-famous Hay Festival at the end of May.

As you would expect, there is music everywhere. Get with the beat at the renowned Brecon International Festival of Jazz or immerse yourself in all things Welsh at the National Eisteddfod, both in August. For ballet, opera, dance and musicals you can't do better than that the Wales Millennium Centre.

Useful regional contacts

For information before you travel, check out the useful regional contacts below. Local Tourist Information Centres will also be able to give you information on accessible attractions and accommodation.

VisitWales
t 0870 830 0306
t 0870 121 1255 (textphone)
w visitwales.com

Brecon Beacons National Park Authority

Plas y Ffynnon, Cambrian Way, Brecon LD3 7DP
t (01874) 624437
e enquiries@breconbeacons.org
w breconbeacons.org
Produces Places to Visit With Easier Access, a guide to short walks and trails, and places of interest suitable for people with limited mobility.

British Red Cross North Wales Branch

Oxford Road, Llandudno LL30 1DH
t (01492) 877885
Provides wheelchairs and equipment on short-term loan across North Wales, and transport and escort services in North West Wales only.

Cadw: Welsh Historic Monuments

Welsh Assembly Government, Plas Carew,Unit 5/7 Cefn Coed, Parc Nantgarw, Cardiff CF15 7QQ
t (01443) 336000
e Cadw@Wales.gsi.gov.uk
w cadw.wales.gov.uk
Responsible for protecting the built heritage of Wales, including over 130 historic sites. A guide to Cadw

sites for disabled visitors is available to download from the website.

Disability Wales

Wrenddu Court, Caerphilly Business Park, Van Road, Caerphilly CF83 3ED
t (029) 2088 7325
t 0800 731 6282 (Helpline Mon-Fri 10am-1pm)
w disabilitywales.org
A national association of disability groups in Wales

Pembrokeshire Coast National Park Authority

Llanion Park, Pembroke Dock SA72 6DY
t 0845 345 7245
e info@permbrokeshirecoast.org.uk
w pembrokeshirecoast.org.uk
Produces Easy Access Routes, a guide to 20 walks on the coast, along with other information about the area, views and beaches. Available by post or to download from the website.

Snowdonia National Park Authority

Penrhyndeudraeth LL48 6LF
t (01766) 770274
e parc@eryri-npa.gov.uk
Produces Enjoying Eryri, a booklet, available in print or braille, on the national park and attractions in Snowdonia.

Tourist Information Centres

When you arrive at your destination, visit a tourist information centre for help with accommodation and information about local attractions and events, or email your request before you go.

Aberaeron	The Quay	(01545) 570602	aberaerontic@ceredigion.gov.uk
Aberdyfi*	The Wharf Gardens	(01654) 767321	tic.aberdyfi@eryri-npa.gov.uk
Abergavenny	Monmouth Road	(01873) 853254	abergavenny.tic@breconbeacons.org
Aberystwyth	Terrace Road	(01970) 612125	aberystwythtic@ceredigion.gov.uk
Bala*	Pensarn Road	(01678) 521021	bala.tic@gwynedd.gov.uk
Bangor*	Deiniol Road	(01248) 352786	bangor.tic@gwynedd.gov.uk
Barmouth*	Station Road	(01341) 280787	barmouth.tic@gwynedd.gov.uk
Barry Island*	The Promenade	(01446) 747171	tourism@valeofglamorgan.gov.uk
Beddgelert*	Canolfan Hebog	(01766) 890615	tic.beddgelert@eryri-npa.gov.uk
Betws y Coed	Royal Oak Stables	(01690) 710426	tic.byc@eryri-npa.gov.uk
Blaenau Ffestiniog*	High Street	(01766) 830360	tic.blaenau@eryri-npa.gov.uk
Blaenavon*	North Street	(01495) 792615	blaenavon.ironworks@btopenworld.com
Borth*	Cambrian Terrace	(01970) 871174	borthtic@ceredigion.gov.uk
Brecon	Cattle Market Car Park	(01874) 622485	brectic@powys.gov.uk
Bridgend	McArthur Glen Design Outlet (Wales)	(01656) 654906	bridgendtic@bridgend.gov.uk
Builth Wells	The Groe Car Park	(01982) 553307	builtic@powys.gov.uk
Caerleon	5 High Street	(01633) 422656	caerleon.tic@newport.gov.uk
Caernarfon	Castle Street	(01286) 672232	caernarfon.tic@gwynedd.gov.uk
Caerphilly	Lower Twyn Square	(029) 2088 0011	tic@caerphilly.gov.uk
Cardiff	The Old Library	0870 121 1258	visitor@cardiff.gov.uk
Cardigan	Bath House Road	(01239) 613230	cardigantic@ceredigion.gov.uk
Carmarthen	113 Lammas Street	(01267) 231557	carmarthentic@carmarthenshire.gov.uk
Chepstow	Bridge Street	(01291) 623772	chepstow.tic@monmouthshire.gov.uk
Conwy	Castle Buildings	(01492) 592248	conwytic@conwy.gov.uk
Dolgellau	Eldon Square	(01341) 422888	tic.dolgellau@eryri-npa.gov.uk
Fishguard Harbour	The Parrog	(01348) 872037	fishguardharbour.tic@pembrokeshire.gov.uk
Fishguard Town	Town Hall, Market Square	(01348) 873484	fishguard.tic@pembrokeshire.gov.uk
Harlech*	High Street	(01766) 780658	tic.harlech@eryri-npa.gov.uk
Haverfordwest	Old Bridge	(01437) 763110	haverfordwest.tic@pembrokeshire.gov.uk
Holyhead	Terminal 1	(01407) 762622	holyhead@nwtic.com
Kilgetty*	Kingsmoor Common	(01834) 814161	info@kilgettytic.fsnet.co.uk
Knighton	West Street	(01547) 529424	oda@offasdyke.demon.co.uk

Lake Vyrnwy*	Vyrnwy Craft Workshops	(01691) 870346	laktic@powys.gov.uk
Llanberis	41b High Street	(01286) 870765	llanberis.tic@gwynedd.gov.uk
Llandovery	Kings Road	(01550) 720693	llandovery.ic@breconbeacons.org
Llandrindod Wells	Memorial Gardens	(01597) 822600	llandtic@powys.gov.uk
Llandudno	1-2 Chapel Street	(01492) 876413	llandudnotic@conwy.gov.uk
Llanfairpwllgwyngyll	Station Site	(01248) 713177	llanfairpwll@nwtic.com
Llangollen	Castle Street	(01978) 860828	llangollen@nwtic.com
Machynlleth	Canolfan Owain Glyndwr	(01654) 702401	mactic@powys.gov.uk
Merthyr Tydfil	14a Glebeland Street	(01685) 379884	tic@merthyr.gov.uk
Milford Haven*	94 Charles Street	(01646) 690866	milford.tic@pembrokeshire.gov.uk
Mold	Earl Road	(01352) 759331	mold@nwtic.com
Monmouth	Agincourt Square	(01600) 713899	monmouth.tic@monmouthshire.gov.uk
Mumbles	Mumbles Road	(01792) 361302	info@mumblestic.co.uk
New Quay*	Church Street	(01545) 560865	newquaytic@ceredigion.gov.uk
Newport	John Frost Square	(01633) 842962	newport.tic@newport.gov.uk
Newport (pembs)*	2 Bank Cottages	(01239) 820912	info@newporttic.fsnet.co.uk
Newtown	Back Lane	(01686) 625580	newtic@powys.gov.uk
Oswestry Mile End	Mile End Services	(01691) 662488	tic@oswestry-bc.gov.uk
Oswestry Town	2 Church Terrace	(01691) 662753	ot@oswestry-welshborders.org.uk
Pembroke Ferry*	Ferry Terminal	(01646) 622753	pembrokedock.tic@pembrokeshire.gov.uk
Pembroke*	Commons Road	(01646) 622388	pembroke.tic@pembrokeshire.gov.uk
Pont Nedd Fechan*	Pontneathvaughan Road	(01639) 721795	pnf-tic@btconnect.com
Porthcawl	John Street	(01656) 786639	porthcawltic@bridgend.gov.uk
Porthmadog	High Street	(01766) 512981	porthmadog.tic@gwynedd.gov.uk
Presteigne*	Broad Street	(01544) 260650	presteignetic@powys.gov.uk
Pwllheli	Station Square	(01758) 613000	pwllheli.tic@gwynedd.gov.uk
Rhayader	North Street	(01597) 810591	rhayader.tic@powys.gov.uk
Rhyl	West Parade	(01745) 355068	rhyl.tic@denbighshire.gov.uk
Saundersfoot*	Harbour Car Park	(01834) 813672	saundersfoot.tic@pembrokeshire.gov.uk
St Davids	1 High Street	(01437) 720392	enquiries@stdavids.pembrokeshirecoast.org.uk
Swansea	Plymouth Street	(01792) 468321	tourism@swansea.gov.uk
Tenby	The Gateway Complex	(01834) 842402	tenby.tic@pembrokeshire.gov.uk
Tywyn*	High Street	(01654) 710070	tywyn.tic@gwynedd.gov.uk
Welshpool	Church Street	(01938) 552043	weltic@powys.gov.uk
Wrexham	Lambpit Street	(01978) 292015	tic@wrexham.gov.uk

seasonal opening

ABERAERON, Ceredigion Map ref 8A2 — SELF CATERING

★★★
SELF CATERING

Units **1**
Sleeps **2–16**

Low season per wk
£455.00–£625.00
High season per wk
£750.00

ACCESS
STATEMENT

Ty Glyn Davis Trust, Nr Aberaeron

The Ty Glyn Davis Trust, c/o Hafod, Llanarth SA47 0QB t (01545) 580708
e enquiries@tyglyndavistrust.co.uk w tyglyndavistrust.co.uk

Fully accessible self-catering holiday centre for family gatherings and groups, ideal for those with special needs. Sleeps up to 16 people, fully equipped. Beautiful, peaceful location, close to the coast.

open All year
nearest shop 2 miles
nearest pub 0.5 miles

Access	♿
General	⊃ P ✂ ▣ ⑤
Unit	🛁 ⚏ ▣ 🖥 ⚏ ▣ ...
Payment	Cash/cheques

ABERSOCH, Gwynedd Map ref 8A2 — SELF CATERING

★★★★–★★★★★
SELF CATERING

ACCESS
STATEMENT

Crugeran Farm Holidays, Pwllheli
contact Crugeran Farm Holidays, Sarn, Pwllheli LL53 8DT
t (01758) 730375
e post@crugeran.com w crugeran.com

BORTH, Ceredigion Map ref 8A2 — SELF CATERING

★★★★★
SELF CATERING

Units **5**
Sleeps **2–10**

Low season per wk
£179.00–£309.00
High season per wk
£369.00–£785.00

ACCESS
STATEMENT

Aberleri Farm Cottages, Borth

Aberleri Farm Cottages, Maramba, Cliff Road, Borth SY24 5NN
t (01970) 871722 f (01970) 871856
e maramba@btinternet.com w aberlericottages.co.uk

General	⊃ ▥ ♿ P
Leisure	🎣
Unit	🛁 ▥ ▣ ⚏ ...
Payment	Credit/debit cards, cash/cheques

Wales Tourist Board-approved. Accessibility Statement on request.

Peacefully situated adjoining nature reserve, golf course and few minutes from sandy beaches. Farmhouse and four cottages, superbly appointed. Luxury bathrooms, three with jacuzzi. Sky Digital and Free-air satellite TVs, DVD, some bedrooms have TV. Convenient for places of interest, restaurants, pubs, shopping. Owners' personal supervision.

open All year
nearest shop 1.5 miles
nearest pub 1.5 miles

From A487 take B4350 to Borth. Shared entrance with Swn-y-Mor Holiday Park at northern end of village at Ynyslas. Adjoining golf course.

BUILTH WELLS, Powys Map ref 8B2 — HOTEL

★★★
COUNTRY HOUSE HOTEL

ACCESS STATEMENT

Caer Beris Manor Hotel Builth Wells LD2 3NP
t (01982) 552601 f (01982) 552586
e caerberis@btconnect.com w caerberis.co.uk

CARDIGAN, Ceredigion Map ref 8A2 — SELF CATERING

★★★–★★★★★
SELF CATERING

Units **5**
Sleeps **4–9**
Low season per wk
£220.00–£250.00
High season per wk
£485.00–£650.00

ACCESS STATEMENT

The Mews, Saddleback, Ladderloft, The Mansion & Granary, Boncath

contact Mr Jim Bowen, Clynfyw, Abercych, Boncath SA37 0HF
t (01239) 841236
e jim.clynfyw@virgin.net w clynfyw.co.uk

Access abc •: 🐾 ⛨

General 🛋 ▥ P ☉ Ⓢ

Unit ♿ ⛽ ▥ , ☐ ▦ ▭ ♨ ⚒ ▨
      🗄 ☍ 🚿 ⁄ ✱

Payment Cash/cheques

We have provided award-winning accommodation on our family's organic farm here in Pembrokeshire for over 20 years. Some guests have revisited us almost every year since then. Set in converted Victorian farm buildings, the sensitively designed all-access cottages provide a wonderfully peaceful base for a countryside holiday. Service dogs welcome.

open All year
nearest shop 2 miles
nearest pub 1 mile

Clynfyw is on the B4332 between Boncath and Cenarth at the top of the hill above Abercych, North Pembrokeshire.

COLWYN BAY, Conwy Map ref 8B1 — CAMPING & CARAVANNING

★★★★★
TOURING PARK

ACCESS STATEMENT

Bron Y Wendon Touring Caravan Park Wern Road, Llanddulas,
Colwyn Bay LL22 8HG t (01492) 512903 f (01492) 512903
e stay@northwales-holidays.co.uk w northwales-holidays.co.uk

CONWY, Conwy Map ref 8B1 — CAMPING & CARAVANNING

★★★
TOURING PARK

🚐 (320) £4.85–£17.60
🚛 (25) £4.85–£17.60
⛺ (50) £4.85–£17.60
320 touring pitches

ACCESS STATEMENT

Conwy Touring Park

Trefriw Road, Conwy LL32 8UX t (01492) 592856 w conwytouringpark.co.uk

Set in spectacular scenery, the perfect location for touring Snowdonia and coastal resorts. Sheltered, wooded site with splendid views. Excellent children's facilities. Special offers. Storage and servicing available. Open Easter to September.

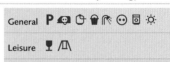

General P 🚐 🕒 👕 🍴 ☺ 📵 ☼

Leisure 🍸 ⛗

Payment Credit/debit cards, cash/cheques

At-a-glance symbols are explained on the flap inside the back cover.

LLANDEILO, Carmarthenshire Map ref 8A3 — SELF CATERING

SELF CATERING
ACCESS STATEMENT

Maerdy Cottages, Llandeilo **t** (01550) 777448
e enquiries@maerdyholidaycottages.co.uk **w** maerdyholidaycottages.co.uk

LLANDUDNO, Conwy

See entry on p290

LLANFAIR CAEREINION, Powys Map ref 8B2 — SELF CATERING

★★★–★★★★★★
SELF CATERING

Units **3**
Sleeps **2–6**

Low season per wk
£110.00–£320.00
High season per wk
£280.00–£495.00

Madog's Wells, Llanfair Caereinion

contact Ann Reed, Madog's Wells, Llanfair Caereinion, Welshpool SY21 0DE
t (01938) 810446 & (01938) 810446 **e** info@madogswells.co.uk
w madogswells.co.uk

Compact cosy two-bedroom bungalow (one double, one single) and two spacious three-bedroom bungalows (one double, two twins) in beautiful secluded valley; bird-watching, walking, steam trains, lakes and mountains nearby. Access statement available.
open All year
nearest shop 3 miles
nearest pub 3 miles

General ⬆ ▦ ♿ **P** ✂ S

Unit ♨ ▦ S ▭ ▱▫ ♨ ▱ ▱▱
▱ ❄

Payment Cash/cheques

SWANSEA, Swansea Map ref 8B3 — HOTEL

★★★
HOTEL
ACCESS STATEMENT

Best Western Aberavon Beach Hotel Neath Port Talbot, Swansea Bay SA12 6QP
t (01639) 884949 **f** (01639) 897885
e sales@aberavonbeach.com **w** aberavonbeach.com

Accessible accommodation

Establishments in Wales are not inspected under the National Accessible Scheme, however they are required to provide Access Statements describing their facilities.

Key to symbols

Symbols at the end of each entry help you pick out the services and facilities which are most important for your stay. A key to the symbols can be found inside the back-cover flap. Keep this open for easy reference.

LLANDUDNO, Conwy Map ref 8B1   **HOTEL**

West Shore

HB per person per night
£33.00–£57.00

Awaiting
NAS rating

West Parade, Llandudno LL30 2BB   **t** (01492) 876833   **f** (01492) 875461
e westshorehotel@johngrooms.org.uk   **w** groomsholidays.org.uk

Access   ☺ abc ♿

General   ⌂ P♿ 👓 ✂ ♟ 🛏 ⊞ ❄

Rooms   ♨ 📺 🖳 ♨ ☕ 🛏 🗄

Payment Credit/debit cards,
cash/cheques, euros

*Turkey and Tinsel breaks (Nov).
Taste of Wales breaks (Mar-Apr).
Valentine breaks (Feb).*

Grooms Holidays property specially adapted for disabled holidaymakers. Seventeen bedrooms with roll-in shower rooms. Some equipment available including hoists, but guests needing personal help should be accompanied or arrange care from a recommended local agency. Tail-lift bus for outings.

open All year
bedrooms 2 double, 8 twin, 7 single, 1 family
bathrooms All en suite

From A55, A546 (Ffordd 6G road), roundabout exit to Gloddaeth Avenue. Right at West Parade. Collection from Llandudno station can be arranged.

     At-a-glance symbols are explained on the flap inside the back cover.

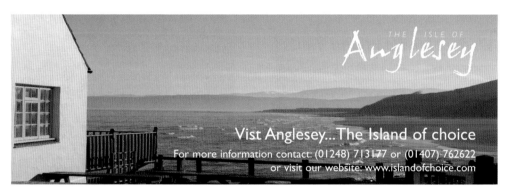

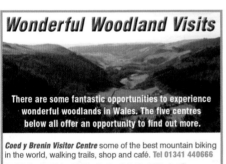

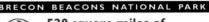

Further
information

Start Point Lighthouse,
near Kingsbridge, Devon

National **organisations**

National tourism organisations

Caravanable

43 Playfield Road, Oxford, OX1 5RS
t (01865) 739653
e info@caravanable.co.uk
w caravanable.co.uk

The website provides details of caravan sites in the UK which have the minimum requirements for disabled people of a shower, basin and toilet with ramped access, or more. The sites have all been recommended by other campers and caravan users. It is advisable to contact the park owners before making your booking. There is also a section on accessible beaches in the UK.

Disabled Holiday Information

PO Box 185, Oswestry, Shropshire SY10 1AF
e info@disabledholidayinfo.org.uk
w disabledholidayinfo.org.uk

An organisation providing information on holidays for people with disabilities including wheelchair accessible visitor attractions, activities and accommodation.

Disabled Ramblers

c/o 14 Belmont Park Road, Maidenhead, Berkshire SL6 6HT
t (01628) 621414
e chairman@disabledramblers.co.uk
w disabledrambers.co.uk

An organisation with a programme of one- and two-day supported rambles in a variety of settings mainly for users of mobility vehicles including wheelchairs, scooters and buggies.

English Heritage

Customer Services Department, PO Box 570, Swindon, Wiltshire SN2 2UR
t (01793) 414878
t 0800 015 0516
w english-heritage.org.uk

English Heritage manage sites of historical interest, including around 400 properties that are open to visitors. It produces an *Access Guide* giving information on access, parking and available services, such as audio tours, tactile exhibitions and sensory gardens. The guide is available online, or from customer services in different formats.

Holidays for All

c/o Tourism for All @ Vitalise, Shap
Road Industrial Estate, Shap Road,
Kendal LA9 6NZ

t 0845 124 9971

e info@tourismforall.org.uk

Holidays for All is a consortium of
disability organisations offering
accommodation and holidays for
people with disabilities. For a brochure,
contact Tourism for All (see page 8).

National Caravan Council

Catherine House, Victoria Road,
Aldershot GU11 1SS

e info@nationalcaravan.co.uk

w thecaravan.net

The representative trade body for the
UK caravan industry. You can search
their website of caravan sites for
'disabled access'.

National Federation Of Shopmobility UK

PO Box 6641, Christchurch BH23 9DQ

t 0845 644 2446

e info@shopmobilityuk.org

w shopmobilityuk.org

NFSUK is the national body for UK-
wide Shopmobility schemes which hire
out manual and powered wheelchairs
and scooters to people with mobility
impairments for shopping and visits to
leisure and commercial facilities. Some
schemes are free and some make a
charge; all welcome donations. You do
not have to be registered disabled to
use a scheme and, with advance notice,
many schemes can arrange an escort
around their locality. Ask for a copy of
the NFSUK Directory or check the
website for the online version.

National Trust

Access for All office, PO Box 39,
Bromley, Kent BR1 3XL

t 0870 458 4000

e accessforall@nationaltrust.org.uk

w nationaltrust.org.uk

The National Trust welcomes all
visitors to its properties. It produces a
free annual booklet *Information for
Visitors with Disabilities* which
contains details of access to properties
throughout the country. The booklet is
also available online.

National voluntary organisations offering assistance

British Red Cross

44 Moorfields, London EC2Y 9AL

t 0870 170 7000

e information@redcross.org.uk

w redcross.org.uk

Some county branches will advise on,
or even help arrange, holidays, and
have members willing to accompany
you on holiday. Look in the phone book
for your local Red Cross branch or visit
the website.

Carers Information

w carersinformation.org.uk

A website site providing up-to-date
resources and information on issues
relevant to informal carers and those
professionals who assist them in
their role.

Carers UK

20-25 Glasshouse Yard, London
EC1A 4JT

t 0808 808 7777
   (CarersLine freephone, Weds and
   Thurs 10am-12pm and 2-4pm)
e info@ukcarers.org
w carersuk.org

A campaigning organisation with a free
advice line for carers, staffed by welfare
rights, community care and benefit
advisers. It has a UK-wide network of
offices, branches and individuals
offering support to carers.

DIAL UK

St Catherine's, Tickhill Road, Doncaster
DN4 8QN

t (01302) 310123
w dialuk.info

A national network of approximately
130 local disability advice services
run by and for disabled people.
For local branch contact details, visit
the website.

Disabled Living Foundation

380-384 Harrow Road, London,
W9 2HU

t (020) 7289 6111
t 0845 130 9177 (helpline)
t (020) 7432 8009 (textphone)
e advice@dlf.org.uk
w dlf.org.uk

A national charity providing impartial
information and advice on disability
equipment and suppliers. It provides
free fact sheets on a variety of
equipment and related topics. You can
visit the equipment demonstration
centre by appointment.

Help With ME

w helpwithme.com

Help With ME is a support site which
supplies adaptive technology products
to help people with Myalgic
Encephalomyelitis/Chronic Fatigue
Syndrome (ME/CFS).

Jubilee Sailing Trust

Hazel Road, Woolston, Southampton
SO19 7GB

t 0870 443 5781
e info@jst.org.uk
w jst.org.uk

A charity enabling both able-bodied
and disabled people to sail on two tall
ships, Lord Nelson and Tenacious.

MENCAP

Mencap National Centre, 123 Golden
Lane, London EC1Y 0RT

t (020) 7454 0454
t 0808 808 1111 (helpline)
e information@mencap.org.uk
w mencap.org.uk

The society provides support to people
with a learning disability and their
carers and families through its national
network. Contact the helpline for a
copy of their holiday grant and holiday
information factsheet.

New Jumbulance Travel Trust

Delaport Coach House, Lamer lane,
Wheathampstead, St Albans AL4 8RQ

t (01582) 831 4444
w jumbulance.org.uk

Jumbulance have a fleet of adapted
coaches enabling severely disabled,
sick and dependent elderly people to
travel on holiday and take day trips.

RADAR

12 City Forum, 250 City Road, London
EC1V 8AF
t (020) 7250 3222
t (020) 7250 4119 (minicom)
e radar@radar.org.uk
w radar.org.uk

A national organisation working with
and for disabled people. It produces a
number of publications, including
Holidays in Britain and Ireland.

Royal National Institute for the Blind (RNIB)

105 Judd Street, London WC1H 9NE
t (020) 7388 1266
t 0845 702 3153 (Customer Services)
w rnib.org.uk

The RNIB promotes equal opportunities
in leisure for people with visual
impairments. It produces information
sheets on the arts and heritage, sport
and recreation, music, broadcasting
and holidays. Their customer services
offer products, advice and publications,
including a guide to hotels
recommended by blind or visually
impaired people.

Royal Society for the Protection of Birds UK (RSPB)

The Lodge, Sandy, Bedfordshire
SG19 2DL
t (01767) 680551
w rspb.org.uk

The RSPB produces leaflets for visitors
with disabilities or visit their website
for information on accessible reserves
and facilities.

SCOPE

Scope Response, PO Box 833, Milton
Keynes, Buckinghamshire MK12 5NY
t 0808 800 3333
e response@scope.org.
w scope.org.uk

Scope is a national disability charity
focussing on cerebral palsy. It
provides in-depth information and
advice on all aspects of cerebral palsy
and disability issues. The Helpline is
open from 9am-7pm weekdays and
10am-2pm on Saturday.

Calling Britain from overseas

Telephone numbers in this guide can be used if you
are dialling from within Britain. If you are an
overseas visitor and wish to call Britain from another
country, start with the international dialling code 00.
Next, dial the country code for the UK, which is **44**.
Finally, dial the UK number, **without the first 0**.

Getting around Britain

To help you on your way contact the organisations listed below and refer to the sections on travelling by rail, car, coach and air.

For comprehensive advice on all forms of travel in the UK see the Department of Transport's Door to Door website **dptac.gov.uk/door-to-door**.

The Automobile Association (AA)

Member Administration Contact Centre, Lambert House Stockport Road, Cheadle SK8 2DY
t 0870 600 0371
t 0800 262 050 (disability helpline)
t 0800 328 2810 (textphone)
w theaa.com

The AA's disability helpline provides advice to members on mobility issues, including home touring and route requests, motorway service area facilities, wheelchair maintenance and driving schools. Written information also available.

Directenquiries
w directenquiries.com

Directenquiries has online information on a range of businesses with accessible facilities, and includes detailed information on the London Underground and on the National Key Scheme for accessible toilets.

The Disabled Motorcyclists Association
Ada House, 77 Thompson Street, Manchester M4 5FY
t (0161) 833 8817
w thedma.org.uk

The Disabled Motorcyclists Association supports disabled people who wish to try motorcycling, or return to it, by offering discounts, member services, a magazine and guidance.

Eurotunnel
UK Terminal, PO Box 2000, Folkestone, Kent CT18 8XY
t 0870 535 3535 (call centre)
t 0800 096 9992 (information line)
w eurotunnel.com

Eurotunnel operates the Channel tunnel car shuttle. Book via telephone or online. Terminals in the UK and France are accessible. Passengers with disabilities are requested to alert check-in staff to ensure assistance if an evacuation is necessary.

Forum of Mobility Centres
Providence Chapel, Ashford, Kent TN26 2JX
t 0800 5593636
e mobility@rcht.cornwall.nhs.uk
w mobility-centres.org.uk

A UK-wide network of 17 independent organisations offering car adaptation information, advice and assessment.

Gatwick Travel-Care

Room 3014B Village Level, South Terminal, Gatwick Airport, Gatwick RH6 0NP
t (01293) 504283
f (01293) 503317

Gatwick Travel-Care offer information, advice and practical help. The office is open weekdays from 9am-5pm and weekdays 9am-4pm.

Green Flag Group

Green Flag House, Cote Lane, Leeds, West Yorkshire LS28 5GF
t 0845 246 1557
t 0800 800 610 (textphone)
w greenflag.com

Green Flag can recover specially modified road vehicles and disabled drivers, from anywhere in the UK.

Heathrow Travel-Care

Room 1308 Queens Building, Heathrow Airport, Hounslow, Middlesex TW6 1B6
t (020) 8745 7495
t (020) 8745 7950 (minicom)
e heathrow_travel_care@baa.co.uk

Provides 24-hour information, advice and counselling for people using facilities at Heathrow. There is a meet and assist service for passengers with special needs available via the office (9am-5pm Monday to Friday), Heathrow information desks, or by phoning (020) 8745 6011.

Mobilise

23 Cottingham Way, Thrapston, Northamptonshire NN14 4PLT
t (01832) 734724
w ddmc.org.uk

Offers transport information to its members and provides motoring concessions on a number of travel services including ferries, RAC membership and parking.

Motorhome Information Service

Maxwelton House, Boltro Road, Haywards Heath RH16 1BJ
t (01444) 458889
e info@motorhomeinfo.co.uk
w motorhomeinfo.co.uk

Information for disabled people on motorhomes or campervans, including addresses of dealers who are experienced in alterations.

Newick Packers

Unit 7, Gatwick Metro Centre, Balcombe Road, Horley RH6 9GA
t (01293) 772473
e enquiries@newick-packers.com
w homepage.ntlworld.com/paul. neilson/newick

Provides a service for packing fully-sealed electric wheelchair batteries for transport by air. Rates vary depending on size, weight and type of battery.

Transport Direct

w transportdirect.info

An online journey planning service for travel by car, train, coach or air. Features also include car park locations, a day trip planner and live travel information.

Travel by rail

National Rail (the train companies) produce *Rail Travel for Disabled Passengers*, a booklet giving details of the minimum level of service that you can expect throughout Britain's rail network and how to request assistance with a rail journey. The booklet is available from most staffed railway station ticket offices, Citizen's Advice Bureaux, some libraries and, in case of difficulty, a copy can be requested from the Disabled Persons Railcard Office address, below.

UK residents with disabilities are entitled to purchase a Disabled Persons Railcard, which allows you to buy discounted rail tickets (generally one third off) with the same discount for an accompanying carer. For qualifying and application details visit the website at disabledpersons-railcard.co.uk, call the application helpline on 0845 605 0525 or textphone 0845 601 0132, or write to Disabled Persons Railcard Office, PO Box 163, Newcastle-Upon-Tyne NE12 8WX.

For advice on planning your journey, or for contact details of your local train company, please telephone National Rail Enquiries on 08457 48 49 50 (textphone 0845 60 50 600) for assistance.

Assistance on trains

Most of train operators publish guides for disabled passengers, giving details about their route and the facilities available at the stations they use. Assistance can be arranged for you at your departure, destination and connecting stations should you need to change trains.

Useful tips

To ensure the best service, it is essential that you communicate your travel requirements at least 24 hours before you travel. If you are unable to give adequate notice, staff will help you as much as possible but they cannot guarantee to provide the normal level of service.

- So that you can be met by station staff, inform the train operator how you will travel to and from the mainline stations.

- Check whether you need to change train during your journey. If you do, ensure that station staff have been notified so that you can be assisted from one train to the other.

- Let the station know if you will need to borrow a wheelchair.

- Tell staff whether you are travelling alone or with a companion.

- If you have booked your journey in advance, train companies will help if your journey is disrupted, or if you have any other problems. If you do not book in advance, they will still help where possible. Train companies will give a refund if they cannot provide the arrangements you booked in advance.

Britrail Pass

If you live abroad and plan to visit Britain, the BritRail Pass gives the freedom to travel on all National Rail services. Ask for details from your travel agent before leaving. BritRail Passes can normally be bought from travel agents outside Britain or by visiting the BritRail website, britrail.net.

Useful contacts

National Rail Enquiries	nationalrail.co.uk	0845 748 4950
		0845 605 0600 (textphone)
Train operating companies	rail.co.uk	
The Trainline	trainline.co.uk	
Arriva Trains	arriva.co.uk	0845 606 1660
		0845 300 3005 (assisted travel)
		0870 410 0355 (textphone)
c2c	c2c-online.co.uk	0845 601 4873
		(01702) 357640 (assisted travel)
		0845 712 5988 (textphone)
Chiltern Railways	chilternrailways.co.uk	0845 600 5165
		0845 707 8051 (textphone)
CrossCountry	crosscountrytrains.co.uk	0845 748 4950
		0845 605 0600 (textphone)
East Midlands Trains	eastmidlandstrains.co.uk	0845 748 4950
		0845 605 0600 (textphone)
First Capital Connect	firstcapitalconnect.co.uk	0845 748 4950
		0800 058 2844 (assisted travel)
		0800 975 1052 (textphone)
First Great Western	firstgreatwestern.co.uk	0845 700 0125
		0800 197 1329 (assisted travel)
		0800 294 9209 (textphone)
First ScotRail	firstgroup.com/scotrail	0800 912 2901
		0845 605 7021 (assisted travel)
		0800 912 2899 (textphone)
Gatwick Express	gatwickexpress.co.uk	0845 850 1530
Heathrow Express	heathrowexpress.com	0845 600 1515
Hull Trains	hulltrains.co.uk	0845 071 0222
		0845 678 6967 (textphone)
Island Line	island-line.co.uk	0800 528 2100
		0800 692 0792 (textphone)
London Midland	londonmidland.com	0845 748 4950
		0845 605 0600 (textphone)
Merseyrail	merseyrail.org	0870 055 2681
		(0151) 702 2071 (textphone)

Phone numbers listed are for general enquiries unless otherwise stated.
*Booking line only.

Northern Rail	northernrail.org	0845 748 4950	
		0845 600 8008	(assisted travel)
		0845 604 5608	(textphone)
One	onerailway.com	0800 028 2878	
		0845 606 7245	(textphone)
South Eastern Trains	southeasternrailway.co.uk	0845 000 2222	
		0800 783 4524	(assisted travel)
		0800 783 4548	(textphone)
South West Trains	southwesttrains.co.uk	0845 600 0650	
		0800 528 2100	(assisted travel)
		0800 692 0792	(textphone)
Southern	southernrailway.com	0845 127 2920	
		0800 138 1016	(assisted travel)
		0800 138 1018	(textphone)
Stansted Express	stanstedexpress.com	0845 600 7245	
Transpennine Express	tpexpress.co.uk	0800 107 2149	
		0845 600 1672	(assisted travel)
		0800 107 2061	(textphone)
Virgin Trains	virgintrains.co.uk	0845 722 2333*	
		0845 744 3366	(assisted travel)
		0845 744 3367	(textphone)

Bank holiday
dates for your diary

holiday	2008	2009
New Year's Day	1 January	1 January
January Bank Holiday (Scotland)	2 January	2 January
Good Friday	21 March	10 April
Easter Monday (England & Wales)	24 March	13 April
Early May Bank Holiday	5 May	4 May
Spring Bank Holiday	26 May	25 May
Summer Bank Holiday (Scotland)	4 August	3 August
Summer Bank Holiday (England & Wales)	25 August	31 August
Christmas Day	25 December	25 December
Boxing Day Holiday	26 December	28 December

Travel by car

For information on driving, visit dptac.gov.uk/door-to-door/04/02.htm.

Parking

The Blue Badge scheme provides a range of parking benefits for disabled people who travel either as drivers or as passengers. The scheme operates throughout the UK. There are Blue Badge parking bays in 64 towns and cities across the UK. For information visit parkingforbluebadges.com.

Some Central London boroughs, including City of London, Westminster, Kensington, Chelsea and Camden, are regulated differently. They generally issue a special parking permit, which restricts mobility around the capital. For more information, contact the Association of Local Government Transport, New Zealand House, 80 Haymarket, London SW1Y 4TG or telephone (020) 7747 4767.

If you are travelling from abroad and are a member of a disabled badge scheme, check whether your badge is valid in the UK with the issuing authority. Although there are no reciprocal arrangements between Britain and the USA, most places (with the exception of Central London) will honour the US sticker, providing the car is safely parked.

Essential documents

If you are travelling from abroad ask the Automobile Association (AA) what documents you will need. Call their disability helpline on 0800 262 050.

Breakdown assistance

The Green Flag Group offers a recovery service for modified vehicles and disabled drivers. See page 299 for contact details.

Car hire companies

Alamo	alamo.co.uk	0870 400 4562*
Avis	avis.co.uk	0844 581 0147
Budget	budget.co.uk	0844 581 2231
Easycar	easycar.com	0906 333 3333
Enterprise	enterprise.com	0870 350 3000*
Hertz	hertz.co.uk	0870 844 8844*
National	nationalcar.co.uk	0870 400 4581
Wheelchair Travel	wheelchair-travel.co.uk	(01483) 233640

Cars with special features are not common and need to be requested well in advanced.
**Booking line only.*

Travel by coach

Confederation of Passenger Transport UK

Imperial House, 15-19 Kingsway, London WC2B 6UN

t (020) 7240 3131
e cpt@cpt-uk.org
w cpt-uk.org

Produces *Access*, a publication on accessible facilities provided by UK bus and coach companies.

National Express customer support

Disabled Persons Travel Helpline, P.O. Box 9854, Birmingham B16 8XN

t (0121) 423 8479 (Disabled Persons Travel Helpline)
t (0121) 455 0086 (textphone)
e DPTH@nationalexpress.com
w nationalexpress.com

It is advisable to contact National Express at least 24 hours in advance of travel to discuss available assistance. Lightweight wheelchairs (weighing less than 20kg) are accepted, but heavier wheelchairs, powered wheelchairs and scooters cannot be carried. Service dogs are accepted and travellers requiring oxygen may carry supplies in hand held bottles. Contact the Disabled Persons Travel Helpline for a copy of their information leaflet (also available in large print or audio format).

Sixt Rent a Car (Sixt Kenning Ltd)

Durrant House, 47 Holywell Street, Chesterfield S41 7SJ

t (01246) 220111
w e-sixt.co.uk

Sixt has wheelchair-accessible minibuses available nationally at over 80 of their branches with short- and long-term rates.

Victoria Coach Station

164 Buckingham Palace Road, London SW1 9TP

t (020) 7824 0000
w tfl.gov.uk/vcs

Operates a mobility assistance service 10am-6pm which can be booked 24 hours in advance by telephone or online. The station is fully accessible including the toilets. There is a help point in the station.

Wheelchair Travel

1 Johnston Green, Guildford, Surrey GU2 9XS

t (01483) 233640
e info@wheelchair-travel.co.uk
w wheelchair-travel.co.uk

Hires out accessible mini-vans and hand controlled cars throughout the country and can provide airport transfers, city tours, wheelchair-accessible taxis, chauffeurs and guides.

Travel by air

If you have special travel requirements, it is important to notify the airline when you book, and advisable to re-check that these have been noted a day or so before travel.

Display your Blue Badge at airport car parks, for a discounted rate at both short- and long-stay car parks. If you are a non-European visitor, you will not be eligible for discounted parking rates and may sometimes be required to pay a long-stay fee regardless of the length of your stay. We recommend you check at the airport before travelling.

For further advice, see the Door to Door website at dptac.gov.uk/door-to-door/06/index.htm. Alternatively, ask DPTAC (Disabled Persons Transport Advisory Committee) for a copy of their Access to Air Travel guidance by calling (020) 7944 8011 or textphone (020) 7944 3277.

The consumer body, Transport Users Council, also offers advice. Contact them at Room K705, CAA House, 45-59 Kingsway, London WC2B 6TB, telephone (020) 7240 6061 or visit caa.co.uk/auc.

Useful contacts

Airport information	a2btravel.com/airports	0870 888 1710
Air Southwest	airsouthwest.com	0870 043 4553
Blue Islands	blueislands.com	0845 620 2122
BMI	flybmi.com	0870 607 0555
BMI Baby	bmibaby.com	0871 224 0224
British Airways	ba.com	0870 850 9850 0845 700 7706 (minicom)
British International (Isles of Scilly to Penzance)	islesofscillyhelicopter.com	(01736) 363871*
Eastern Airways	easternairways.com	0870 366 9100 *
Easyjet	easyjet.com	0871 244 2366
Flybe	flybe.com	0871 522 6100
Jet2.com	jet2.com	0871 226 1737*
Ryanair	ryanair.com	0871 246 0000
Skybus (Isles of Scilly)	islesofscilly-travel.com	0845 710 5555
VLM	flyvlm.com	0871 666 5050

*Booking line only.

Quality assessment schemes

When you're looking for a place to stay, you need a rating system you can trust. Quality ratings are your clear guide to what to expect, in an easy-to-understand form.

National tourist board professional assessors pay unannounced visits to establishments that are new to the rating scheme and stay overnight where appropriate. Once in the scheme establishments receive an annual pre-arranged day visit, with an overnight stay generally every other year for hotel and B&B guest accommodation. On these occasions the assessors book in anonymously, and test all the facilities and services.

Based on internationally recognised star ratings, the system puts great emphasis on quality, and reflects exactly what consumers are looking for. Ratings are awarded from one to five stars – the more stars, the higher the quality and the greater the range of facilities and services provided. They are the sign of quality assurance, giving you the confidence to book accommodation that meets your expectations.

Look out, too, for VisitBritain's Gold and Silver Awards, which are awarded to hotels and guest accommodation achieving the highest levels of quality within their star rating. While the overall rating is based on a combination of facilities and quality, the Gold and Silver Awards are based solely on quality.

Hotels

All hotels that are awarded a star rating will meet the minimum standards – so you can be confident that you will find the basic services that you would expect, such as:

- All bedrooms with an en suite or private bathroom
- A designated reception facility and staff members who will be available during the day and evening (24hrs in case of an emergency)
- A licence to serve alcohol (unless a temperance hotel)
- Access to the hotel at all times for registered guests
- Dinner available at least five days a week (with the exception of a Town House Hotel or Metro Hotel)
- All statutory obligations will be met.

Hotels have to provide certain additional facilities and services at the higher star levels, some of which may be important to you:

TWO-STAR hotels must provide:
- Dinner seven nights a week.

THREE-STAR hotels must provide:
- All en suite bedrooms (ie no private bathrooms)
- Direct dial phones in all rooms
- Room service during core hours
- A permanently staffed reception.

FOUR-STAR hotels must provide:
- 24-hour room service
- 50% of all en suites with bath **and** shower.

FIVE-STAR hotels must provide:
- Some permanent suites
- Enhanced services, such as concierge.

Sometimes a hotel with a lower star rating has exceptional bedrooms and bathrooms and offers its guests a special welcome, but cannot achieve a higher rating because, for example, it does not offer dinner every evening (two star), room service (three star) or does not have the minimum 50% of bathrooms with bath **and** shower (four star).

Quality

The availability of additional services alone is not enough for an establishment to achieve a higher star rating. Hotels have to meet exacting standards for quality in critical areas. Consumer research has shown the critical areas to be: cleanliness, bedrooms, bathrooms, hospitality and service, and food.

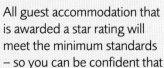

Guest accommodation

All guest accommodation that is awarded a star rating will meet the minimum standards – so you can be confident that you will find the basic services that you would expect, such as:

- A clear explanation of booking charges, services offered and cancellation terms
- A full cooked breakfast or substantial continental breakfast
- At least one bathroom or shower room for every six guests
- For a stay of more than one night, rooms cleaned and beds made daily
- Printed advice on how to summon emergency assistance at night
- All statutory obligations will be met.

TWO-STAR accommodation provides all of the above but the rating reflects a higher quality of services and facilities than one-star accommodation.

Proprietors of guest accommodation have to provide certain additional facilities and services at the higher star levels, some of which may be important to you:

THREE-STAR accommodation must provide:
- Private bathroom/shower room (cannot be shared with the owners)
- Bedrooms must have a washbasin if not en suite.

FOUR-STAR accommodation must provide:
- 50% of bedrooms en suite or with private bathroom.

FIVE-STAR accommodation must provide:
- All bedrooms with en suite or private bathroom.

Sometimes guest accommodation has exceptional bedrooms and bathrooms and offers visitors a very special welcome, but cannot achieve a higher star rating because, for example, there are no en suite bedrooms, or it is difficult to put washbasins in the bedrooms (three star). This is sometimes the case with period properties.

Quality

The availability of additional facilities alone is not enough for an establishment to achieve a higher star rating. Guest accommodation has to meet exacting standards for quality in critical areas. Consumer research has shown the critical areas to be: cleanliness, bedrooms, bathrooms, hospitality and food.

Self-catering accommodation

All self-catering accommodation that is awarded a star rating will meet the minimum standards – so you can be confident that you will find the basic services that you would expect, such as:

- Clear information prior to booking on all aspects of the accommodation including location, facilities, prices, deposit, policies on smoking, children, etc
- No shared facilities, with the exception of a laundry room in multi-unit sites
- All appliances and furnishings will meet product safety standards for self-catering accommodation, particularly regarding fire safety
- At least one smoke alarm in the unit and a fire blanket in the kitchen
- Clear information on emergency procedures, including who to contact
- Contact details for the local doctor, dentist, etc

- All statutory obligations will be met including an annual gas check and public liability insurance.

Certain additional facilities and services are required at the higher star levels, some of which may be important to you:

TWO-STAR accommodation must provide:
- Single beds which are a minimum of 3ft wide and double beds a minimum of 4ft 6in.

THREE-STAR accommodation must provide:
- Bed linen (with or without additional charge).

FOUR-STAR accommodation must provide:
- All sleeping space in bedrooms, unless a studio (bed settees cannot be advertised)
- Bed linen included in the hire charge and beds are made up for arrival.

FIVE-STAR accommodation must provide:
- At least two of the following items: tumble-dryer, telephone, Hi-Fi, video, DVD.

Some self-catering establishments offer a choice of accommodation units that may have different star ratings. In this case, the entry shows the range available.

Quality

The availability of additional facilities, such as a dishwasher or DVD, is not enough to achieve a higher star rating. Self-catering accommodation with a lower star rating may offer some or all of the above, but to achieve the higher star ratings, the overall quality score has to be reached and exacting standards have to be met in critical areas. Consumer research has shown these to be: cleanliness, bedrooms, bathrooms, kitchens and public areas.

Camping and Caravan Parks

The British Graded Holiday Parks Scheme, operated jointly by the national tourist boards for England, Scotland, Wales and Northern Ireland, was devised in association with the British Holiday and Home Parks Association and the National Caravan Council. It gives you a clear guide of what to expect in an easy-to-understand form.

The star rating process is very thorough to ensure that when you make a booking you can be confident it will meet your expectations. Professional assessors visit parks annually and take into account over 50 separate aspects, from landscaping and layout to maintenance, customer care and, most importantly, cleanliness.

Strict guidelines ensure that every park is assessed to the same criteria. A random check is made of a sample of accommodation for hire but the quality of the accommodation itself is not included in the grading assessment.

In addition to The British Graded Holiday Parks Scheme, VisitBritain operates a rating scheme for Holiday Villages. The assessor stays on the site overnight and grades the overall quality of the visitor experience, including accommodation, facilities, cleanliness, service and food.

So you can rest assured that when you choose a star-rated park or holiday village you won't be disappointed.

Star ratings

Parks are required to meet progressively higher standards of quality as they move up the scale from one to five stars:

ONE STAR Acceptable

To achieve this grade, the park must be clean with good standards of maintenance and customer care.

TWO STAR Good

All the above points plus an improved level of landscaping, lighting, refuse disposal and maintenance. May be less expensive than more highly rated parks.

THREE STAR Very good

Most parks fall within this category; three stars represent the industry standard. The range of facilities provided may vary from park to park, but they will be of a very good standard and will be well maintained.

FOUR STAR Excellent

You can expect careful attention to detail in the provision of all services and facilities. Four-star parks rank among the industry's best.

FIVE STAR Exceptional

Highest levels of customer care will be provided. All facilities will be maintained in pristine condition in attractive surroundings.

For information on the Caravan Holiday Home Award Scheme, see page 314.

Advice and information

Making a booking

When enquiring about accommodation, make sure you check prices, the quality rating and other important details. You will also need to state your requirements clearly and precisely, for example:

- Arrival and departure dates, with acceptable alternatives if appropriate
- Accessible requirements
- The type of accommodation you need – for example, room with twin beds, en suite bathroom
- The terms you want – for example, room only, bed and breakfast
- The age of any children with you, whether you want them to share your room or be next door, and any other requirements, such as a cot
- Any particular requirements you may have, such as a special diet or a ground-floor room.

Confirmation

Misunderstandings can easily happen over the telephone, so do request a written confirmation, together with details of any terms and conditions.

Deposits

If you make a hotel or guest accommodation reservation weeks or months in advance, you will probably be asked for a deposit, which will then be deducted from the final bill when you leave. The amount will vary from establishment to establishment and could be payment in full at peak times.

Proprietors of self-catering accommodation will normally ask you to pay a deposit immediately, and then to pay the full balance before your holiday date. This safeguards the proprietor in case you decide to cancel at a late stage or simply do not turn up. He or she may have turned down other bookings on the strength of yours and may find it hard to re-let if you cancel.

In the case of camping and caravan parks the full charge often has to be paid in advance. This may be in two instalments – a deposit at the time of booking and the balance by, say, two weeks before the start of the booked period.

Payment on arrival

Some establishments, especially large hotels in big towns, ask you to pay for your room on arrival if you have not booked it in advance. This is especially likely to happen if you arrive late and have little or no luggage.

If you are asked to pay on arrival, it is a good idea to see your room first, to make sure it meets your requirements.

Cancellations

Legal contract

When you accept accommodation that is offered to you, by telephone or in writing, you enter a legally binding contract with the proprietor. This means that if you cancel your booking, fail to take up the accommodation or leave early, the proprietor may be entitled to compensation if he or she cannot re-let for all or a good part of the booked period. You will probably forfeit any deposit you have paid, and may well be asked for an additional payment.

At the time of booking you should be advised of what charges would be made in the event of cancelling the accommodation or leaving early. If this is not mentioned you should ask so that future disputes can be avoided. The proprietor cannot make a claim until after the booked period, and during that time he or she should make every effort to re-let the accommodation. If there is a dispute it is sensible for both sides to seek legal advice on the matter. If you do have to change your travel plans, it is in your own interests to let the proprietor know in writing as soon as possible, to give them a chance to re-let your accommodation.

And remember, if you book by telephone and are asked for your credit card number, you should check whether the proprietor intends charging your credit card account should you later cancel your reservation. A proprietor should not be able to charge your credit card account with a cancellation fee unless he or she has made this clear at the time of your booking and you have agreed.

However, to avoid later disputes, we suggest you check whether this is the intention.

Insurance

A travel or holiday insurance policy will safeguard you if you have to cancel or change your holiday plans. You can arrange a policy quite cheaply through your insurance company or travel agent. Some hotels also offer their own insurance schemes and many self-catering agencies insist their customers take out a policy when they book their holidays.

Arrival time

If you know you will be arriving late in the evening, it is a good idea to say so when you book. If you are delayed on your way, a telephone call to say that you will be late would be appreciated.

It is particularly important to liaise with the owner of self-catering accommodation about key collection as he or she will not necessarily be on site.

Service charges and tipping

These days many places levy service charges automatically. If they do, they must clearly say so in their offer of accommodation, at the time of booking. The service charge then becomes part of the legal contract when you accept the offer of accommodation.

If a service charge is levied automatically, there is no need to tip the staff, unless they provide some exceptional service. The usual tip for meals is 10% of the total bill.

Telephone charges

Establishments can set their own charges for telephone calls made through their switchboard or from direct-dial telephones in bedrooms. These charges are often much higher than telephone companies' standard charges (to defray the cost of providing the service).

Comparing costs

It is a condition of the national tourist board's quality assessment scheme that an establishment's unit charges are on display by the telephones or with the room information. It is not always easy to compare these charges with standard rates, so before using a telephone for long-distance calls, you may decide to ask how the charges compare.

Security of valuables

You can deposit your valuables with the proprietor or manager during your stay, and we recommend you do this as a sensible precaution. Make sure you obtain a receipt for them. Some places do not accept articles for safe custody, and in that case it is wisest to keep your valuables with you.

Disclaimer

Some proprietors put up a notice that disclaims liability for property brought on to their premises by a guest. In fact, they can only restrict their liability to a minimum laid down by law (The Hotel Proprietors Act 1956). Under that Act, a proprietor is liable for the value of the loss or damage to any property (except a car or its contents) of a guest who has engaged overnight accommodation, but if the proprietor has the notice on display as prescribed under that Act, liability is limited to £50 for one article and a total of £100 for any one guest.

The notice must be prominently displayed in the reception area or main entrance. These limits do not apply to valuables you have deposited with the proprietor for safekeeping, or to property lost through the default, neglect or wilful act of the proprietor or their staff.

Bringing pets to the UK

Dogs (including service dogs), cats, ferrets and some other pet mammals can be brought into the UK from certain countries without having to undertake six months' quarantine on arrival provided they meet all the rules of the Pet Travel Scheme (PETS).

For full details, visit the PETS website at **w** defra.gov.uk/animalh/quarantine/ index.htm or contact the PETS Helpline
t +44 (0)870 241 1710
e pets.helpline@defra.gsi.gov.uk
Ask for fact sheets which cover dogs and cats, ferrets or domestic rabbits and rodents.

What to expect

Hotels, guest and self-catering accommodation, holiday villages

The proprietor/management is required to undertake the following:

- To maintain standards of guest care, cleanliness and service appropriate to the type of establishment;

- To describe accurately in any advertisement, brochure or other printed or electronic media, the facilities and services provided;

- To make clear to visitors exactly what is included in all prices quoted for accommodation, including taxes, and any other surcharges. Details of charges for additional services/facilities should also be made clear;

- To give a clear statement of the policy on cancellations to guests at the time of booking ie by telephone, fax, email, as well as information given in a printed format;

- To adhere to and not to exceed prices quoted at the time of booking for accommodation and other services;

- To advise visitors at the time of booking, and subsequently if any change, if the accommodation offered is in an unconnected annexe or similar and to indicate the location of such accommodation and any difference in comfort and/or amenities from accommodation in the establishment;

- To register all guests on arrival (except self-catering accommodation);

- To give each visitor on request details of payments due and a receipt, if required;

- To deal promptly and courteously with all enquiries, requests, bookings and correspondence from visitors;

- To ensure complaint handling procedures are in place and that complaints received are investigated promptly and courteously and that the outcome is communicated to the visitor;

- To give due consideration to the requirements of visitors with disabilities and visitors with special needs, and to make suitable provision where applicable;

- To provide public liability insurance or comparable arrangements and to comply with all applicable planning, safety and other statutory requirements;

- To allow a national tourist board assessor reasonable access to the establishment on request, to confirm the VisitBritain Code of Conduct is being observed.

What to expect

Holiday, touring and camping parks

In addition to fulfilling its statutory obligations, including having applied for a certificate under the Fire Precautions Act 1971 (if applicable) and holding public liability insurance, and ensuring that all caravan holiday homes/chalets for hire and the park and all buildings and facilities thereon, the fixtures, furnishings, fittings and decor are maintained in sound and clean condition and are fit for the purposes intended, the management is required to undertake the following:

- To ensure high standards of courtesy, cleanliness, catering and service appropriate to the type of park;

- To describe to all visitors and prospective visitors the amenities, facilities and services provided by the park and/or caravan holiday homes/chalets whether by advertisement, brochure, word of mouth or other means;

- To allow visitors to see the park or caravan holiday homes/chalets for hire, if requested, before booking;

- To present grading awards and/or any other national tourist board awards unambiguously;

- To make clear to visitors exactly what is included in prices quoted for the park or caravan holiday homes/chalets, meals and refreshments, including service charge, taxes and other surcharges. Details of charges, if any, for heating or for additional services or facilities available should also be made clear;

- To adhere to, and not to exceed, prices current at time of occupation for caravan holiday homes/chalets or other services;

- To advise visitors at the time of booking, and subsequently if any change, if the caravan holiday home/chalet or pitch offered is in a different location or on another park, and to indicate the location of this and any difference in comfort and amenities;

- To give each visitor, on request, details of payments due and a receipt if required;

- To advise visitors at the time of booking of the charges that might be incurred if the booking is subsequently cancelled;

- To register all guests on arrival;

- To deal promptly and courteously with all visitors and prospective visitors, including enquiries, requests, reservations, correspondence and complaints;

- To allow a national tourist board representative reasonable access to the park and/or caravan holiday homes/chalet whether by prior appointment or on an unannounced assessment, to confirm that the VisitBritain Code of Conduct is being observed and that the appropriate quality standard is being maintained;

- The operator must comply with the provision of the caravan industry Codes of Practice.

Caravan Holiday Home Award Scheme

VisitBritain, VisitScotland and Visit Wales run award schemes for individual holiday caravan homes on highly graded caravan parks.

In addition to complying with standards for Holiday Parks, these exceptional caravans must have a shower or bath, toilet, mains electricity and water heating (at no extra charge) and a fridge (many also have a colour TV).

Comments and complaints

The law

Places that offer accommodation have legal and statutory responsibilities to their customers, such as providing information about prices, providing adequate fire precautions and safeguarding valuables. Like other businesses, they must also abide by the Trades Description Acts 1968 and 1972 when they describe their accommodation and facilities. All the places featured in this guide have declared that they do fulfil all applicable statutory obligations.

Information

The proprietors themselves supply the descriptions of their establishments and other information for the entries, (except national tourist board ratings and awards). VisitBritain cannot guarantee the accuracy of information in this guide, and accepts no responsibility for any error or misrepresentation. All liability for loss, disappointment, negligence or other damage caused by reliance on the information contained in this guide, or in the event of bankruptcy or liquidation or cessation of trade of any company, individual or firm mentioned, is hereby excluded. We strongly recommend that you carefully check prices and other details when you book your accommodation.

Quality Rose signage

All establishments/parks displaying a Quality Rose sign have to hold current membership of an Enjoy England Quality Rose assessment scheme or The British Graded Holiday Parks Scheme. When an establishment is sold the new owner has to reapply and be reassessed.

Problems

Of course, we hope you will not have cause for complaint, but problems do occur from time to time. If you are dissatisfied with anything, make your complaint to the management immediately. Then the management can take action at once to investigate the matter and put things right. The longer you leave a complaint, the harder it is to deal with it effectively.

In certain circumstances, VisitBritain may look into complaints. However, VisitBritain has no statutory control over establishments or their methods of operating. VisitBritain cannot become involved in legal or contractual matters, nor can they get involved in seeking financial recompense.

If you do have problems that have not been resolved by the proprietor and which you would like to bring to our attention, please write to:

England
Quality in Tourism
Farncombe House
Broadway
Worcestershire WR12 7LJ

Scotland
Quality and Standards
VisitScotland
Thistle House
Beechwood Park North
Inverness IV2 3ED

Wales
VisitWales
Ty Glyndwr
Treowain Enterprise Park
Machynlleth
Powys SY20 8WW

Entries

All the establishments/parks featured in this guide have been assessed or have applied for assessment under a national tourist board quality assessment scheme or The British Graded Holiday Parks Scheme.

Proprietors have paid to have their establishment/ park featured in either a standard entry (includes description, facilities and prices) or enhanced entry (photograph and extended details).

Locations

Places to stay are generally listed under the town, city or village where they are located. If a place is in a small village, you may find it listed under a nearby town (providing it is within a seven-mile radius).

Place names are listed alphabetically within each regional section of the guide, along with the ceremonial county they are in and their map reference. Complete addresses for self-catering properties are not given and the town(s) listed may be a distance from the actual establishment. Please check the precise location at the time of booking.

Map references

These refer to the colour location maps at the front of the guide. The first figure shown is the map number, the following letter and figure indicate the grid reference on the map. Some entries were included just before the guide went to press, so they do not appear on the maps.

Addresses

County names, which appear in the place headings, are not repeated in the entries. When you are writing, you should of course make sure you use the full address and postcode.

Telephone numbers

Telephone numbers are listed below the accommodation address for each entry. Area codes are shown in brackets.

Prices

The prices shown are only a general guide; they were supplied to us by proprietors in summer 2007. Remember, changes may occur after the guide goes to press, so we strongly advise you to check prices when you book your accommodation.

Prices are shown in pounds sterling and include VAT where applicable. Some places also include a service charge in their standard tariff, so check this when you book.

Bed and breakfast: the prices shown are per room for overnight accommodation with breakfast. The double room price is for two people. (If a double room is occupied by one person there is sometimes a reduction in price.)

Half board: the prices shown are per person per night for room, evening meal and breakfast. These prices are usually based on two people sharing a room.

Evening meal: the prices shown are per person per night.

Some places only provide a continental breakfast in the set price, and you may have to pay extra if you want a full English breakfast.

According to the law, establishments with at least four bedrooms or eight beds must display their overnight accommodation charges in the reception area or entrance. In your own interests, do make sure you check prices and what they include.

Self catering: prices shown are per unit per week and include VAT.

Camping: touring pitches are based on the minimum and maximum charges for one night for two persons, car and either caravan or tent. (Some parks may charge separately for car, caravan or tent, and for each person and there may be an extra charge for caravan awnings.) Minimum and maximum prices for caravan holiday homes are given per week.

Children's rates

You will find that many places charge a reduced rate for children, especially if they share a room with their parents. Some places charge the full rate, however, when a child occupies a room which might otherwise have been let to an adult. The upper age limit for reductions for children varies from one hotel to another, so check this when you book.

Seasonal packages and special promotions

Prices often vary through the year and may be significantly lower outside peak holiday weeks. A number of establishments taking an enhanced entry have included special offers and themed breaks.

Bathrooms
(hotels and guest accommodation)

Each accommodation entry shows you the number of en suite and private bathrooms available. En suite bathroom means the bath or shower and wc are contained behind the main door of the bedroom. Private bathroom means a bath or shower and wc solely for the occupants of one bedroom, on the same floor, reasonably close and with a key provided. If the availability of a bath, rather than a shower, is important to you, remember to check when you book.

Meals
(hotels and guest accommodation)

It is advisable to check availability of meals and set times when making your reservation. Some smaller places may ask you at breakfast whether you want an evening meal. The prices shown in each entry are for bed and breakfast or half board, but many places also offer lunch.

Chalets/villas for hire
(camping and caravan parks)

Where a site has chalets or villas for hire this is indicated by this symbol ⚑. Please note that this type of accommodation is not necessarily included within the official quality rating for the park and it is advisable that you contact the proprietor directly if you require further information.

Opening period

If an entry does not indicate an opening period, please check directly with the establishment.

Symbols

The at-a-glance symbols included at the end of each entry show many of the services and facilities available at each establishment. You will find the key to these symbols on the back-cover flap – open it out and check the meanings as you go.

Smoking

In the UK, it is illegal to smoke in enclosed public spaces and places of work. This means that smoking is banned in the public and communal areas of hotels, guesthouses and B&Bs, and in restaurants, bars and pubs.

Some hotels, guesthouses and B&Bs may choose to provide designated smoking bedrooms, and B&Bs and guest houses may allow smoking in private areas that are not used by any staff. Smoking may also be allowed in self-contained short-term rental accommodation, such as holiday cottages, flats or caravans, if the owner chooses to allow it.

If you wish to smoke, it is advisable to check whether it is allowed when you book.

Alcoholic drinks

All hotels (except temperance hotels) hold an alcohol licence. Some guest accommodation may also be licensed, however, the licence may be restricted – to diners only, for example. If a bar is available this is shown by the ♟ symbol.

Pets

Many places accept guests with dogs, but we do advise that you check this when you book, and ask if there are any extra charges or rules about exactly where your pet is allowed. The acceptance of dogs is not always extended to cats and it is strongly advised that pet owners contact the establishment well in advance. Some establishments do not accept pets at all. Pets are welcome by arrangement where you see this symbol ♞.

The quarantine laws have changed in the UK, and dogs, cats and ferrets are able to come into Britain from over 50 countries. For details of the Pet Travel Scheme (PETS) please turn to page 312.

Payment accepted

The types of payment accepted by an establishment are listed in the payment accepted section. If you plan to pay by card, check that the establishment will take your particular card before you book. Some proprietors will charge you a higher rate if you pay by credit card rather than cash or cheque. The difference is to cover the percentage paid by the proprietor to the credit card company. When you book by telephone, you may be asked for your credit card number as confirmation. But remember, the proprietor may then charge your credit card account if you cancel your booking. See under Cancellations on page 311.

Awaiting confirmation of rating

At the time of going to press some establishments/parks featured in this guide had not yet been assessed for their rating for the year 2007/8 and so their new rating could not be included. Rating Applied For indicates this.

Accessible Schemes
index

Establishments participating in accessible schemes are listed below. At the front of the guide you can find information about the different schemes. Establishments listed have a detailed entry in this guide.

England

♿ Mobility level 1

🔖 Mobility level 1 continued

🔖 Mobility level 2

Establishments listed here have a detailed entry in this guide.

♿ Mobility level 2 continued

Torquay South West England	Atlantis Holiday Apartments ★★★	197
Veryan South West England	Trenona Farm Holidays ★★★★	198
Yelverton South West England	Overcombe House ★★★★	202
Chale South East England	Atherfield Green Farm Holiday Cottages ★★★★	229
Heathfield South East England	Spicers ★★★★	231
Lewes South East England	Heath Farm ★★★★	232
Sandwich South East England	The Old Dairy ★★★★	235
Witney South East England	Swallows Nest ★★★★	236

♿ Mobility level 3 Independent

Henley Central England	Damerons Farm Holidays ★★★★	132
Malvern Central England	Hidelow House Cottages ★★★★–★★★★★★	137
Stafford Central England	Swan Hotel	149
Wigsthorpe Central England	Nene Valley Cottages ★★★★★	145
Ashwater South West England	Blagdon Farm Country Holidays ★★★★–★★★★★★	177
Blandford Forum South West England	Houghton Lodge ★★★★★	179
Broadclyst South West England	Hue's Piece ★★★★	181
Colyton South West England	Smallicombe Farm ★★★★	183
Looe South West England	Tudor Holiday Lodges ★★★★	186
St Just-in-Penwith South West England	Swallow's End ★★★★	194
Shaftesbury South West England	Hartgrove Farm ★★–★★★★	195
West Bexington South West England	Tamarisk Farm Cottages ★★★★	199
Weston-super-Mare South West England	Royal Hotel ★★★	200

♿ Mobility level 3 Assisted

Cockfield Northern England	Stonecroft and Swallows Nest ★★★★	70
Pickering Northern England	Rawcliffe House Farm ★★★★	82
Sandringham Central England	Park House Hotel ★★ SILVER	141
Ashwater South West England	Blagdon Farm Country Holidays ★★★★–★★★★★★	177
Blandford Forum South West England	Houghton Lodge ★★★★★	179
Looe South West England	Tudor Holiday Lodges ★★★★	186
Lostwithiel South West England	Brean Park ★★★★★	187
Chale South East England	Atherfield Green Farm Holiday Cottages ★★★★	229

♿ Access Exceptional Independent

Tugford Central England	Tugford Farm B&B ★★★★	144
Lostwithiel South West England	Hartswheal Barn ★★★–★★★★	188

♿ Access Exceptional Assisted

Mablethorpe Central England	Grange Cottages ★★★★	137
Tugford Central England	Tugford Farm B&B ★★★★	144
Lostwithiel South West England	Hartswheal Barn ★★★–★★★★	188

🔊 Hearing impairment level 1

Broughton Mills Northern England	Swallows Nest ★★★★	68
Cornriggs Northern England	Cornriggs Cottages ★★★★★	72
Ashbourne Central England	Ancestral Barn ★★★★–★★★★★	121
Boston Central England	Elms Farm Cottages ★★★★–★★★★★	124
Brassington Central England	Hoe Grange Holidays ★★★★	125
Weston-super-Mare South West England	Royal Hotel ★★★	200

👁 Visual impairment level 1

Broughton Mills Northern England	Swallows Nest ★★★★	68
Boston Central England	Elms Farm Cottages ★★★★–★★★★★	124
Brassington Central England	Hoe Grange Holidays ★★★★	125

Scotland

♿ Mobility level 1

♿ Mobility level 2

♿ Mobility level 3

Wales

♿ Mobility level 2

Access Statement

Quick reference index

If you're looking for a specific facility use this index to see at-a-glance detailed accommodation entries that match your requirements.

▦ Level entry shower continued

Establishments listed here have a detailed entry in this guide.

⚠ Hoist available

♿ Adapted kitchen

♿ Adapted kitchen continued

🐕 Facilities for service dogs

Establishments listed here have a detailed entry in this guide.

Index to display advertisers

All display advertisers are listed below.

Index to display advertisers

Index by place name

The following places all have detailed accommodation entries in this guide. If the place where you wish to stay is not shown, the location maps (starting on page 22) will help you find somewhere to stay in the area.

Index by property name

All accommodation with a detailed entry in this guide is listed below.

Index by property name

Establishments listed here have a detailed entry in this guide.

Bank holiday
dates for your diary

holiday	2008	2009
New Year's Day	1 January	1 January
January Bank Holiday (Scotland)	2 January	2 January
Good Friday	21 March	10 April
Easter Monday (England & Wales)	24 March	13 April
Early May Bank Holiday	5 May	4 May
Spring Bank Holiday	26 May	25 May
Summer Bank Holiday (Scotland)	4 August	3 August
Summer Bank Holiday (England & Wales)	25 August	31 August
Christmas Day	25 December	25 December
Boxing Day Holiday	26 December	28 December

Published by: Tourism for All UK, c/o Vitalise, Shap Road Industrial Estate, Kendal LA9 6NT and VisitBritain, Thames Tower, Blacks Road, London W6 9EL in partnership with Britain's tourism industry visitbritain.com

Publishing Manager: Jennifer Littman

Production Manager: Iris Buckley

Compilation, design, copywriting, production and advertisement sales: Jackson Lowe, 3 St Andrews Place, Southover Road, Lewes, East Sussex BN7 1UP

t (01273) 487487 jacksonlowe.com

Typesetting: Marlinzo Services, Somerset and Jackson Lowe

Maps: Based on digital map data © ESR Cartography, 2006

Printing and binding: Emirates Printing Press, Dubai, United Arab Emirates

Cover design: Jackson Lowe

Front cover: Hidelow House, Worcester

Photography credits: Bournemouth Oceanarium; britainonview/David Angel/Daniel Bosworth/Martin Brent/ East of England Tourism Rod Edwards/Jakob Ebrey/ Eden Project/Rod Edwards/Adrian Houston/Leicester Shire PR/Pawel Libera/McCormick-McAdam/Eric Nathan/ Tony Pleavin/Grant Pritchard/Ingrid Rasmussen/David Sellman/Andy Sewell/Ian Shaw/Thanet District Council Rod Edwards/Worcestershire County Council Daniel Bosworth; Iris Buckley; Cardiff Millennium Centre; Zac Macaulay; NTPL/ Rob Judges; scottishviewpoint.com/Paul Tomkins; visitlondonimages/britainonview; Vitalise

A VisitBritain Publishing guide